THE
MAKING OF AMERICA
SERIES

ATLANTIC
HIGHLANDS

FROM LENAPE CAMPS
TO BAYSIDE TOWN

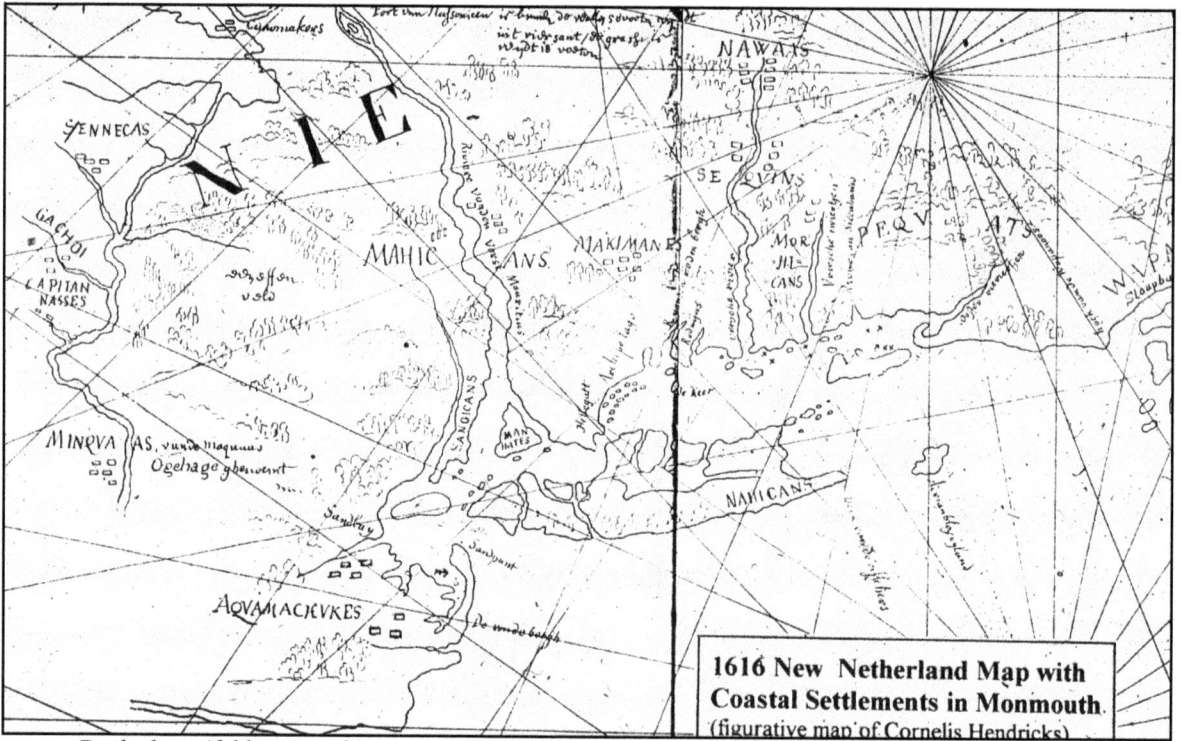

1616 New Netherland Map with Coastal Settlements in Monmouth. (figurative map of Cornelis Hendricks)

By the beautiful bay. *Part of the summertime amusement park that existed from 1915 to 1941, a long sandy beach stretched between Avenues A and D. Swimmers and sunners changed clothes in the "Pavilion" building's cubicles. Kiddies scampered and the unathletic lazed in the wide band of shallow bay water, while the more energetic took to the ladder-diving-sliding float farther offshore.*

Dedication

For Esther and Vic

THE
MAKING OF AMERICA
SERIES

ATLANTIC HIGHLANDS

FROM LENAPE CAMPS TO BAYSIDE TOWN

PAUL D. BOYD

ARCADIA
PUBLISHING

Published by Arcadia Publishing
Charleston, South Carolina

For all general information contact Arcadia Publishing at:
Telephone 843-853-2070
Fax 843-853-0044
E-Mail sales@arcadiapublishing.com
For customer service and orders:
Toll-Free 1-888-313-2665

Visit us on the Internet at www.arcadiapublishing.com

Front caption: This legendary house was the home of Thomas Henry Leonard, the first mayor of Atlantic Highlands, located on the west side of First Avenue between Center and Mount Avenues. He stands at the far right with his wife, Maria. From left are his daughters Marianna, Mabel, and Edith Maria; an unidentified woman; and Dr. Harry Hendrickson and his wife (the fourth daughter, Clara), who were given the house at their marriage in 1893. In 1900 they moved most of it to the northeast corner of Second and Mount Avenues. At its former location on First Avenue commercial buildings were erected known as the Homestead Block.

CONTENTS

ACKNOWLEDGMENTS

The institutional "parent" of this book project is the Atlantic Highlands Historical Society, which has long seen the need for a narrative town history of readable length. The society's archives are the main source of images in the book.

Local historians were vital fact sources. Prime among them is Thomas Henry Leonard. His 1923 book, *From Indian Trail to Electric Rail*, radiates enthusiastic town boosterism and is like the town attic: full of past details both essential and ephemeral. Others include antiquarian writers Hornor, Ellis, Salter and Beekman, and the instant historians of the *Atlantic Highlands Journal* back to the 1890s (see bibliography).

The Civil War narrative draws heavily on work by historian and Arcadia author John S. King, a fellow board member of the Atlantic Highlands Historical Society. John scoured every imaginable record of the conflict and its local participants and generously shared it.

Karl and Susan Brunig provided information on local World War I hero Paul Brunig, via former Mayor Michael Harmon of Atlantic Highlands and directly to the author.

The author's doctoral research on the Lenape, used in chapter one, was mentored by Herbert C. Kraft and Dr. Peter O. Wacker, who have both beautifully interpreted the lifeways of the past. Mary Ann Kiernan at the Monmouth County Archives patiently helped ferret out old deeds and other historic documents.

Randall Gabrielan provided many photographs, especially ones collected for but not published in his Atlantic Highlands *Images of America* book for Arcadia (see it for an additional visual feast). Scanning and producing compact discs of historic images used in this book's center section was done as a friendly contribution by Ray Clark, Jo-Ann Hunt, and Chris DuBarton.

Long-time residents gave hours of information and insight. The main oral historians were Rosemarie Kelly, John Phair, Ann Rosse, Shirley Thorne, and Alma and George Wuesthoff. Elyse Hudacsko Rosati helped analyze and map town growth via building records. Also drawn on was a paper legacy of highly credible notes and foolscap drafts, left in historical society archives by a team of interviewers-researchers that no one remembers, named Overholt, Thomas, White, and Haisser.

Lenape place names were translated by two scholars of Lenape language, James Rementer and Ray Whritenour, specialists in the Southern Unami and Northern Unami dialects, respectively.

Finally, every line of text and caption was reviewed, and edited or questioned where necessary, by veteran writer-editor and friend Victor Zak. Editors Jim Kempert and Rob Kangas at Arcadia Publishing were valuable readers and saw the manuscript through publishing in the form you now see.

INTRODUCTION

Atlantic Highlands: the name says exactly what it is geographically. The town overlooks where the Atlantic Ocean meets the bay at Sandy Hook, and its hills mark the highest point on the eastern seaboard. The town's sheltered bayside location and broad outlook have made it a focal point for the shoreline region, as well as a key meeting point during successive eras of its history.

For thousands of years, the original inhabitants lived along the cliffs and creeks and flatlands of the area, where we still find rich evidence of their fishing, hunting, cooking, and pathfinding. Here the Lenape people first encountered European explorers and then Dutch merchants who docked and traded in the 1600s. In a deed signed with Lenape chief Popamora, English settlers bought the peninsula between the ocean, the bay, and the Navesink River in 1664. They gave the name Portland Poynt to the first town laid out in the area, with ten long home lots taking up most of today's west side.

Colonists convened the first Assembly of New Jersey in Portland Poynt in 1667. Its meetings managed the affairs of three towns. Its leaders also rebelled against the land tax levied by the English colonial "proprietors" for several decades. Town residents and newcomers took up lands in a long westward stretch along the bayshore well beyond today's town boundaries.

During Revolutionary War years, loyalists to the English crown and patriots of the new America clashed in repeated raids and counterattacks across these lands. And here passed English troops after the 1778 Battle of Monmouth with General George Washington's army, heading to the royalist stronghold on Sandy Hook and to New York. In post-war decades, the inhabitants returned to the production and marketing of produce, fish, and logs.

A century later, the peaceful farms, woodlands, and waterfront met an onrush of resort developers, church groups, and town builders. They created the Victorian core of today's larger town, named it Bay View, and attracted thousands of visitors and year-round residents. In a tourist boom, three dozen hotels and boarding houses soon opened, along with bathing beaches and pavilions. Between 1879 and 1890, 153 houses were built, including elaborate "cottages" that climbed the hillside, with each level offering a bay view. Steamboats and the railroad came to town, which had become an independent borough and was renamed Atlantic Highlands.

In the 1900s, the town's ridges and bay edges looked out to a rising Manhattan skyline. In 1915 the town met its manifest destiny in two ways. It annexed a large area of highland hilltops and slopes called Navesink Park, where prime housing eventually was built. It was put on the map by a new bayfront amusement park that, fed by boats and trains and trolleys, drew crowds of fun-seekers every summer. During the Prohibition era of the 1920s, its coves hosted rumrunning—a lucrative, illegal business that was headquartered in a hillside lookout house. Starting with a small lagoon in the teens and then building a seawall, landfill, bulkhead, and piers project in the 1940s, the town became a key boating center on the Jersey shore, and parades of fishing, commuter, and pleasure boats sailed its waters.

Much of this overview has opened up to me because of my trustee and historian roles in the Atlantic Highlands Historical Society. From the two hilltop towers of its headquarters in the Strauss Mansion and Museum, the symbol of the town's Victorian core, the outlook is as wide as the town's outreach has long been in its region. The mansion windows watch over the rolling inland hills to the east and south, the long curve of the bayshore on the west, and the bay and the distant cityscape of New York on the north. In fact, the arbitrary, manmade boundaries of today's town were never the limit of its effective scope—not for the local Lenape who derived subsistence from dozens of square miles, or for the late-1600s English settlers who quickly outgrew their 80-acre village plat, or for the late-1700s militiamen, whaleboaters, and other citizens who were caught up in a Revolution waged across wider lands and waters. Exploring this expanded catchment area, this book tries to see Atlantic Highlands in its natural geographic and historical context, which transcends the 1.2 square miles belonging to the borough.

The book also debunks several long-told tales, bringing original research and new insights to bear on old myths. The Lenape were not summer visitors who came to the shore for summer sun and shellfish, as generations of students have been told; they were here as year-round residents, which in-ground and in-archive evidence demonstrates (chapter 1). The story that Portland Poynt did not thrive after the 1600s makes it seem that the settlement disappeared, not just the name; in fact, town families stayed and not only added larger crop and forage lands for themselves west of the village, but also were joined by dozens of new neighbors there (chapter 3). Some old-timers have said that African Americans came to the area after the Civil War and as servants in the Victorian mansions of the late 1800s; the truth is they were here from the 1690s and in increasing numbers, both free and enslaved, over the next two centuries (chapter 3). Finally, the classic town founding father tale portrays Thomas Henry Leonard as a selfless visionary in the 1870s and after, whereas close analysis reveals a more complex figure; his capitalism, churchliness, geocentrism, and sense of self-importance also were major driving forces of his accomplishments (chapter 7).

For the first time, complete or corrected accounts have been assembled from both new research and existing materials about six topics. First, Dutch involvement in the area was mainly for trading rather than colonization, but now receives full attention for what it actually was (chapter 2). Second, where exactly were the first ten lots laid out by the English settlers in 1667? Much misinterpretation and mystery has now been wiped out by a far-reaching analysis of every shred of evidence (chapter 3). Third, previous accounts make it seem that those settlers were all from Long Island, but they were also from Rhode Island and Barbados, which also has several other connections with Portland Poynt. Fourth, the central position of Many Mind Creek in our geography is no excuse for the abuse it has endured—getting dredged, channeled, straightened, neglected, dumped in, and bad-mouthed since the 1880s as now reported herein (chapter 8). Fifth, some of the silence and embarrassment about liquor bootlegging in the 1920s and the locals who engaged in it has rolled back with the passage of time. That story is now told more comprehensively than was possible before (chapter 8). Sixth, on a lighter note, the former bayside amusement park, source of fond childhood memories for local old-timers, can now be seen in its entirety as both a word picture and an aerial photo (chapter 8, illustration no. 46).

Though such improvements continue to be made, history-telling remains an inexact, even haphazard activity. What you discover and uncover is what you write about, but much remains buried. Interpretations depend on such qualifiers as "apparently" and "reportedly" when evidence is not conclusive. Personal narratives full of human drama and stories about the commanding sweep of social forces at work are only occasionally, with luck, part of the historian's tool kit. Still, it is a great pleasure to move forward through the eras and try to save the past for the future.

For the sake of those times to come, this is an appeal to those with historical materials and memories of important events, trends, and people left out of this account to make them available for preservation and use. Because, to adapt a proverb about protecting the earth:

"We have not inherited our history from our parents;
we have borrowed it from our children."

Chapter One

LENAPE CAMPS

Eight men propelled the long dugout canoe along the wooded shore of the bay, moving almost noiselessly except for the dip and swish of their paddles. In the hollowed out center of the canoe were coiled coarse-grass baskets lined with seaweed that contained their haul of shellfish from the morning. They had gone to the beds just offshore from Chingarora Creek to gather oysters by hand at the low tide, and now they were heading home.

The sun was more than halfway down the sky from its noontime high as they passed coastal clumps of reeds and sedge and glided into a small cove. They steered the canoe around a sand bar, where waterbirds were pecking at strands of washed up eelgrass and sea lettuce. In front of them was the mouth of the creek their people called Cupanickinu, meaning "obstructed stream." Today, its channel was free of clutter and blockage; it had been cleared the day before when a long downpour had been followed by an in-rushing storm tide and a downstream surge of rainwater from the steep hills to the east.

The men paddled upstream past the sandy beach, the dunes, and the broad saltmarsh behind them. They navigated several curves of the creek until the great chestnut tree trunk that had been carved into a canoe reached a gentle slope on the east bank. The boat slid on to the land and came to a stop at a campsite on the edge of a clearing. Women and children came out of several huts made from hickory sapling posts stuck in the ground and covered with bark from oak trees. The women took the baskets from the hull and carried them over to a flattened pile of blackened stones. The women laid the seaweed into holes in this hearth, while the men pounded the large oysters—as big as their feet—with the beaks of clamshells. When the oysters were cracked open, they were laid into the hearth-holes and fires were lit on top to roast the catch.

The scene is a "shellfish restaurant" along Many Mind Creek, one of the cooking and eating places used by the Lenape people living on the peninsula bounded by Sandy Hook Bay, the Atlantic Ocean, and the Navesink River. After consuming the meat of the oysters, or on other days from clams, the shells were discarded on the land in gradually accumulating layers or mounds that archaeologists dug up centuries later. Such shell middens, as they're called, have been found in Atlantic Highlands. One specific location, as described above, was about 400 feet from today's bayshore edge, along the bank of Many Mind Creek in the stretch between Bay and Center Avenues. There, the creek's original west bank had a boomerang-shaped curve until a drainage project in the 1920s straightened its course and uncovered the shell middens on the former east bank. The area was raised in elevation by deposits of landfill and then covered with expanses of blacktop to make parking lots for two apartment houses that were built there.

The shell midden at Many Mind Creek is only one of 93 mounds, piles, or heaps of shells deposited by Native Americans over the centuries along the coasts of Raritan Bay and Sandy Hook Bay and the New Jersey shores of the Atlantic Ocean. Sixteen of these deposits are on the New Jersey side of the bay, and 13 more are on the Staten Island side.

Commuters, Not Nomads

There is a long-held belief that the shells at these many sites were mainly discarded by large numbers of Native Americans from the interior, who supposedly visited the coast each summer to feast on shellfish, swim in the ocean, and sunbathe just like modern tourists. Tradition has it that they hiked to the shore from year-round habitations as far as Trenton, eastern Pennsylvania, and the upper Delaware Valley (a seven-day walk)—and also that Mohawk Indians traveled there from upper New York state. As the warm months waned, the visitors reportedly headed back to their inland homes, carrying dried shellfish for winter consumption. Why would they make such long round-trips when, back at home, plenty of freshwater shellfish with similar nutritional value were available and eaten by them? If they did go to the seashore and bring home shellfish, why is there no evidence of marine shells in inland areas?

Underlying the tale is the idea that the bay and ocean coastal areas of New Jersey had a mostly temporary summer population and few if any permanent Lenape residents. In colonial times, the white settlers saw that the Lenape did not practice European-style land ownership, build houses, fence fields, keep livestock, or have other settled-residence behaviors. They described Lenape life as highly transient and nomadic, the population as small, scattered, and little identified with any kind of home territories. Whether caused by ethnocentric "blinders" or by limited observations, such an empty-land interpretation also suited the territorial ambitions of colonists.

Through varying versions over time, the trek tale has survived. Today it is still taught in some schools, included in new books, and reported in the media. It has been so often repeated and so nearly ritualized that it lives in the realm of folklore, where familiarity takes over from fact and frequency of telling becomes its own source of truth.

It is bunk. There are no eyewitness accounts by the 15 authors who wrote about the area between 1625 and the 1740s when most Lenape had left New Jersey. In the early 1900s, the tale was credited to unnamed "early authorities," a "persistent tradition among many descendants of early settlers of New Jersey," and the stories told by "gran'daddies"—in other words, hand-me-down oral transmission. Almost all the historians and archaeologists specializing in the Lenape omit the trek altogether from their writings, claim it has no factual basis, or provide contrary evidence. Even the first writer to describe a summer trek—a local historian named Charles D. Deshler, in an 1880 speech in New Brunswick, New Jersey—admitted he was fictionalizing: "We may indulge the fancy that this [Minisink] Path was devised to enable the 'upper ten' among the aborigines to enjoy 'the season' at Long Branch, and to "lay up stores of shells and fish." He was projecting the seasonal behaviors of an American beachgoing elite (the "upper ten" percent of the population) of the late 1800s on to Indians of the 1600s and before. Many later writers simplistically claimed that, since there were shell piles along the coast and there were trails and paths running from far inland to the shore, the shells had to have been deposited by people who traveled from inland.

Contradicting the empty land idea, the coastal zones in Monmouth County have strong evidence of year-round habitation by fair numbers of Lenape people who were hunting, fishing, cooking, and eating along the shores of their own homelands. The evidence comes from many sources: archaeological studies and amateur collectors' finds, historical accounts by European writers, oral histories of the Lenape themselves, deeds from Lenape land sales, information about trail and path networks, and geographical place names. There was even an early map of the coastal zone, made by Dutch explorer Adriaen Block in 1614, that shows three settlements or villages in the form of rectangles above the Navesink River. The combined weight of these data, which have been analyzed and correlated by the author for his doctoral dissertation at Rutgers University, requires that the trek tale be relegated to a file labeled "charming fables of questionable validity."

The ancestors and descendants of the people who roasted and ate shellfish along the bank of Many Mind Creek lived in the northeastern coastal corner of New Jersey for thousands of years before Europeans arrived. The first Americans reached the mid-Atlantic coast about 12,000 years ago. Evidence of Native Americans in Monmouth County is 11,000 years old, and the Atlantic Highlands area has artifacts dated to 8,000 years ago.

The native people on the Navesink peninsula, themselves known as the Navesink band of the Lenape, survived and thrived by adopting a number of strategies. An understanding of how they lived their lives and how they made their livelihoods can be gained by looking at different types of evidence from their times that have been found in and around Atlantic Highlands. They were dependent on a wide range of resources, all of which they had to obtain by their own efforts. Since no area as small as the 1.2 square miles of today's Atlantic Highlands could possibly contain everything needed for survival, they had to travel and scout over a fairly broad territory. In fact, according to two authorities, the defined hunting territory regularly used by an extended family of Lenape people could be as large as 200 square miles.

Theirs was a purposeful search, undertaken not as wandering nomads (the stereotypical image), but as commuters with regular, selected destinations. They went to known sites—where resources they needed were located, and when it was the right season. In effect, the Navesinks and other Lenape bands had to maintain an unwritten catalog and mental map of their resources for living.

For fishing, this meant going to the estuaries when the shad began their spring runs from the ocean and bay and up the coastal streams; knowing where in the bay they could take a harvest from clam beds; and going to the Chingarora offshore reef (today's Union Beach) or the eastern end of the Navesink River when the oysters were mature. After spring migration was the time for snagging waterbirds in marshlands. They hunted deer during winter in deep protected hollows where they gathered (called "yarding"), like the one between Sears/ Washington Avenues and East Highland Avenue in Atlantic Highlands; here, the deer were sheltered against northern winter winds off the bay, and provided with acorns to eat in the forest and drinking water in the spring-fed creek. The rest of the year the Lenape went after deer at browsing grounds on woodland edges and clearings, and year-round they made ingenious use of all deer parts for many subsistence needs.

For health needs, they spotted where to find sumac plants, whose roots they boiled for a tea to control dysentery, and berries that they made into a sore throat gargle, and plantain that helped fight inflammations. They had to be alert to the times and places for the growth of edible wild plants in the meadows, woods, and swamps. In the woods, they noted where trees with acorns and other edible nuts were located. They took fresh water from nearby hillside springs, such as the "spout" (today called Henry Hudson Springs), but also remembered sources for getting drinks elsewhere on their regular routes. Where good local clays were available was another point, since pottery was important for cooking, food storage, and water transport. They made special, far-ranging reconnaissance for sources of stone that would withstand chipping and pecking into tools and projectile points, since local "peanut stone" was too brittle and local ironstone too dense to reshape. And they blazed trails and navigated by canoe far and wide in order to procure raw materials available elsewhere, to trade for needed commodities produced by other native bands, and to make social connections and political alliances.

Shellfish, Stone Tools, and Hunting Gear

Unfortunately, the shell midden that surfaced along Many Mind Creek near the bay was not studied in any way before being buried by landfill and covered over with macadam. This happened in the days before laws were passed to protect our archaeological heritage, at the least by retrieving all possible data on prehistoric and historic sites threatened by construction. If the Many Mind Creek midden were discovered today, many revealing studies could be done, thanks to advances in scientific research techniques. For example, analysis of radiocarbon in charcoal from the cooking hearth could determine when the site was used. Also, shell growth can be analyzed to determine the season of harvest. Such studies have shown that the Lenape were present and consuming shellfish all year long, clearly challenging the assumption in the trek tale that they were only harvested in the summer.

Near the junction of Wagner Creek and Bowne Creek abutting today's western border of Atlantic Highlands was a second local shell site. Here a house was built in the 1660s by James Bowne, an original European settler in Portland Poynt and the "Indian interpreter" for early land sale deeds. In the mid-1900s, many shells surfaced on the slope between the house and the creeks, suggesting that local Lenape also held shellfish feasts here. In addition, the immediate area of the house yielded 18 projectile points or arrowheads and some stone tools.

In the area surrounding Atlantic Highlands, the eastern end of the Navesink River near the ocean has long had extensive oyster and clam beds. In the 1890s, George H. Fountain located a "great number of Indian shell heaps" on the banks of gullies and ravines opening into tributaries on the river's northern bank. He found four holes lined with seaweed and filled with shells in compact masses. One hole contained oyster, hard-shell clam, mussel, and bay scallop shells, all showing fire marks. Under them was a skeleton, buried two feet, three inches down, on its right side with legs drawn. The other holes contained oyster shells up to 10 and 11 inches long. They also included fragments of clay pipes, several bone tools, and a pottery fragment made from native clay and ornamented with a "basket" design. The assemblage lends itself to an interpretation that a burial ceremony and feast took place there. Based on the pottery, this site probably dates to between 1000 and 1600 A.D. Pottery also means at least semi-sedentary living, as required by the logistics of ceramics manufacture and the relatively fragile nature of clay pots.

Another large shell deposit was found before the 1970s on the Hartshorne estate along the Navesink River north bank by Godfrey Horn, an amateur archaeologist who was born in and lived in Atlantic Highlands (illustration no. 6). Owned by the Hartshorne family since the 1670s, these lands were largely undisturbed for centuries; even today, over 700 acres remain natural lands as part of the county-owned Hartshorne Woods park. Here, beyond the Atlantic Highlands border, Horn found a kitchen midden or "camping and dining place" of the Lenape, with "vast mounds of clam, oyster and other shells." This is a south-facing slope, apparently preferred for Lenape settlement since it provided protection from the northeast wind.

Above the Clay Pit Creek estuary, in the hamlet of Navesink, Fred Romenko bulldozed land in 1962 and uncovered five-foot-thick deposits of shells at several locations. It made the land "absolutely white," he said. Discarded over many years, the shellfish would have been brought by canoe from oyster beds in the Navesink River. Or, Romenko believes, the Lenape could have brought shellfish there by canoe from Sandy Hook Bay about 1.5 miles to the northwest. In fact, some old maps show a water passageway from the bay, via Many Mind Creek at Sears Avenue, and across low land there to Clay Pit Creek; the area linking the two creeks contains evidence of oyster shell beds, river bottom, and tidal flow, suggesting this connection once existed.

Continuing westward, there were seven shell sites between Union Beach and Cliffwood in a wide arc circling around the bay indentation formed by the mouths of the Chingarora, Luppatatong, and Matawan Creeks (all Lenape names). The one at Conaskonk Point (another Lenape name), which was carefully investigated by professional archaeologist Charles Rau in 1863, contained not only oyster and clam shells, but also pottery, stone knives, axes, arrowheads, and many other implements. Based on the pottery, the site was used sometime in the Woodland period between 400 and 3,000 years ago.

When they found suitable raw materials, the Navesink people chipped, pecked, and flint-knapped stones to make a large variety of tools and weapons for specific roles in hunting, fishing, and food processing. Stone artifacts they created, since found and identified, include projectile points or arrowheads, broadspears, netsinkers, mortars and pestles, mullers and grinding stones, choppers, anvil stones and hammerstones, knives and scrapers, drills, axes, nutting stones, etc.

Two sites along Many Mind Creek have yielded stone artifacts of Lenape manufacture. One site, as shown by an axehead found there, was in use between 4,000 and 6,000 years ago, in a period that archaeologists call the Late Archaic. The Lenape fitted a wooden handle to this type of stone axehead, binding them together by sinew or rawhide that was wrapped around a groove in the stone. But the groove on this axehead went only three-quarters of the way around it—a modification made in the Late Archaic so that a piece of wood could be wedged in on the ungrooved flat side to tighten the fit of the handle. This is the only Lenape artifact found inside Atlantic Highlands that yields information on dating.

In the 1970s, an archaeologist and two collectors and analysts of Lenape artifacts found some east of Many Mind Creek near Lincoln Avenue. The New Jersey State Museum officially listed their findings as site "28MO73."

Farther east in the borough are two sites where stone artifacts have also been discovered. At the spot now called Henry Hudson Spring, a find of two projectile points or arrowheads was reported in 1978 by Michael Gimigliano, a professional archaeologist. It's not surprising to find arrowheads at this spot whose ample fresh-water supplies drew Lenape for frequent visits. It also was, and still is, a location for animals and birds to obtain water, especially the many birds who migrate on the saltwater routes of the Atlantic coastal flyway. One can easily picture an Indian coming there with a bow and arrows in a quiver, finding edible wildlife present, and letting loose with the well-aimed shots of an everyday hunter.

Also in the eastern part of the borough, Ocean Boulevard—bounded by very steep slopes at Point Lookout—is carried across what old-time locals call "Landslide Bridge." A first span was built on pilings here after 1920 when a tremendous piece of the cliff fell to the shore below with a noise so loud it was heard all around. The marl soil here is very slippery, rich in fossils, and held many arrowheads that were collected in the 1960s. Also on this slope were found natural geodes called "paint cups." Using pebbles, the Lenape ground them to a cup shape and mixed the powdered mineral pigment or ocher with water or animal grease to make red body paint. Red was a favorite color for ceremonial and other paint uses by the Lenape (see box).

South of Atlantic Highlands in the Clay Pit Creek area, a major collection of projectile points, 44 in all, was gathered by a student group led by local artist and resident Travers Neidlinger. Included was a Lackawaxen type point, which dates to the Late Archaic period 4,000 to 6,000 years ago. They also found debitage left from chipping stones to make points.

West of Atlantic Highlands, in neighboring Leonardo, the farms of the Leonard family produced large crops of asparagus in the 1800s, and many projectile points or arrowheads surfaced in those fields during cultivation.

A farmer named Martin Matula had fields in Belford and Navesink at different times from the 1920s–1960s, and in both places his plows often turned up stone artifacts. Among the more than 100 items he retained were numerous projectile points in varied styles, as well as a sinew stone, scraper, pestle, chisel, celt, and axes—all now exhibited in the Strauss Mansion "Lenape Room" in Atlantic Highlands. Significantly, the point types that were diagnostic of specific periods ranged from 2,000 to 8,000 years in age.

Camps, Pots, and Burials

No pottery has been unearthed within the borders of Atlantic Highlands, but there have been significant finds of pottery mixed with other artifacts in camp-size settlements along Compton's Creek and Ware Creek in nearby Belford. The presence of pottery means a site was used after 1000 B.C. in the so-called Woodland period

A small hunting-gathering camp is the archaeologists' interpretation of the

Uses of Red Paint

For various social and ceremonial events, a common practice was to paint the entire head and face red with some black dots, or one side red and the other black, or only the central part along the crown of the head.

In the 12-day Big House ceremony, attendants painted everyone with red paint (*olàmàn* in the Lenape language). They also painted the drum and drumsticks used in the ceremonies and the right half of the carved Mësingw faces mounted on the walls and centerpost of the House (Mësingw is the guardian spirit of the game animals); the left half of the faces were painted black.

In Lenape funerals, the face of the deceased was painted with *olàmàn* so that when he stood before the Creator he would be recognized as a true Lenape. For a woman, a spot the size of a nickel was dotted on each cheek; for a man three lines were drawn from the outer side of the eye back almost to the hairline. During the funeral, red paint was applied to a notch cut into the head end of the coffin as a means for the soul to come to and leave the body.

When wooden grave markers were used, they were painted with *olàmàn* to help the deceased find the way to the afterlife. Since it served as a mark of passage for the dead, red face paint used for the Big House ceremony had to be removed by people before going to sleep so that the "spirits of the departed" would not try to take them into the other world.

Compton Creek site, where pottery sherds as well as stone tools and a cooking site were found (28MO272). Ronald Mason from Atlantic Highlands located ceramic pieces that had been impressed with a net design before drying. Some undecorated ceramics were recently dated to around 100 A.D. by measuring the radioactivity in grains of the potter's clay using thermoluminescence methods. Adjacent to the camp was rock that had been cracked from the heat of cooking fires, and flakes of jasper and other stone materials left from making arrowheads. The significance of jasper is that this stone does not exist locally and had to be imported from eastern Pennsylvania, indicating a long-distance procurement or trading effort.

The largest discovery in the bayshore area was 50 pot sherds in another camp in Belford, in lowlands between Ware Creek and Shoal Harbor. Curated by Travers Neidlinger, these ceramic pieces had been impressed, incised, or stamped with a sort of herringbone pattern in a style named Bowman's Brook. The same site also contained 43 projectile points, some of which date to between 1,100 and 4,000 years ago. Included were points called Susquehanna Broadspears, which were used as harpoons for spearing large fish, and two triangular jasper points. The site also contained such tools as a drill, knives, celts, axes, bannerstone, and scrapers. Along the same creek in Belford was a large prehistoric site near its headwaters, as reported by several sources.

In Port Monmouth's former Lorillard Farm, numerous finds by the Montenat brothers included 13 pot sherds as well as 170 projectile points, numerous knives, scrapers and drills, a couple of spear points and celts, and the stem of an Indian pipe (often smoked during ceremonies and negotiations)—all stored in the New Jersey State Museum.

The presence of burials in an area suggests that Lenape people had more than a transitory association with the land. Burials usually took place near a settlement site, but only rarely was a special tract set aside for multiple burials like in European cemeteries. An apparent exception is an Indian burial ground, still identified as such and unbuilt, in the Fair View section of Middletown.

In coastal areas, some burials were made in beds of shells. The shells perhaps had some special use in burial ceremonies, represented "food" for use in the journey of the deceased, or helped stabilize burial sites that were marshy or subject to coastal flooding.

Starting in 1897, three burial sites were found in the Navesink hamlet/Clay Pit Creek area. The earliest site was the one discovered by George Fountain, with a skeleton buried under shells, as described earlier. The other two burials were a skeleton that was dug up when a road was being excavated for a sewer installation, and a human skull found when digging the foundation for a cold-frame in the early 1900s on land that became the Bridle & Latham florist property.

In neighboring Leonardo is "Old Woman Hill," reportedly the grave site of a Lenape woman sometime before the Revolutionary War. One story is that she was killed by white men and buried by Indians who placed stones on the grave and added more whenever they passed. Another version is that she was the wife of an Indian sachem or chief and died during a spring migration along the Minisink Trail that goes to Navesink. The grave, now inside the Earle Naval Weapons Station, is a short way downhill from that trail, which became King's Highway. Marking a grave with a cairn—a pile of stones—was a fairly common Native-American custom. It provided a route marker and a place to meditate along a trail used for seasonal migration, sacred pilgrimage, or resource gathering. Passing travelers said prayers, added more rock for good luck, and showed respect for ancestors in the belief that cairns contain the essence of their elders.

Reinforcing the fact that the Lenape had a number of lasting settlements in the area, there is information on 27 of their burial sites in Monmouth County, including 14 sites with multiple burials. The largest concentration of burials so far reported was at Red Bank, which had six burials at three nearby sites.

Also indicating lasting settlements, post molds have recently been discovered at three sites in Monmouth County. These are circular spots in the ground where posts were driven into the ground as the framework for a residential structure, such as a wickiup (a three-sided shelter) or a wigwam (a round structure with a door and a smoke-hole in the roof). The locations are at the Monmouth Battlefield site in Manalapan, near the Navesink River in Little Silver, and overlooking Timber Swamp Brook in western Howell Township.

Inevitably, of course, reports of archaeological finds can tell only a small part of the story about how the Lenape lived in past centuries and millennia in any section of their territory. Still hidden away in unexcavated lands are many additional artifacts and features that have not yet come to light, and may never do so, given the entirely random way in which archaeologists are brought to a site. Other forms of "digging" in archives in order to study place names, trails and paths, maps, deeds, histories, tribal tales, and other records also contribute valuable data.

Naming the Lands and Waters

> A creek engulfed by mists. A crooked river. A very sandy place. A clay
> trail. A village with rabbits. A place you can see from afar.

These evocative images come from names the Lenape gave to some places in the Atlantic Highlands area before the Europeans arrived. Those names are among 106 former and current Lenape place names in Monmouth County that the author has identified through research in deeds, town records, colonial documents, and published histories back to the 1600s. The sheer number of these place names suggests a more dense pattern of land use and settlement than had previously been assumed in most studies of Lenape life and locations.

When translated, the place names provide solid information about characteristic features and natural resources of these locations that had value for the Lenape. That is why, for the author's doctoral dissertation, suggested translations have now been developed in team work by two scholars of Lenape language: James Rementer and Ray Whritenour, specialists in the Southern Unami and Northern Unami dialects, respectively. They succeeded in interpreting 81 of the Monmouth County place names.

The act of naming has to reflect some type of attachment to the places by the Lenape name-givers of the time. Among the reasons for affixing a name label were to recall these places as locations for lasting settlements or repeated stays, procurement sites for needed resources (fish and wildlife, plants, wood, water, stone for weapons and tools), places with notable physical characteristics (topography, hydrography, vegetation, etc.), guidance or landmarks for navigation of waterways and for wayfinding on land, and as sites for ceremonial, ritual, or sacred events or materials used in such events, in a few special cases.

Lenape settlements were often located near bodies of water, which served as means of canoe transport, sources of fish, and locales for hunting water-fowl and water-seeking animals. Because of this close association, the Lenape often named the waters; usually aptly describing hydrological, physical, or geographical characteristics. The same name might apply to the Lenape settlement itself, the surrounding land area, or the local band of Lenape people.

Nine of the place names now catalogued for Monmouth County are from a map (illustration no. 5) covering 35 square miles that accompanied the land sale deed signed by the Lenape and arriving Europeans on March 25, 1664. The map and deed covered the entire Navesink peninsula, stretching east-west from the oceanfront to Keansburg and western Middletown, and north-south from the bay to the Navesink River.

The most used local name is *Navesink*, shown by an oval on the map as Navesant at the oceanside overlook from the Navesink Highlands hills. It's also the name of a river, a village, and the local Lenape band that inhabited a wide swath of Monmouth County and neighboring areas. Forty variant spellings were shown in 1996 to the then oldest living native speaker of Lenape, Lucy Parks Blalock in Oklahoma, who had never visited New Jersey or studied its map. At once, she selected Newasink as authentic and said it means "place you can see from afar." This matches the coastal prominence of the Navesink Highlands, which early sailors anglicized to Neversink because it seems to never sink from view as seen from the ocean.

The hamlet of Navesink, neighboring the Navesink River on one side and Atlantic Highlands on the other, was the site of two other Lenape place names. The village of *Usquaanunk* at the head of the Clay Pit Creek estuary translates as "place of the clay trail, muddy stream, or muddy place." This was a point on the Lenape's long-distance Minisink-to-Navesink trail, and the soil is very clayey. Clay Pit Creek is named *Paskahunge*, indicating "divided shallows" or a blocked place on a stream. The creek today is still very shallow, with mud flats showing at low tide and divides into two branches at the estuary consistent with the Lenape meaning of its name.

Many Mind Creek in today's Atlantic Highlands is *Cupanickinu*. Its interpretation, "obstructed stream," may refer to logs, debris, or sediment blocking its channel, a sedge island or sand bar across the creek mouth, or reeds and bank-side vegetation making creek access difficult from land and vice versa. The widened lake-like channel inland on the map may represent the formerly swampy area between today's South Avenue and Jackson Bridge behind Foodtown.

Another creek flowing into the bay farther west is Compton's Creek in Belford. On the 1664 map it is labeled Cowwarranisland. The root word *Cowwarran* is probably a corruption of Corrawa Brook, which appears in later deeds and means "it mists, smokes, is damp." Salt marshes there are definitely damp, and mists roll in from the ocean and bay and hover above the low coastal lands.

Racko Rumwaham is the name of Sandy Hook on the map, and next to it is the word "beach" in English. Racko, a variant of *lekau* in Lenape, means sand, but linguists could not translate *Rumwaham*.

Among the other names is a Lenape village named *Shaquasit*, shown as a circle on the map and later spelled *Cháquasitt*. It's today's historic old Middletown center. A recent upscale subdivision along Kings Highway East was sign-posted as Cháquasitt, together with the supposed translation "land of paradise" (helpful for marketing). The correct, more mundane meaning found by the Lenape linguists is "short foot" from *tschachkw-sit*. This may refer to short-footed rabbits, raccoons, opossums, or other small animals that offered meat and fur supplies.

Trails and Paths

Long before European settlers came to these shores, the Lenape had created a well-ordered system of trails and paths. These crisscrossed the Lenape territory in all directions, with so many inter-connecting routes that the Indians' travel network was almost as complete as today's road maps. In addition to following routes that animals had trampled, the Lenape had multiple reasons for creating their own trails, pathways, local branches, and tributary routes leading to resources needed for subsistence. Each settlement had its own universe of local procurement places for daily survival and seasonal needs, as well as special purposes.

For various purposes the Lenape also needed land connections between major villages in a wider district or region. These trail links allowed for exchange of raw materials and goods, procurement of special, locally unavailable resources such as jasper, mating beyond the immediate clan and related local bands, consultations for mutual definition of hunting territories, and conflicts or negotiations with more distant groups. These trails were usually segments in long-distance routes. Many existing Lenape trails came into use by European settlers and were eventually transformed into horse paths, carriage roads, and modern streets or highways.

One such route in the Atlantic Highlands area was the eastern end of the Minisink-to-Navesink Trail. It exists today as Linden and Navesink Avenues, Hartshorne Road, Monmouth Avenue, and King's Highway, and passes such well-known local landmarks as the Stone Church and the red corner store. From this area the trail ran northwest through New Jersey, reaching Minisink 75 miles away, near the corner where New Jersey, Pennsylvania, and New York come together. Where the trail crossed the Middletown village center of today was a major switching point for Lenape trails in the region. There were three long-distance trails: the Minisink-Navesink Trail's coastal branch coming in from the northwest, the inland branch from the west, and the Burlington Trail from the southwest. Also three shorter trails were there, heading for the coast: the Waackaack Trail going north to today's Keansburg, the Shoal Harbor Trail northeast to today's Belford, and the continuing Minisink-Navesink Trail going to the Navesink Highlands along the ridge facing Sandy Hook Bay and ending at the Atlantic coast.

The trail to and from the Navesink Highlands was a fairly straight route as shown on the simplistic Lenape-English land deed map in 1664 (illustration no. 5), though in reality it had many curves and turns. It went along today's King's Highway/Monmouth Avenue until it reached the head of the Clay Pit Creek three miles short of the Atlantic Ocean. From that point, it branched out three ways to the coast.

One was to turn northeast and climb today's Navesink Avenue to the hilltop, and then down today's Linden Avenue to the bay. This route, as well as other local paths, were attractive because they lead to the calm waters of the bay that are protected from ocean storms and provide rich oyster, clam, and fish resources.

Another ran along the Navesink River north bank to the ocean. Numerous archaeological finds there suggest significant use of this riverside route, which led to the valued shellfish resources in the river mouth, as well as to the ocean. Until 1778 there was a land connection from the river bank to Sandy Hook and the shorefront.

A final way went halfway along the riverside route before turning uphill and ending at the coastal outlook plateau of Rocky Point. This peninsula tip at the corner of the ocean, bay, and Navesink River has an amazing overview of "the Great Waters," one of the Lenape terms of awe and respect for the Atlantic Ocean.

In addition to this mainly east-west trail and its branches, other shorter north-south paths transected the narrow Navesink peninsula, connecting the ridge-top Minisink-Navesink route with bayshore and river-edge locations. Such spurs leading to Keansburg and Belford are documented by old deeds, maps, and historical accounts. Other local routes would have gone down to the bayshore at such landing places as the cove at the mouth of Many Mind Creek and the end of Avenue D. There were trails to the three springs used by Indians and colonists alike: one at today's Henry Hudson Springs by the bay, another near the southwest corner of Ocean Boulevard and Grand Avenue, and a third at the headwaters of Many Mind Creek in the deep hollow north of Sears and Washington Avenues.

The path along Many Mind Creek would have crossed the peninsula, heading south to the Lenape village of Usquaanunk at today's hamlet of Navesink, to its valuable resources of clay and marsh life, and to the shellfish beds in its neighboring river. The road that became Avenue D appears on the earliest maps white men made in the area, probably adopting a Lenape route; the same is true for its southward continuation, Portland Road, which rises to an intersection with the Lenape trail that became King's Highway. The path to the spout may have continued along the beachfront westward to the fossil bank and paint-pot site below today's Landslide Bridge. And it's likely that another path destination was the top of Mount Mitchill because of its beautiful, strategic overview to the bay and ocean.

Land Sale Deeds

A wealth of information about Lenape locations comes from land sale deeds. The author has collected and analyzed 70 of them that were signed in Monmouth County by Indians and Europeans between 1650 and 1743. As discussed above, they often contain the Lenape names of districts, chiefdoms, villages, fields, streams, and other locations. They also describe Lenape trail segments as boundary markers for properties being conveyed. Among the villages of the Navesink band thus identified in northeastern Monmouth County were Cháquassit (Middletown's old village center), Usquaanunk (today's hamlet of Navesink), and Ramezing.

Ramezing seems to have been the central place of the entire district of the Navesink people, including the bayshore region from Sandy Hook to as far west as today's Laurence Harbor. Ramezing or variants of the name are mentioned in no less than eleven deeds, including ones that call it a "town." Its importance is also seen in old historical accounts back to 1663 and in modern archaeological studies of the site. It was located about 2.5 miles southwest of Red Bank, where four waterways come together (Swimming River, Hop River, Yellow Brook, and Pine Brook). Evidence from a cluster of seven registered archaeological sites and other sources shows its domestic settlement area extended about a half-mile from east to west; there were also shell middens, at least two toolmaking areas, an "Indian field" for crops, and four related camps for hunting and gathering forays, work on tools related to these activities, and some initial food processing. Five long-distance Lenape trails are in the immediately surrounding district, and two of them go through the town's activity areas. The site appears to have been occupied continuously or repeatedly from 6,000 years ago until the late 1600s (between the Late Archaic and Late Woodland periods as designated by archaeologists). This body of evidence far outweighs what is known about *Cháquasitt* and *Usquaanunk*, which were much smaller settlements.

That people in the Atlantic Highlands area and the wider Navesink peninsula were in Ramezing's zone of influence is clear from the role of the key "sachem of Ramezing"—the chief named Popamora. He was the principal signatory of the first deed signed with the

English settlers conveying the Navesink peninsula in 1664. This indicates that he exercised political and physical control of that land on behalf of the native inhabitants, or at least was the spokesman for their collective decision. He went on to sign still more deeds, until he had more deeds over more years than any other chief—15 of them during 17 years. Associated with him in the 15 deeds were ten other sachems, more than joined with any other Lenape signatory. On eight deeds his name came first on the list, indicating seniority in years or rank and occurring more than for any other sachem.

The Atlantic Highlands area was part of the district falling within the realm of Ramezing and its chief Popamora, and its main economic role was probably as a site for hunting-gathering camps and for fishermen launching into the bay. More important, high elevations and outlook platforms of the Navesink Highlands hills may also have served as a space for community gatherings, annual ceremonies, seasonal celebrations, native councils, or even sacred rituals. Exploring that possibility requires a look into the oral history of the Lenape people.

Oral History

Many specific details about the arrival of Henry Hudson's ship, the *Half Moon*, give evidence of a strong and lasting presence of Lenape people in this area at the time. On September 2, 1609, the ship was off the New Jersey coast of the Atlantic Ocean, heading north toward the Navesink Highlands peninsula. That night, officer Robert Juet wrote in his journal, "we saw a great fire" in the "high hills." The only topography matching that description along the entire flat New Jersey ocean shore is the Navesink Highlands; in fact, its topmost elevation of 272 feet at Mount Mitchill in Atlantic Highlands is the highest point on the Eastern seaboard. Beyond that oft-told story about the whites arriving, it is essential to see the event from the standpoint of the histories and traditions of the Lenape people.

They had enormous reverence for the great ocean, which added to the importance of the *Half Moon*'s arrival on its waters. The ocean has a significant presence in a number of narratives and events that are recounted in Lenape oral history, for example: the creation of the earth out of the ocean, the formation of the North American continent from the ocean, and the origin of the Lenape people from the ocean. At the most basic level, the ocean contributed to the daily subsistence and ultimate survival of the Lenape.

The various names given to the ocean by the Lenape suggest—not surprisingly even today—that their thinking about it was inspired by respect and full of awe. The main reasons for this are its size, tidal movement, and saltiness, and the sun's daily emergence over the water. Among their names for it, as translated into English, are the Big Water, the Great Waters, the Eastern Tide Water, the Great Salt Water Lake, and the Big Water Where the Daylight Appears.

There is also an element of the spiritual and the sacred in the ocean as seen by the Lenape. In their tradition, the Great Creator (*Kishëlemukòng*) is helped by a number of spirit beings (*manëtuwàk*) in managing affairs in the world and everyday issues of survival. One such being watches over the east and the ocean, and is called "Our Grandfather where the daylight begins" (*Mùxumsa Wehènjiopangw*). It is even possible that the Lenape defined key points along the coast as sacred spaces because they are physically impressive locations, face one of the cardinal directions, have a view to the east and the first rays of daylight, and serve as religious "portals" to the world beyond. Sites for the spiritual vision quest that Lenape and other Native American young men traditionally undertook were often on precipices with panoramic 360-degree views—a description not far off from fitting the Navesink Highlands coastal outlook.

Based on their traditions and needs, the Lenape people could have had several possible purposes for setting a fire on these hills in 1609: to drive deer and other game into a circle of waiting hunters; to burn off vegetation in preparation for planting crops; to generate warmth on a chilly night in early September; or to accompany and illuminate a community ceremony.

A more specific interpretation is that they were having a very special ceremony and had especially built a fire in preparation for a feast and entertainment to mark the arrival of the *Half Moon*. According to Lenape oral tradition, some coastal Lenape spotted on the horizon what appeared to be "a huge bird with white wings" (sails), "an uncommonly large fish or a huge canoe," or "a very big house floating on the sea." Nearby chiefs and people were summoned to come and see this ship of awesome size. They thought it must be the house of the Great Spirit and Creator, *Kishelëmukòng*, who was coming to pay a visit. So they prepared a great celebration with "the best of foods, meat was brought for sacrifice, and arrangements were made for a dance and for entertainment"—preparations that would normally include a large fire.

The highest eastward point in these hills, which is closest to the *Half Moon*'s approach and the first promontory visible from the south, is today called Rocky Point. Here, on a bluff-top gently sloping from 220 feet above sea level toward steep eastern and southern cliffs, is where the fire was most likely built and the ceremony prepared. Overlooking the Navesink River, Sandy Hook, and the ocean, it stands above a vast seascape and varied landscape. The panorama from this point had to have special impact for the Lenape, as it does for anyone who sees it today.

Whatever its purpose, the fire on the Navesink Highlands clearly signalled that people were living there. From these heights, they could see the great masted ship far down the ocean shore as it sailed northward, and then as it rounded the Hook, and finally on September 4, as it put down anchor in the bay. Juet's journal says that on September 5 the ship was brought in "hard by the souther shoare" of Sandy Hook Bay, and crew members "went on land" and "saw great store of Men, Women and Children". They climbed up into the woods, with its "great store of very goodly Oakes."

Most significant, on the hilltop the crew members were taken to "the great council house or house of worship" of the Lenape where they offered the Lenape some cups of liquor to drink. The existence of a council house on top of the Navesink Highlands would be consistent with its location as the ocean-side ending of the Minisink-to-Navesink Trail; the trail was the route to a gathering point for people from around the district. Its existence could also explain why, even 55 years later when the Lenape sold the entire peninsula to arriving English settlers, they held back or reserved a tract in the Navesink Highlands and stayed there for 14 more years. In fact, a total of 106 years would pass between Hudson's 1609 visit and the last historical evidence of Lenape activity in the area in 1715 (see box on next page).

Also, virulent diseases brought in by Europeans killed off many Lenape who had never been exposed to such illnesses and had no natural immunity to them. They suffered high mortality from measles, smallpox, typhus, venereal diseases, malaria, influenza, tuberculosis, and other respiratory diseases. One observer wrote that not one-tenth or even one-thirtieth of their 1609 population was alive in 1679. Records show at least 14 disease epidemics between 1633 and 1702. Another cause of death was malnutrition due to removals, being denied their hunting grounds, and being subjected to unaccustomed conditions. At the start of the 1600s, the thousands of Lenapes had far out-numbered the few hundred Europeans, but less than 100 years later the ratio was reversed.

The Lenape people were largely gone from Sandy Hook and the Navesink peninsula by the 1680s, though a number lingered until 1715 and a few stragglers never left. By the 1750s almost all the Lenape were gone from all of New Jersey, including Lappawinsoe, who became a leader of his exiled people when they moved to Pennsylvania (illustration no. 4).

Timeline

1664: March 25, 1664 was the date when Popamora sold the neck of land stretching from Sandy Hook and Rocky Point to Keansburg on the west to the Navesink Highlands on the east, and from the Raritan Bay shore on the north to the Navesink River banks on the south. With it came the map – actually a simplistic line-drawing or sketch – of the territory and a few of its main features. On the mainland facing the ocean is an oval which the English map-makers labeled "Navesant," sufficiently inland from the coastline to be on the Rocky Point hilltop.

Three historians document that the Lenape did not all leave the area after this deed was signed. One writes that in the early times of the English settlers, "the Indians often encamped" at a place near the Navesink River that later became the site of the house of the English Quaker Richard Hartshorne; "Indian relics" were "still turned up by the plow" in the 1880s.

1671: The easterly end of the Navesink hills was sold by William Goulding, the nominal English title-holder under the 1664 deed, to Hartshorne. At this time a Lenape "encampment" was still on the Navesink hills, perhaps in the same area as the ceremonial fire of 1609.

1675: Lenape were still present and trading food for European gunpowder. This is detailed in Hartshorne's letter to a "Dear Friend" in England, giving his impressions of life in the area. He wrote that the Indians sold fish big enough to serve "6 or 8 men" at a cost of only half a pound of gunpowder; "a fat buck...much bigger than the English deer" for a pound and a half of powder; and a peck of strawberries for 6 pence.

1678: The Lenape had long used the resources of Sandy Hook for a number of purposes. Their traditional concept was that land and other resources are natural gifts for use by all people, not commodities for sale. While the Lenape were knowingly selling land in the 1670s, they still assumed they could take wild animals and vegetation they needed to survive, including dry trees for making dugout canoes. In 1678, still present in the area, they continued to exercise usage rights on the Hook. In order to obtain clear jurisdiction and maintain peace, Hartshorne entered into an agreement with Lenape chiefs Vowavapon and Tocus on August 8, 1678 to buy these usage rights for 13 shillings and exclude the Lenape from going there at all.

1685: Still the Lenape did not leave and were providing beaver, mink, and raccoon furs to be shipped to England.

1703: Two Lenape chiefs named Shawmose and Mariblark were present, but probably left soon after signing a sale deed for bayside land running two or three miles inland along Compton's Creek in Belford.

1715: Lenape hunters were still catching local game and trading furs and skins for export to English markets. In the same year, ten local Indians were listed as current debtors in the estate inventory of Captain John Bowne, grandson of a 1667 original settler at Portland Poynt (today's Atlantic Highlands).

Chapter Two

EARLY EXPLORERS AND THE DUTCH

The first semi-serious visit by European explorers to the bayshore and neighboring lands and waters was by the Englishman Henry Hudson in 1609 and his crew, with Dutch sponsorship and ship, aboard the *Halve Maen* (Half Moon). He had been preceded along this coast by expeditions captained, staffed, and sponsored by people of at least six European nationalities.

There is disputed evidence that some Viking ships may have passed by around 1000 A.D. Later, occasional fishing boats from Viking lands and France supposedly wandered briefly southward from Canadian waters. The pace picked up in the early 1500s, when European commercial powers competed to find a shortcut "northwest passage" along the mid-Atlantic coast that would lead to the trading treasures of east Asia, just as Columbus had tried to do via the Caribbean. During less than 50 years, several deliberate voyages of discovery were launched.

In 1498 Giovanni Caboto, an Italian working for the English as John Cabot, is believed to have passed these shores during his second voyage that ranged from Newfoundland to Florida. A map reportedly depicting his observations was drawn by the Spaniard Juan de la Cosa (owner of the *Santa Maria* that Columbus chartered in 1492), including what some see as New York's lower bay.

In 1523 Giovanni da Verrazzano, an Italian working for the French, sailed into Sandy Hook Bay in his ship *La Dauphine* and was the first European explorer to do more than take soundings. He observed the Highlands of Navesink and named it *"Monticello di St. Polo"* (little mountain of St. Paul). In a letter to the French King, François I, he gave what clearly seems to be a description of the area, including references to the Navesink Highlands ("steep hills"), the Hudson ("a very large river"), Sandy Hook/Raritan Bays, and the Indians:

> We found a very pleasant situation among some steep hills, through which a very large river, deep at its mouth, forced its way to the sea; from the sea to the estuary of the river any ship heavily laden might pass without the help of tide, which rises eight feet. But as we were riding at anchor in a good berth, we would not venture up in our vessel without a knowledge of the mouth; therefore we took the boat, and entering the river we found the country on its banks well peopled, the inhabitants not differing much from the others, being dressed out with the feathers of birds of various colors. They came towards us with evident delight, raising loud shouts of admiration and showing us where we could most securely land with our boat.

In 1524–1525 Estevao Gomes, a Portuguese employed by Spain who had served as Magellan's pilot in 1519, made a seven-month survey of the Atlantic coast from the Chesapeake Bay to Newfoundland. A map depicting what he saw was the earliest to delineate the eastern coast of North America and to name Sandy Hook ("Cabo de Arenas" or Cape of Sand). This was the 1525 "Castiglione World Map" by Diogo Ribeiro, another Portuguese who was the royal cartographer of Spain and who maintained its official record of discoveries.

In 1541 Jean Alfonce de Saintonge (sometimes called only Alfonce), probably a Portuguese who had obtained French nationality, explored the area and produced a map. He reported seeing "a great river of fresh water and in its entry a sandy island," which describes the Hudson River, its bay and estuary, and the approach to it from the ocean.

Hudson and the Opening of Trade

Like the explorers who preceded him, Henry Hudson made his 1609 voyage across the Atlantic and down the east coast of America to search for a "northwest passage." Looking for its entrance, he sailed into and around Sandy Hook/Raritan Bay and up the Hudson River between September 2 and October 4 (illustration no. 8).

When his ship arrived inside Sandy Hook on September 4, it came in "hard by the souther shoare" of the bay. It put down anchor at a spot gauged as five fathoms deep, matching the depth offshore from the coastal springs called the spout. The ship's visit during the next six days started off with friendly meetings the first two days, but the third day there was a fight and a crew member was killed. What went wrong?

Only part of the answer comes from the journal kept by Robert Juet, an officer on the *Half Moon*, and from other Dutch accounts published in 1611 and 1625. In those sources, the six-day visit is described in detail.

On the first day, the Lenape "came aboord of us, seeming very glad of our comming," traded tobacco for knives and beads, and "are very civill."

On the second day, several peaceful mutual exchanges of visits and goods took place. Crew members went on land and "saw great store of Men, Women and Children" who gave them tobacco and dried currants. The crew members were led to "the great council house or house of worship" and offered the Lenape some cups of liquor. Tradition has it that the visitors were also shown the spout, where the crew refilled the ship's water casks. Later, many Lenape paddled dugout canoes in the bay and climbed aboard Hudson's ship.

The 13 Dutch merchants who sponsored Hudson's trip were naturally interested in new trading opportunities it might reveal, so Hudson's people were always on the lookout for valuable resources. On this second day, they noted three interesting potential assets:

- Magnificent high and thick oaks, together with poplars, linden trees, and various other kinds of wood useful in ship-building.
- The natives had copper, including tobacco pipes and "other things of Copper they did weare about their neckes," and the land reportedly contained deposits of iron.
- Some natives wore "divers sorts of good Furres." (As soon as 1611, this attracted more Dutch ships and soon generated a thriving fur trade, with Indians catching animals and trading pelts for Dutch goods.)

On Hudson's second night there, the crew stayed "very quiet" on their ship and "durst not trust" the natives. Why? Had the crew tried to get the furs and copper, threatening or using some force and causing hostility among the natives? Juet's journal does not explain, but both before and after the Sandy Hook stop the crew stole furs from other natives.

On the third day, Hudson sent five men in a boat to reconnoiter upper New York Bay. Heading back toward the ship that evening, "they were set upon by two canoes" carrying 26 native men. John Colman "was slaine in the fight . . . with an Arrow shot into his throat." No cause or reason for the fight is given, which reads like an unprovoked Indian attack in the European report.

On the fourth day, Hudson set defensive boards on his ship's portholes, kept close watch all night, and made his men carry firearms.

On the fifth day, natives came aboard again to trade tobacco and grain for knives and beads, "offered us no violence," and gave no indication of being aware of Colman's death.

On the sixth day, natives came aboard, some with bows and arrows, others making a "show of buying of knives, to betray us, but we perceived their intent" (no evidence is cited). The crew took two natives hostage against possible attack, and treated them like clowns by putting red coats on them and parading them on the deck. When they let one go, the other escaped by leaping overboard. The *Half Moon* pulled up anchor, sailed north, and never returned to the bayshore.

The rest of the answer is in reports of nasty behavior by Hudson's crew toward other Native Americans in July and October. This pattern makes it not unlikely that the crew also misbehaved in Sandy Hook Bay, explaining why hostilities also broke out there.

At Hudson's first landfall in July in Penobscot Bay, Maine, the Indians brought him "many Beaver skinnes and other fine Furres" to trade. But his crew, armed with large guns called "Murderers" and muskets, ransacked a Penobscot village, "took spoyle" of the natives, and wrote shameless reports of their action. If Hudson disapproved of his men's actions, he made no effort to control or punish them, or to make them return the stolen goods. The next morning he made off with the loot, setting sails to depart at 5 a.m.

After leaving Sandy Hook Bay in October and heading north, Hudson encountered natives upriver from Manhattan. Again he distrusted them, "perceived their intent to betray us," and refused to receive them on board. Using muskets and guns against bows and arrows, his men killed eight to ten natives. After the battle he sailed down river. Still looking for riches, he spotted a "white greene Cliffe" that he thought contained copper or silver.

It was furs and minerals that Hudson wanted, and the natives were apparently just in the way or just a way of getting the wealth he sought. His mission did not locate a northwest passage, but it succeeded in carrying home wonderful furs (better than those in Europe), which whetted the appetites of his sponsors.

In 1611, responding to reports from Hudson's trip, the venturesome Dutch merchants sent out five ships to scout North America's eastern coast for trading opportunities. One ship captain, Adriaen Block, sailed along the middle Atlantic coast, stopped along the southeastern shore of Sandy Hook Bay/Raritan Bay at the same cove in Atlantic Highlands as Hudson's crew had done, and drew an anchor on his map at that spot (illustration no. 1). He did fairly accurate but somewhat exaggerated mapping of the area and its coastline, and drew small rectangles portraying three Lenape settlements along Sandy Hook Bay. In 1614 Block returned to Holland, bearing a large load of furs and his map with "*Niev Nederlandt*" written out over a large territory, portraying a potentially extensive colony.

During 1614–1616, a second captain, Cornelis Hendricks, who had been Block's mate and succeeded him, made a repeat trip along the bayshore. His team produced a map three feet long that provided a more precise guide for safe navigation. It was reported that they stopped to "trade with the Inhabitants. . . . Found the country full of trees . . . in some places covered with vines," and saw "bucks and does, turkeys and partridges." They sent out *uytlopers* (scouts), led by a man named Kleynties, to tap Native-American sources of information and explore the country. As a result of Block's and Hendricks' exploration reports, the Dutch governing body granted a monopoly for four trading expeditions to a group formed by the merchants called the United New Netherland Company.

In 1619 another Dutch captain, Thomas Dermer, sailed inside Sandy Hook. He wrote that "In this place I talk with many Saluages [savages]" who "offered me Pilots." Also, "one of them drew mee a Plot with Chalke upon a Chest"—a map showing the Narrows, Long Island, Hell Gate north of Manhattan, and other land and water features.

In 1621, a year after the original trade monopoly expired, the Dutch government incorporated the Dutch West India Company to run a quadrangular trade between Dutch ports, west Africa, Brazil and the Caribbean, and New Netherland. As the trading monopoly and de facto governing authority in the region, the new company controlled New Netherland until the English took over in 1664. But the few Dutch settlements it fostered in all that time were basically trading posts rather than towns. A few farms were established in Hoboken and Pavonia (today's Jersey City), and there were settlement attempts in Staten Island, but below the Raritan River and along the bayshore there were perhaps only some scattered trading huts at most.

Trading, Woodchopping and Watering of Ships

While New Jersey was under Dutch control until 1664, it was part of the wider American province of New Netherland, which in turn was only a small part of the worldwide operations of the Dutch mercantile enterprise. The interest of the few Dutch present in the territory was trade and profit, settlement, and farming. Most came for a tour of duty with the company. Those who traveled to the Navesink peninsula were looking for furs, venison, timber, or water for their ships, and then left. They may have built small piers as landing places or small shelters as trading bases, but not Dutch villages. In 1624 the standing instruction for the resident director of the company was:

> to increase the trade in skins and other articles that are obtained in the country and at the place of trading with the Indians have a cabin erected so that the goods may be stored therein, and at a suitable time he shall send one or more sloops thither to carry on trade.

He was also instructed "to load the ships with all sorts of wood as far as it is possible so that the ships do not come home empty" when leaving New Netherland.

The company's interest in the Navesink peninsula and surrounding area is evident from pre-1630 maps that name four geographic features after merchants, company directors, and other Dutch officials. This suggests that trade here by the Dutch was more than light and fleeting and that they paid attention to the topography and assumed possession:

• Sandy Hook, then half as long as today, was mapped as Godyn's Point, named for Samuel Godyn, a Company director in Amsterdam and neo-feudal patroon or overlord of large tracts of land in New Netherland up to 1636. He sent his own agents to buy land from the Indians as well as pelts for the highly profitable fur trade. The other Dutch name for Sandy Hook was "Sant punt," meaning sand point.

• Along the Atlantic Ocean coast just south of Sandy Hook, the land was marked De rondebergh or Rodenburgh hoeck on early maps. This was named for Johan or Lucas von Rodenburgh who later were senior officials in Curaçao, a Caribbean post of the Dutch West Indies Company.

• Lower New York Bay was labeled Coenraets Bay, including the portion later known as Sandy Hook Bay. The namesake was Albert Coenraets, who became a Company director and patroon in 1622.

• Rensselaer's Hoeck was the name given to the Navesink Highlands, after Kiliaen van Rensselaer, a Company director and patroon. He sent import-export ships from Amsterdam to Manhattan and up the Hudson to his fur-trading settlement near Albany and back to Amsterdam again via Sandy Hook. The word "Hoeck" is seventeenth century Dutch for pier, meaning that Rensselaer's agents had a ship pier or landing place here.

A 1656 Dutch source reported that "the outward bound vessels usually stop at the watering-place" where they took on "a sufficient supply of wood and water, which are easily obtained at that place." A specific example is a transatlantic trading ship named *Rensselaerswyck*, which was owned by van Rensselaer and made a 1636–1637 round trip. The journal of captain Jan van Schellinger shows his ship stayed 18 days on the bay side of Navesink Highlands (see box).

The six days of work by the carpenters, perhaps imported from Manhattan, were to repair and refit the ship to return across the Atlantic. On the way over months before, it had been damaged in heavy storms. The work was done here because the carpenters could get wood needed for the ship from supplies that had been cut from the "great store of goodly oakes" and other trees on these shores, as described by Henry Hudson's crew in 1609. The seven days at "the watering place" undoubtedly meant taking barrels to be filled at today's Henry Hudson Spring, as also used by Hudson's ship in 1609. At the same time, the crew chopped away at trees on the northern slope to produce firewood.

Hudson had also admired, and reported enthusiastically about, the gray fox furs worn and offered in trade by the Lenape who met his ship. For Dutch traders following his lead, beaver quickly became the favorite pelt because of its use in the "felt hats" so popular in Europe. Already by 1620, a Company ship named *Bever* (Dutch for beaver), returned from New Netherland with a cargo of furs. The official seal of New Netherland was a beaver, surrounded by a necklace of wampum used in trade with local Indians. The fur traders

> ## From Ship's Log,
> ## July 16–August 4, 1637
>
> **July 16**: Sailed north to "rinselaers hoeck" and "tacked into the bay."
>
> **July 20**: "The carpenters came on board."
>
> **July 25**: "The carpenters finished their work."
>
> **July 27**: Mate Hendrick de Freest (died the 26th) and a child were buried—on land? in water?
>
> **July 29**: "We sailed to the watering place."
>
> **July 30**: "Our casks were filled with water."
>
> **July 31 and August 1**: "We cut firewood."
>
> **August 4**: "We got our water and wood on board" and set sail in the evening.

looked for otter; muskrat, used for making felt hats; and marten, mink, raccoon, and bear. Deer and elk skin were in great demand in Europe for making shoes, leather pants, vests, jackets, aprons, bags, and other leather products.

One Dutch trader along the Navesink River in the 1640s was Aert Theunisen, a farmer and brewer from Hoboken who probably traded his homemade brew for furs hunted by the Indians. He came in his trading sloop along the ocean to the then-existing Navesink River inlet called *Beeregat* in Dutch, which means "bear hole," conceivably to get bearskins from the Lenape; the Lenape shell midden at nearby Red Bank contained bones of black bear, among other animals wanted for their fur or skin. In October 1643, on a trading expedition on the Navesink River south of Atlantic Highlands, Theunissen was killed by local Indians. This was probably part of the widespread attacks then being made by many Lenape bands, including the Navesinks, in retaliation for a Native-American massacre that Dutch governor Kieft had ordered at Pavonia (Jersey City). Later, following the Native Americans' sale on the Navesink peninsula, a Derick Theunissen/Tunissen came to settle and in 1672 bought a lot in Portland Poynt, today's Atlantic Highlands.

Another Dutch trader, Jacob Couwenhoven, pulled his sloop in at bayshore inlets and traded with the Lenape for furs and venison, sometimes accompanied by another Dutchman, Peter Lawrensen, as interpreter. Their trading territory covered lands of the Navesink and Raritan bands of the Lenape. In the late 1600s members of both their families also settled along the bayshore, including some Couwenhovens who anglicized their name as Conover and continued running boats between there and Manhattan into the 1700s.

Bayside Probes

These involvements were commercial in motive and transitory in nature. Not until 1650 did the Dutch administration seriously try to purchase land from Native Americans south of the Raritan River and along the lower bay. The population of the entire New Netherland was only about 2,000 in 1650, and most of that was in New Amsterdam. That year, Amsterdam announced a new policy of encouraging Dutch citizens to settle the territory. The enticement was free land, tax exemptions on products of farming, hunting, and fishing, and ability to trade along the Atlantic coast by paying a small duty at New Amsterdam.

Some wealthy men saw this as an investment opportunity, hoping to cash in on a settler boom. Three buyers—a merchant, a nobleman, and a government figure—soon entered into land sale deeds with the Navesink band of the Lenape who controlled the southern shore of Raritan Bay and Sandy Hook Bay, including the Atlantic Highlands area (see box). Now that official policies and land purchases were finally in place, it seemed the arrival of Dutch settlers could not be far behind.

Of the three buyers, a Bohemian named Augustin Heerman (the merchant), had perhaps the best prospect of achieving colonization in the area. A surveyor by profession, he was the only one who came to the Navesink region to negotiate with the Lenape chiefs for land purchases and assess the territory directly. He was in the area in March and again in December 1651, when he signed two deeds with the Lenape sachem Mattano and seven other Lenape. He even mapped the area with high accuracy, producing what some say is the manuscript for the so-called Jansson-Visscher map published in 1651.

The Land Purchase Attempts

• In August 1650, an agent for the nobleman Baron Hendrick van der Capellen signed a deed with a Lenape chief for a large swath of "land about the Nevesinck," including ten Lenape-named places on the south side of the bay. The agent, Govert Lockermans, reportedly made a fortune in gun-running, selling liquor to Indians, and sometimes in legal trade (and returned to the Navesink region in 1663—see below). But after a few years, the controlling Dutch Company objected to the Baron's Indian purchases and, tired of the dispute, he sold out in 1661.

• In March 1651, the merchant Augustin Heerman signed a deed with six Lenape, for extensive lands along the south shore of the bay. The sale was done with the agreement of Oringken, "sachem of Nevesinca" (Navesink). However, the deed was revoked two years later by Governor Peter Stuyvesant, claiming that acquisition of such large territory would lead to land speculation. A different reason may have been that Stuyvesant wanted revenge on Heerman, who had been one of the main protest petitioners to the Dutch government in 1649 against Stuyvesant's totalitarian rule.

• In November 1651, the Dutch government at Amsterdam issued a patent to Cornelis van Werckhoven, a member of the Dutch government. He got two large colonies—one "to begin at Nevesing" near Sandy Hook and proceed northwards to the west side of the Hudson, and the other at Tappan. However, the granting of the "Nevesing" colony led to a protest by Baron van der Cappellen, who claimed it duplicated his own earlier purchase. Werckhoven's numerous intended settlers did not materialize.

The lands of the Navesink band of the Lenape were now the focus of a struggle between the nobleman, Baron van der Capellen, and the government man, Cornelis van Werckhoven, who claimed the same land. The controversy is not surprising because no one band of the Lenape controlled all the territory between the Navesink and Raritan Rivers, territorial definitions in deeds and patents were imprecise and mapping was almost nonexistent, and Dutch policies on land purchases and settlement were in flux. In any case, the company directors in Amsterdam were firm on one point: their august persons and their powers and rights must not be ignored. They expressed outrage that "invaders" were taking "the best land . . . without formality and without determination by survey, as if the company and its officers had nothing to say about it." They demanded a close check that people wanting land "will be able and intend shortly to populate, cultivate and bring [it] into a good state of tillage."

How far Werckhoven was able to develop his patroonship is not known. He claimed to have taken possession of it, which infers some sort of occupancy. As shown by a 1663 Dutch report, a man who became a tutor to his children, the surveyor Jacques Cortelyou, was quite familiar with the territory, which he had "visited and inspected formerly."

If Werckhoven planted any settlers in Navesink territory, which is unlikely, they were in danger by 1655 when war with the Native Americans flared up again. In September, 2,000 Indian fighting men took up arms and terrorized all white settlements within reach. The Navesink Indians were much involved in this war and, for years after the uprising had been stopped, the Dutch continued to hunt down some they identified as participants.

By 1660, Van Werckhoven abandoned the Navesink region and his intended colonies in today's New Jersey. Instead he began a settlement on Long Island at New Utrecht. Clearly intending to become a resident, he installed his children there with Cortelyou as their tutor. However, he soon decided to return to Holland, leaving Cortelyou in charge of his lands, but with colonization plans, if any, remaining unclear.

Rival Dutch and English Expeditions

"Buy Lenape land"—this was the order given in December 1663 in New Amsterdam. Moving out beyond Manhattan and the Hudson region, the Dutch now wanted to buy from the Lenape the territory "from Barnegatt to the Raritan" in today's New Jersey. Part of their motivation was colonial rivalry with England. In addition to controlling and colonizing New England, the English also claimed the mid-Atlantic coastal region based on Cabot's exploration in 1498, ahead of Hudson's 1609 visit. Following the restoration of Charles II to the throne in 1660, the predominant English faction wanted to crush the international commercial power of the Dutch, overcome them as rivals in the money-making slave trade, and take over New Netherland.

By 1663, English residents of Gravesend at the southeastern corner of Long Island were aware of this ambition, impatient with Dutch rule, and looking for an English takeover. At the minimum they wanted to escape from Dutch control. This led them to be interested in moving to the southern bayshore, where more fertile land and larger landholdings were potentially available and Dutch involvement was between minimal and non-existent. Tradition has it that, for several years, some of them had sailed across the bay from their homes in Gravesend to fish for the shad and alewives that swarmed in bayside creeks in springtime. Some of them reportedly even stayed all summer with their families to plant and harvest crops. In December 1663, 20 Englishmen, mostly from Gravesend, decided to make a reconnaissance of the southern bayshore for land they could buy and permanently settle. Their leader for this sailing expedition—and during their later settlement of the new lands—was John Bowne of Gravesend, who became a founder of the village of Portland Poynt where today's Atlantic Highlands stands; also present was Randall Huet, another founder of that village.

For their part, the Dutch wanted to buy lands and preempt their English competitors from settling the bayshore and ocean coast of New Netherland. To repair relations with the Lenape and discourage English attempts to purchase land, the Dutch were even authorized to forgive former Lenape offenses if they pledged to sell land only to the Dutch. The offenses were many, since the Navesink and Raritan bands of the Lenape had resisted Dutch authority for over 40 years through two prior wars and supported a current Indian uprising along the Hudson River. The English, too, had repeatedly been involved in wars with the Dutch, and shared a distaste for them with the Lenape.

A few days after the English group left Long Island, a Dutch party sailed south from New Amsterdam. In the boat were Govert Lockermans and Jacques Cortelyou, with their history in bayside land acquisition. Captain Lieutenant Martin Crigier was commander of 12 soldiers and sailors. Crigier, a Hudson River trader and sloop captain, had led military expeditions against the Indians up the Hudson River and against another colonial rival—the Swedes on the lower Delaware River. Accompanying the group was a Lenape named Piewecherenoes, but called "Hans, the savage" or "our savage" in the Dutch record of the trip.

At the mouth of the Raritan River, this Dutch group encountered fellow Dutchman Jacob Couwenhoven in his trading sloop with Peter Lawrenson. He informed them that Navesink and Raritan Indians at a meeting three miles inland had been joined by Englishmen from Long Island the previous day. The Dutch wanted to chase the English upriver, but were stuck at the river mouth for two days because of severe opposing winds. Instead, they sent Hans on foot to warn the Lenape chiefs against selling land to the English.

When the English sloop came downriver to the bay, the Dutch accused them of "unbecoming" anti-government activity. The English gave an evasive and dismissive reply and continued sailing. Next came Hans arriving with the Lenape chiefs, who told the Dutch that the English had given them rum and wampum as gifts and asked to buy some land.

Determined to catch up with the English and prevent them from making a purchase, the Dutch group sailed across the bay to its southern shore near Sandy Hook. The English had already arrived, after stopping at creeks between Matawan and Sandy Hook, looking for suitable places to settle. The Dutch saw them at a cove under the Navesink Highlands and pulled their boat in to land. The location, a creek between "Rensselaer pier and the point," is difficult to pinpoint; different sources describe it as the cove that used to exist at the mouth of Many Mind Creek in Atlantic Highlands, or a small creek that used to exist near the base of Sandy Hook.

The Dutch were accompanied by a Lenape, Quikems, who knew the Navesink lands and lived in the Lenape village of Ramezing on the Swimming River near today's Tinton Falls. The English also had a Lenape guide with them, another resident of Ramezing whose name was Sukkurus in Dutch records (Sackarois in the English). Though living in the same village, the two Lenape were from different factions, pro-Dutch on Quikems' side and pro-English with Sukkurus. The Dutch, already angered by the English scouting for land, had additional reason for fury when Quikems told them that Sukkurus, originally from western Long Island in the Gravesend area, had taken part several years ago in killing some Dutch inhabitants of Queens during an Indian uprising. He had fled to the Navesink region where his militant hatred for the Dutch won him high status, and he became something of an agent for the English. As Sackarois some years later, still favoring the English, he sold them three tracts of land in Monmouth County.

At the cove, the rival colonists realized their missions were at complete cross-purposes and their loyalties were in opposition. They launched into a long, bitter, and mutually unyielding discussion, with John Bowne doing most of the talking for the English. Reaching a complete stand-off, eventually they parted peacefully without using the weapons they all carried and as enemies, with neither side able to overpower the other.

The next day, December 12, the Dutch met the Lenape chief Mattano, who had put his signature mark on two deeds with Augustin Heerman in 1651 and on a Staten Island sale deed with five other Lenape for Baron van der Capellen in 1657. In this new negotiation, the Dutch preempted the English by obtaining a promise that Mattano and his people would sell the unsold lands of the Navesinks to the Dutch, for a price not determined. Two weeks later on December 26, Mattano told the Dutch his sale price for the Navesink lands was 4,000 guilders. The price was so high and so angered the Dutch authorities that they decided to use force to get better terms. They began planning to send a garrison of 30 soldiers to the area under Crigier, but soon found that, because of Dutch military battles with Lenape in the lower Hudson valley, no troops could be spared for the expedition. This left the path open for a purchase by the English, who then invited the Navesink chief Popamora for a visit to Long Island in February 1664. Popamora now changed his mind and promised to sell land only to the English, not the Dutch.

Chapter Three

ENGLISH SETTLERS

The year 1664 began over a century of English control of the bayshore, New Jersey, and the mid-Atlantic region. It lasted until the Revolutionary War broke out in 1776 and colonial Americans won their independence from Britain.

In August 1664, an English fleet of four frigates with 450 soldiers and 92 guns under Colonel Richard Nicolls sailed into the East River and demanded the surrender of the town of New Amsterdam and the wider territory of New Netherland. In giving up power without firing a shot, the Dutch governor, Peter Stuyvesant, negotiated a guarantee from Nicolls that the colonists "shall enjoy the liberty of their consciences in divine worship and church discipline." This freedom of religion was also built into the 1665 charter for settlement of the bayshore region, and ultimately into the United States Constitution. The English soon divided New Netherland into colonies known as New York and New Jersey. Nicolls became the governor of both and quickly began to encourage English settlement.

Settlers aiming for the shores of Sandy Hook Bay already had a head start. In December 1663, twenty of them had made a reconnaissance along the bayshore for possible settlement (see chapter 2). Then three of them led by John Bowne made return trips to negotiate with the Lenape for purchase of land on the Navesink peninsula. They brought gifts of clothing to help smooth negotiations and seal a deal with Popamora, the chief of the Navesink band of the Lenape, and his people. The gifts were three pairs of breeches and three coats, and the visitors also offered them "wine at times."

On March 25, 1664, six Englishmen from Long Island signed a land sale deed with Popamora, including John Bowne and three others from the December 1663 scouting party. It covered the entire Navesink peninsula, an area of around 35 square miles. Accompanying the deed, a "drawn out Figure further Explained" this territory and a few of its main features—in other words, a map (illustration no. 5). Coastlines, river banks, and creeks were drawn as straight or gently curved lines, without including the numerous bends, turns, or squiggles that these features have. The mapped peninsula is shown as rectangular in shape, though in reality it is more nearly triangular. These are typical of Native-American mapping techniques based on length of travel time rather than geographical distances and shapes. There may have been mapping contributions by the five Englishmen listed as "interpreters" in the deed, meaning that they must have had previous knowledge of the area; three of them became original settlers at Portland Poynt (James Bowne, John Horabin, and Randall Huet).

Nine place names on the map are in the Lenape language, often accompanied by an English identifying word (i.e. beach, creek, river, path); some are translated and interpreted in chapter 1. Between the Navesink River and the bay, the mainland has an east-west trail line that joins two circles representing Lenape villages and an oval designating an area that probably had less intensive use as a chiefly or ceremonial place.

For all the land shown on the map, the English buyers paid the Lenape 200 fathoms of wampum, five coats, one shirt, one clout capp (cloth cap), one gun, 12 pounds of tobacco, and one anker of liquors (the equivalent of 10 gallons). To assess whether this price was fair, a bargain, or a rip-off, you have to realize these products were novelties or high-end technologies that had particular value for the Lenape. Guns and liquors were prized for their use in hunting and drinking, and because the Lenape lacked the means to make them. The tobacco might be a year's supply for one man, but it also had a ceremonial value in Lenape rituals. As for the ordinary coats, shirt, and cap, the Lenape did not have woven cloth, sewing thread, or needles. Their normal clothing was fur pelts, or pieces of deerskin, sometimes joined by rawhide into leggings. Tailored clothing that breathes (unlike animal skins) and has different colors must have had luxury appeal. Popamora may have gained favor by giving four of the five coats to others in his band.

As for wampum, the coastal Lenape obviously had the raw material, sea shells, for making it. Yet they didn't have iron drills to make holes in the shells so they could be strung as beads and the strings sewn together as belts. Dutch, Swedish, and English traders brought drills and made wampum a medium of exchange with the Native Americans. The standard measure for wampum strings was the fathom, equal to six feet or the width of extended arms, so the payment of 200 fathoms meant almost a quarter-mile of shell work. Wampum represented about two-thirds of the purchase cost, which the English buyers were to pay in installments—60 percent when signing the deed and the balance in 12 months. Half the wampum had to be black (really blue-black or purple), which was worth twice as much as white.

Soon after the deed was concluded with Popamora, two of its English negotiators, John Bowne and Randall Huet Sr., came to live on the bayshore as pioneer settlers. They located themselves next to a creek that meandered and changed directions so much that they named it Many Mind Creek. More settlers arrived, and they named the area Portland Poynt, which includes today's Atlantic Highlands.

Finally a year later settlers' representatives sailed with Popamora and his men to New York to meet English Colonial Governor Nicolls. There, on April 7, 1665, both parties confirmed the deed, the sale price, and their mutual satisfaction, as required by English law. The next day, the governor signed the Monmouth or Navesink Patent, a document that made a huge land grant to 12 men, including John Bowne. The tract was even larger than the Navesink peninsula covered by the 1664 deed with Popamora. It covered all of today's Monmouth and Ocean Counties and parts of Middlesex and Essex Counties, running along the bayshore all the way to the Raritan River at South Amboy (illustration no. 9). The patent called for at least 100 families to settle and to "manure and plant" the land within three years. For the common protection and good, they were to organize themselves in nucleated villages with houses "not too far distant and scattering one from another." For seven years, the settlers would have to pay no "rents, customs, excise, tax or levy whatsoever," but after 1672 they were to pay the same rate as others in royal territories. Freedom of worship, free elections, local lawmaking power, and civil court trials were provided, but criminal cases had to be tried in New York. The 12 original patentees were each to receive 500 acres of land, with 120 additional acres for each member of the family and 60 for each servant—an incentive to bring black slaves or white indentured servants.

Total costs for the Navesink peninsula land purchase from the Lenape and for related travels and negotiations were finally reckoned five years later on July 5–8, 1670, at a meeting of the white settlers who inhabited Portland Poynt, Middletown, and Shrewsbury. Expenditures were itemized and costed in Dutch guilders and English pounds, including the wampum, clothing, gun, tobacco, and liquor given to the Lenape. To translate this into current values, the Nederlandsche Bank of Amsterdam has calculated that one Dutch guilder in 1626 was worth $11.157 in 1998, with conversion pegged to the quantity of gold in the early seventeenth-century guilder. Using that rate, the total purchase cost came to the equivalent of about $39,584 in 1998 dollars. Of this amount, what Popamora and the Navesinks received was worth $16,177, and the expenses of the English agents for the purchase were $23,407. Popamora's sale was for about 22,400 acres (35 square miles), or the equivalent of 69¢ an acre.

Creating "Portland Poynt"—the Mysterious Layout

There are two important and "landmark" historic facts about Portland Poynt, which includes much of the territory of today's Atlantic Highlands. It was the site of the first legislature that ever assembled in New Jersey, known as the Assembly and sometimes as the general court. Its initial meeting was June 4, 1667, almost a year before the representatives of all towns in the Province met in Elizabethtown together with the governor and his council.

Founding Document for Portland Poynt

"The lotts on Portland Poynt being unto No.10

are Layd out and are in breadth twenty pls [poles] each Lott,

and run up from the banck into the woodes

upon A strait line W. & N [west and north].

with Qornar [corner] as the land is good,

about 60 to 70 poles.

The further Most west Lott on the south side,

No. 1, John Hiribin [Horabin],

No. 2, James Bownes [Bowne],

No. 3, Richard Richardsons [Richardson].

The lotts on the north side of the Swamp or Valley,

No. 4, Randell Huelt [Huet] Senior,

No. 5, Henry Pizsey [Percy],

No. 6, John Binds [Bowne],

No. 7, Randell Huelt [Huet] Junior,

No. 8, William Bowne,

No. 9, William Shakerley [Shackerly]."

Lot no. 10 was assigned to Matthias Howard after this document was drawn up.

Note on interpretation:

The above text in Deed Book A is recorded in an old-style handwriting that is hard to decipher. Moreover, this text became fuzzy over the centuries, as the vellum page was overlaid with linen for preservation and the ink faded. To produce the above text, the archived page was studied by magnifying it six-fold and comparing blurred letters with neighboring pages in the same hand. Original spellings have been retained. To help in understanding and interpretation, the text has been divided to begin each new idea on a new line, abbreviations have been spelled out inside brackets, and standard spellings have been given in italics next to the variant versions of family names.

The Assembly at Portland Poynt consisted of elected representatives from "Newasink and Navarumsunk necks" (the Navesink and Rumson peninsulas), where colonists had begun to settle in Portland Poynt, Middletown, and Shrewsbury. Most meetings were held in Portland Poynt, in the house of either Richard Richardson or Randall Huet. Richardson's was on the west side of today's Avenue D between West Highland and Washington Avenues; Huet's was on the east side of Avenue D between today's Leonard Avenue and Highway 36.

The other important historic fact is that Portland Poynt was the first village to be laid out for settlement by Europeans in the entire territory of today's Monmouth and Ocean Counties. The division of its land into ten lots was agreed on December 14, 1667, 16 days ahead of Middletown village. Their decision was recorded on page 13 of Deed Book A, kept at the Monmouth County Archives. The text is in the box at left.

The location, layout, and pattern of the ten lots on the ground has long been fuel for speculation, badly misinterpreted, and a mystery. However, an authoritative picture can now be drawn, following patient deciphering of the language in the founding document and careful plotting of all relevant evidence. The 1667 pattern that has now been discovered (illustration no. 10) is also borne out by the boundaries shown in an 1844 map (illustration no. 15), an 1879 panoramic painting (illustration no. 18), and an 1884 map showing elevations of the "valley," the extent of marshlands, and the street pattern. These illustrations are in the book's center section. To understand the new findings requires detailed discussion, and there is no way to transform it into light entertainment. Nine items of evidence are examined below, starting by following the sequence in the founding document.

Lot Dimensions. As an inherited long-time practice, English settlers in the American northeast typically adopted a "long lot system of division" of lands. Lots were rectangular, had relatively narrow frontage along the banks of rivers/brooks/creeks, and extended back from there at greater length. This model, which produces rectangular lots, was used at Portland Poynt.

Describing the size of the lots, the Portland Poynt founding document uses an old unit of measure called poles (abbreviated as "pls"). Also known as rods or perches, a pole is 16.5 feet long. Thus, the width of 20 poles is equal to 330 feet, and the length of 60 to 70 poles becomes 990 to 1,155 feet. In square measure, this translates into between 7.5 and 8.75 acres, which is a good match for a 1672 deed describing Randall Huet Jr.'s "home lott" as having eight acres.

Previous writers were evidently not aware of the correct interpretation of "pls" as used in the founding document, assumed the measurement had to be in yards, and so described much smaller lots only 60 feet wide and 180 to 210 feet long. This would be much too little space to accommodate what European settlers typically did on their home lots—build a house, keep livestock, grow corn, plant kitchen gardens, and set up outbuildings such as corn cribs, sheds, barns, or other outbuildings.

Water Frontage. While the founding document never mentions any body of water, it notes that the lots "run up from the banck into the woodes." Use of the term "bank" clearly connotes the bank of a creek. If the bay had been meant, the word used would be "shore" as in "go on shore" or "sail off shore," referring to the edge of a large body of water, not a little creek. The term "run up from the banck" means that the long dimension of the lots was perpendicular to the creek bank. The short side of the lots paralleled the creek, maximizing the number of lots with water access.

A later document, on page 21 of Deed Book A, makes it clear that the bank is on Many Mind Creek. That page reports how the general court, held at Portland Poynt on December 28, 1669, ordered that the town's inhabitants have "full power and liberty to take up thare principall lotts of land . . . at or near a small creek within the limits of this towne of Midltown cal'd Many Mind Spring."

Further evidence for this comes from simple logic. Settlers naturally preferred lots with direct access to a source of fresh water (not salt water) for crops, drinking/bathing by animals, and washing and drinking by people. Many Mind is a fresh water source, originating in springs and surface run-off from upland watersheds.

Finally, the only creek given a name by the first settlers at Portland Poynt was Many Mind Creek, indicating its defining, central role for them. Traditional sources offer two possible reasons for the name. One is that the earliest arriving settlers were of many minds about where to establish their village, but finally agreed on putting it beside the spring-fed creek, which they then labeled Many Mind Creek. The second reason is that, between its source and mouth, the creek itself is of many minds, changing direction three times as it runs south, then west, and finally north.

Long dimension of the lots. The founding document says that the lengthwise orientation of the lots is on a "strait line W. & N"—a straight line that runs northwesterly. The only possible starting point for such a line is the west bank of Many Mind Creek, not from the bayshore or the other creek bank. A line running up from the bayshore would have to head south, southeast, or southwest, and a line running up from the creek's east bank would be heading east, northeast, or southeast.

"Corner" and land quality. The founding document says that the ten lots had a "corner as the land is good." This refers to the northwestern block of land near the bayshore that is not good for cultivation and where the pattern of laid-out lots therefore stopped. The area where the land was unsuitable for settlement can still be clearly seen today. It is contained within the space bounded by Avenue D on the east, Central Avenue on the south, Wagner Creek on the west, and the bay on the north. It includes three kinds of uncultivable land that any farmer would avoid, even today: wetlands/swamp in a wide zone east of the creek; sandy beach and lowland in a band along the bay front; and on the higher elevation in the northeast portion, the land consists of very coarse quartz sand that is weathered and cemented into massive beds of sandstone, which is an outcrop of the deep-seated "Englishtown" geological formation. This area is called the "dead lands" in a 1696 deed between original settlers James and John Bowne.

South side/north side. The document refers to "The further Most west lott on the south side"—in other words, the most southwestern lot—as being lot number 1 of John Horabin. The location of lot number 2 of James Bowne, his neighbor to the north, is well known and easily identified, since it is the land where the "Bowne House" stands today, west of Avenue D and running parallel to Highway 36. This also makes it possible to locate lot number 3 as being north of lot number 2. The three lots had access to fresh water from Bowne's Creek (now Wagner Creek), which bisects them.

The other seven lots are "on the north side of the Swamp or Valley," according to the founding document. As late as 1884, much of the final third of Many Mind Creek as it headed toward the bay was bordered by swamp. The creek and these wetlands made up the area of lowest elevation, a valley, as shown by contour lines on the 1884 map, and represent the only location where the swamp or valley has a north side. Lots 4 through 10 were lined up above this valley. The only other nearby swamp is the wetlands farther west, near the mouth of Wagner Creek; the only possible north side of that swamp is the bay, which obviously is not a place for settlement.

Different lot lengths. The row of lots numbered 4 through 10 ran up from the bank of the creek a distance of 990 to 1,155 feet according to the founding document. The different lengths undoubtedly related to the amount of uncultivable swampland along the creek border of the lots, with compensating extra length for those lots that had a wider band of swampland.

Access road. Along their farthest boundary west of the creek, lots 4 through 10 needed a path, as did lots 1 to 3 farther west, to allow access to the bay where boats could be loaded and unloaded. The previous inhabitants, the Lenape, may already have had a path to a bayside landing here, or the white settlers created one at the dividing line between the two rows of lots laid out in 1667. For 200 years and more, its route, today's Avenue D, was the only local road shown on maps of the settlement area. It appears on a 1777–1778 map made by a British military map-maker, Lieutenant John Hills, during the Revolutionary War.

1844 map. This map (illustration no. 15) shows nine houses and related crop fields and orchards west of Many Mind Creek. While plot maps of the era were still only approximate and not based on field survey, the pattern of lot boundaries broadly follows the 1667 layout discussed above. The 1667 boundary road, today's Avenue D, is still in place and is still the only public roadway in the area (the same is true of the 1851 Lightfoot map). The land west of Many Mind Creek is still the predominant area of settlement as of 1844 (and also in 1851). Only two houses exist east of the creek on the 1844 map—the house of William Brown that later became Thomas Leonard's along First Avenue, and the Hooper estate in the hills farther east.

1879 panorama painting. In the Strauss Mansion and Museum of the Atlantic Highlands Historical Society is an 1879 painting by W.H. Rymer (illustration no. 18). It looks north from the Hillside section toward the central lowlands of today's town and the bay beyond. The tree-bordered fields west of Many Mind Creek at that date still reflect the outlines of the first seven lots north of the Great Swamp or Valley, as laid out in 1667. They also predict today's street grid in western Atlantic Highlands.

Additional Lots

With only eight acres each, the ten house lots had too little land for farming and could not provide adequate subsistence. So, residents of the new little village decided that they would "further enlarge" their holdings "if lands were found fit for planting." To this end, a survey of all the land in "Newasink Neck and Narumson Neck" was made after June 1668 by five appointed settlers of the three towns, including James Bowne and Richard Richardson from Portland Poynt. The surveyors were ordered to "take a full view, both off the upland & meddow of each Neck & and to take good observation off the quantitie and qualities of each, & to give reportt thareoff." The typical categories of land necessary for English-style farming were grassy areas for grazing pastures, salt marshes for cutting hay, fields for planting crops, and forested lands for timber, firewood, etc.

By May 1669, the surveyors gave their report, which was approved by their Assembly, meeting at Portland Poynt. The report recommended the creation and fencing of 36 additional "out-lots and salt meadow lots," with still more lots to be laid out that winter. The lots stretched out along the bayshore in an area called Shoal Harbor, which at the time reached westward from the ten home lots, through today's Leonardo, Belford, and Port Monmouth, as far as Point Comfort in today's Keansburg. In some accounts, the territory known as Portland Poynt is described as encompassing that entire zone, plus the eastward area of the Navesink Highlands extending to Sandy Hook.

The additional Shoal Harbor out-lots and salt meadows went to some of the families living near Many Mind Creek, such as the Bownes, and people from Middletown village also received some. Unlike the nearly identical land allocations in Portland Poynt village, these lots varied in size based on relative ability to "improve" and manage the land. A secondary effect was to perpetuate the English social class system; more acreage went to richer settlers who had servants to work the land and larger numbers of cattle to graze.

The First Landowners

Five of the ten first landowning families in Portland Poynt came from Gravesend, on the southwestern end of Long Island (today's Brooklyn). This was about 12 miles from the bayshore, a trip that would have taken two to three hours in a sailing sloop of the time, depending on the wind. The five landowners were three Bownes (William and his sons John and James) and two Huets (father and son, both named Randall). The other five first landowners included one man whose previous home is unknown, three men from Rhode Island, and one man whose homes were in Rhode Island and, strangely enough, Barbados. Nine of the families settled in Portland Poynt, but the Rhode Island/Barbados man apparently did not.

Lot 1—John Horabin. John Horabin was one of the witnesses, signers, and interpreters of the 1664 deed with Popamora. In 1667, his house lot was "the further Most west lot on the south side," or the most southwesterly lot. He had six cattle and seven hogs in 1669 when he recorded the identifying mark he made on their ears. By 1676 he had apparently left Portland Poynt for Shrewsbury where one neighbor was Henry Leonard, whose descendant later founded Atlantic Highlands. He died by 1677. Presumably his neighbor, James Bowne, obtained this lot since a Bowne family member built a house there that still stands, somewhat redone, south of Highway 36.

Lot 2—James Bowne. Born in 1636, James was the younger son of William Bowne (John was eldest). At 28, he was an "Indian interpreter" in the 1664 negotiations with Popamora and signed the deed. The next year he married Mary Stout, daughter of Richard and Penelope Stout, and came from Gravesend to settle at Portland Poynt. In 1667–1670, the local General Assembly elected him to be overseer, one of its three officers and not unlike today's county freeholders. In 1677 he was selected to represent the settlers in a land rent dispute with the governor of New Jersey.

Some believe he built part of the Historic Register "Bowne House" that still stands on lot number 2 (west of the Leonard Avenue/Bowne Avenue corner). However, preservation experts say the original section was later replaced, as shown by the dating of its construction techniques. In 1678 he recorded his "Hoge & cattle Marks att Portland Point" and also owned horses. In addition to his town lot and outlying lands at Portland Poynt, he acquired 1,352 more acres between 1670 and 1690. When he died in 1695, his son James Jr. administered his estate and took up 150 acres of his land, including seven acres at Shoal

Harbor. When James Jr. died in 1750, he had five black slaves. A second son, Samuel, lived in the Bowne House on lot number 2.

Lot 3—Richard Richardson. Originally from Rhode Island, Richardson was an early arrival in Portland Poynt. In 1667 he became the first clerk of Monmouth County when the local General Assembly elected him to be its "Recorder." He was also made one of the three overseers of Portland Poynt. The same year, his Portland Poynt house was the site of an assembly session. He was a leader in the refusal of most Monmouth County settlers to pay the arrears in land tax claimed by the governor of New Jersey. When that dispute was settled, he received a grant of 150 acres from the proprietors. For unknown reasons, Richardson left the new settlement by 1685 and moved to Barbados. Bownes probably took possession of his lot.

Lot 4—Randall Huet, Sr. (also Hewitt, Hulet). Coming from Massachusetts and then Gravesend, Huet was a trader, merchant, or innkeeper. He was one of the 20 men who took part in the December 1663 reconnaissance of the Navesink peninsula, supplied £1 worth of rum that was shared with the Indians, and was one of the interpreters for the 1664 deed. He and John Bowne were the only men of the 20 who then came to settle in Portland Poynt. His house, like Richard Richardson's, was the site of several meetings of the Monmouth Assembly between June 1667 and 1672. He died in 1670, willed his house and home lot in Portland Poynt to his wife Margaret, and divided the rest of his land among his wife and his three sons Randall, Joseph, and Thomas; Joseph's share alone was 240 acres. Other possessions covered in his will included a red heifer, a young sow, and 260 pounds of tobacco—a product he probably traded.

In February 1671 his widow Margaret Huet married Bernard Smith. In July 1673 she sold her inherited land, cattle, and swine, and "all the iron, pewter and brass which I am possessed with" to Cornelis Steenwyck. The land sale was to pay a 1658 debt her deceased husband owed to Steenwyck (illustration no. 11). In April 1673 her son Thomas took a 3-year lease with Steenwyck for land and livestock his father had owned. Steenwyck was a rich trader whose ships ran to Barbados, elsewhere in the Caribbean, and Africa. Also, he was mayor of Manhattan for five years in the 1670s. He became a partner in the Tinton Iron Works in Shrewsbury with Lewis Morris. Steenwyck purchased land there and in four other New Jersey locations as a real estate investment. There's no evidence he ever lived in Portland Poynt, and he died in 1684.

Lot 5—Henry Percy (also Percey, Pizsey, Picsey). A blacksmith, Percy was from Warwick, Rhode Island. At the Monmouth Assembly in December 1667, he was chosen as one of three overseers for Portland Point. In May 1669 he took on an apprentice blacksmith, seven-year-old Mathew Howard, under an indenture signed by Mathew's widowed mother, Kathern, who lived on lot 10. By January 1672 Percy had died, and his widow sold lot 5 to Christopher Allmey of Shrewsbury, who also bought lot 10 at the same time (see below). The deed reveals that the lot then had at least one house, its land had been cleared and broken up, fencing and fruit trees had been added, and six swine, four head of cattle, and five horses were living there. In addition, Percy had rights to 180 acres of "gift lands" provided by the colonial governor in 1676.

Lot 6—John Bowne (oldest son of William). Coming from Gravesend, John Bowne was an early negotiator for land purchases from the Lenape, beginning in December 1663. He was named as a recipient of land in the March 1664 deed with Popamora, and was a leader in the settlement of Monmouth County and Portland Poynt in particular. In October

1667 at the first meeting of Monmouth settlers, he was elected speaker of the Assembly and custodian of the moneys of the three towns. By 1669 he owned some livestock and recorded his earmark. In 1672, he became the justice of the peace. As of 1675 he had three servants and had acquired over 1,400 acres in Middletown, including two town lots and extensive out plantations, in addition to his eight acres at Portland Poynt.

Lot 7—Randall Huet, Jr. With his wife Dorothy, Randall Huet Jr. moved from Long Island to Portland Poynt, built a house, and planted apple and peach trees. In addition to his lot, he received 240 acres of land from the proprietors and also inherited a share of his father's land. Then in October 1672 he sold to Derick Tunison his "home lott and houseings 8 acres in Portland Point . . . with two acres meadow belonging thereto." Around 1679 Tunison built a nearby house for George Job, a 24- by 16-foot structure and "fit to shingle," and went to court to force Job to pay him. The same year, Tunison added to his land by a grant of 240 acres from the proprietors.

After leaving Portland Poynt, Huet became an entrepreneur. In 1674, he became partners in two businesses with Charles Haynes, an early settler in the Middletown area. One business involved 50-50 shares in the production of pine wood and pine tar. The second business was a sloop that Huet owned and used for unknown purposes; he sold Haynes a one-third share of the "sloop or boat, rigging, cable, anchor, appertenences, & sails" and a one-third share of profits. In 1676 and 1680 he bought extensive tracts of land in Colts Neck and Middletown. In 1679 a charter was issued for a whale-fishing company to him, his brothers Joseph and Thomas, and nine other men. Also in 1679 he received a proprietors' grant of 240 acres and in 1685 sold 240 acres (probably the same) to John Crawford of Middletown; the land was described as adjoining the bay and lands that belonged to Richard Hartshorne and Samuel Culver, placing it west of Portland Poynt village. He died about 1694.

Lot 8—William Bowne. In 1667 William Bowne and his wife moved from Gravesend, to Portland Poynt. In 1668 he had hogs and cattle and officially recorded their earmarks. He took part in at least one general court meeting, held in 1669 in the house of Randall Huet Sr. In addition to lot 8, he received a grant of 240 acres from the proprietors. He died in 1677, and his son John claimed land from his father's estate.

Lot 9—William Shackerly (also Shabeley, Shakely). When William Shackerly bought land in Portland Poynt, he was living in Rhode Island but also had a home in Barbados. His occupation was "mariner." There is no sign that he ever came to live in Portland Poynt, and he sold his lot in September 1672 to John Jay of Barbados, who was a Quaker. In 1673 Jay fell off a horse in Shrewsbury, broke his neck, and probably died on that trip accompanying George Fox, a Quaker emissary traveling from the bayshore, en route to Maryland.

Lot 10—Mathias Howard. Mathias and Hester Howard and their son Mathew were the mysterious family of Portland Poynt and probably the least prosperous. When lots were laid out in 1667, the Howards were not mentioned. Later they received lot number 10, though no records say when or what they paid for it. Their lot was the closest to the bay front where the sandier soil is not good for cultivation, salt air and wind can be harsh, and ground and surface water tends to be brackish. They came from Rhode Island, but the town is unknown; they lived in Portland Poynt as of 1669, but no other year; presumably they built some kind of shelter, but had no known livestock; and they must have worked to survive, but doing what?

We have no idea what happened to the Howards after 1669. In fact, only one document establishes their very existence. On May 26, 1669, Hester Howard signed an "indenture," committing seven-year-old Mathew to a 14-year term as an apprentice blacksmith and servant. Perhaps the father, Mathias, had died or disappeared; such contracts were normally made by men in those days. Hester and her son were probably left destitute and an apprenticeship was the best hope for Mathew's support. The indenture placed Mathew in the "charge and custody" of Henry Percy, blacksmith, and his wife Kathern; they also came from Rhode Island and lived in good circumstances on lot number 5 in Portland Poynt. Young Mathew was to live with the Percys as "a faithful & trusty servant," be fed and clothed by them, receive blacksmith training from Henry, and become "a free man" at age 21. Percy was then to give him "a pair of bellows, one anvill, one hammer," other necessary blacksmith tools, and "two new sutes off apparill, one sute for ordinary days common waring and the other sute for Sabath day waring."

The contract also provided that if Henry Percy should die during the 14 years, his wife would keep Mathew. But if she also died Mathew would then "go free and be at his own liberty." As luck would have it, Henry died by

The Barbados Connection

In its first 29 years, Portland Poynt had Barbados connections that involved five men: Shackerly, Jay, Steenwyck, Morris, and Richardson. This is surprising since all previous histories only say that English settlers came from Gravesend, to Portland Poynt, largely ignoring those who came from Rhode Island and never mentioning anything about so far off a place as Barbados. What was the Barbados connection about?

A lot of English colonists left Barbados in the 1660s. They faced political struggles between British royalists and supporters of Cromwell. Economic difficulties included falling prices for sugar, the main crop, and a growing scarcity of land as large slaveholding planters grabbed more and more space. Lack of opportunity for all but the most wealthy led to out-migration of people like Shackerly, Morris, and Jay that lasted through the end of the 1660s.

The New Jersey/New York region was a familiar place to go, since it had enjoyed trade relations with Barbados since 1650. Barbadian investors like Lewis Morris wanted to try their luck in New Jersey as investors and land speculators. Fertile land, at a premium in the West Indies, was limitlessly available in New Jersey. The area was described as "much cried up of late" (meaning "sought after") since the English took over from the Dutch in 1664. Morris obtained thousands of acres for his iron works in Shrewsbury and had 60 or 70 slaves. Farther north, extensive lands between the Passaic and Hackensack rivers were bought by Barbadians—15,000 and more acres each—and the area became known as "Barbadoes Neck" (illustration no. 9)

By 1680 Barbados turned around, experiencing "explosive development." Big and middle-size planters had turned the island into an amazingly effective sugar-producing machine and "the richest colony in English America." Presumably this wealth is what attracted men like Richard Richardson from Portland Poynt to seek his fortune in Barbados.

January 1672. That's when his widow sold the land to another Rhode Islander, Christopher Allmey. There is no mention of Mathew Howard, by then nine or ten years old. What happened to Hester is nowhere told. Could a guess be that they took one of Allmeys' boats back to Rhode Island to some remaining family there? Perhaps we'll never know—part of the Howards' sad mystery.

Allmey was a boatman, whose sloop had been used in the 1663–1664 negotiations with the Navesink Indians and carried most of the Quaker settlers and their moveable goods to Monmouth County starting in 1665. In the period 1667–1690, his boat made trips with passengers and peltries between Newport and other Rhode Island ports. At times he may have docked it in the mouth of Many Mind Creek beside his lot, as well as at land he owned in northeast Rumson, which he named "Passage Point." Allmey had a wife and three servants as of 1675 and owned over 1,000 acres of land in Monmouth County. He was taken to court on charges of commandeering a boat full of logwood and other goods and transporting tobacco and other goods to other colonies in his sloop without paying customs. A jury found him guilty of taking and keeping a boatload of whale blubber and "converting it to his own use" (not paying the royal tax). He also sued others for killing his cattle, not paying a £50 debt, etc. After 1690, he returned to Rhode Island and lived there until his death.

How the Village Fared

Nine of the ten original owners were actually present in Portland Point during the late 1660s. There were 19 residents in all, counting nine adult males, six with their wives, plus four children. One historian says that "a considerable number of houses were built" on the lots. There is documentation that five landowners built houses, but obviously the other four must also have done so. The owners of six lots kept and registered cattle, pigs, and/or horses.

In addition to their personal affairs, the new residents of Portland Poynt and the two related towns of Middletown and Shrewsbury had a lot of public business to manage. This ranged from surveying and dividing land into lots, to passing local laws, to punishing crimes and regulating behavior. They even dealt with how people in the three towns could kill pigs (see box at right). For such community needs, they created the first representative body in New Jersey, called interchangeably the Monmouth Assembly, General Assembly, or general court, which met at least a dozen times between 1667 and 1672. Its first session in October 1667 and most meetings thereafter were held in Portland Poynt in the houses of Randall Huet or Richard Richardson. John Bowne was elected Assembly speaker and custodian of moneys, Richard Richardson was recorder, and he, James Bowne, and Henry Percy were overseers for Portland Poynt.

The landmark sessions of the Assembly were those of 1667–1672 dealing with the survey and division of lands (reported above), the July 1670 session to settle accounts for the cost of purchasing the land from the Lenape, and a number of sessions up to 1672 concerning the dispute with the governor of New Jersey over his claims for "quit rent" or property tax. (The term comes from feudal times when a tenant was freed, or quit, from other obligations to his landlord by paying a monetary rent.)

At the July 1670 session, a bill was presented for costs incurred by William Reape and others during the Lenape negotiations of 1663–1664, including transporting Native Americans to New York, entertaining them, and paying the agreed land purchase price (covered earlier in this chapter). The bill listed 106 people as purchasers and residents who were to share the total costs amounting to around $39,485 in today's dollars. Of these people, a fair number had not paid their full share and 22 had paid nothing. The Assembly gave the deadbeats a payment deadline of November 30, 1670, and the penalty for missing it was forfeit and seizure of their lands.

The most controversial issues for the Monmouth Assembly arose because of a change of colonial governors. In the 1665 Monmouth Patent, Governor Nicolls had made three key promises: a seven-year tax holiday, security of land titles based on the purchase from the Lenape, and the right of local self-government. In New York, Nicolls had granted the Patent under authority from the Duke of York (brother of King Charles I). But in London, the Duke had already handed over New Jersey to two "Lords Proprietors," Sir George Carteret and Lord John Berkeley. Nicolls only learned about the transfer of power in July 1665 when Philip Carteret, Sir George's cousin, arrived in New Jersey to govern on behalf of the new proprietors. He brought with him The Concessions and Agreements, a document that reversed the three promises Nicolls had given in the Patent. Nicolls did not recognize Carteret's authority and maintained that his principal, the Duke of York, was bound by the acts of his agent, Nicolls, until such time as the agent was notified that his role was revoked.

For the next 37 years, Portland Poynt, Middletown, and Shrewsbury insisted on their rights under the Patent. Leaders in this revolt were three original patentees of Portland Poynt, Richard Richardson, James and John Bowne, and a later landowner there, Richard Hartshorne. As they and other settlers saw it, in 1664 the land had been bought from the genuine proprietors, the Native Americans; why should the new settlers pay for the land again in the form of annual "quitrent" or land tax? What was the basis for the land ownership claim of the English proprietors and the requirement that all landholders re-apply for land titles? If anyone had investment rights in the land, it was the settlers, not only by their purchase from the Indians, but also by the fact that they had themselves cleared and developed the land. After all their trouble, expense and hardship, they were being told that their Patent was worthless and that some people "wee simple creatures never heard of before," called "Proprietors," own their land and also have the right to govern them. By their popular resistance to the claimed prerogatives of largely absentee proprietors, the settlers were in effect foreshadowing what became the American Revolution a century later.

On the other hand, the settlers took on more power of self-government than the Monmouth Patent had intended them to have. They were within their rights to appoint their local officers, adopt local ordinances, and run a local court—all actions taken by their assembly meeting at Portland Poynt beginning in 1667. But in May 1668, when the provincial assembly of New Jersey convened by Governor Carteret decided to levy taxes, the Monmouth decision to challenge this action was really a rebellion. Though Captain John Bowne of Portland Poynt and James Grover of Middletown attended the first provincial assembly, the authorities of the Monmouth towns later repudiated its enactments that ran counter to their interpretation of the Patent. The towns feared that yielding to acts passed by

Swine Wild and Unmark't

There has been some "disorder" recently because people are unlawfully killing swine they say are "running wild and unmark't in ye woodes." The word "unmark't" means not having the owner's mark on the pig's ear.

To stop these "ilegall practizes", the Court now forbids killing unmarked swine within the town limits, even by their owners. In the future, the only way is, first, tell the town officers you're going to do it; then do it, outside the town limits; and finally, bring the dead swine "into the towne after emboweling the whole and intire" and present it "to publique view."

Anyone caught privately killing an unmark't swine will be fined five pounds. The dead animal must be presented as part of the proof, and the corpse shall "be disposed off as the court shall think fitt."

From decision of December 28, 1669, by the Court at Portland Poynt, Monmouth County Deed Book A page 20.

Carteret's assembly meant a surrender of their liberties and prerogatives. Carteret twice sent agents to collect tax levies from Monmouth townspeople; in 1668 they were rebuffed; in 1670, they met open resistance and riotous meetings, and were even beaten. In 1671, the East Jersey Assembly declared the Monmouth towns guilty of contempt of the lawful authorities of the province.

In 1674 the proprietors formally disowned the Nicolls Patent, declaring it "null and void." They ordered the inhabitants at Portland Poynt and the two other Monmouth towns to get new warrants, surveys, and registration for their land from the colonial government or risk being forcibly dislodged. The announcement met with continued violent opposition from the towns.

Finally in 1675 Governor Carteret eased off and sought to make peace with the settlers by issuing the "Grants and Concessions" document. It gave 500 acres each to the men named in the Monmouth Patent, and 120 acres to other early settlers and their wives, plus allowances for children and servants. But all these grants were subject to payment of annual quit rent. This "give-and-take" compromise was nevertheless described by certain historians as a victory for the settlers because it recognized some equity due to them under the Patent and provided compensation for their claims. Also, the governor's assembly began creating a local court system, eliminating the need for the local assembly and court that had often met at Portland Poynt, and John Bowne was appointed to be a justice of the peace in Monmouth. A calming factor was the influx of many new settlers who received their land from the governor and accepted his tax requirements. An uneasy compliance began to replace open controversy in some quarters, but many settlers remained notoriously independent minded and resisted the proprietors' control of civil government right up to 1702 when New Jersey became a royal colony.

Chapter Four

COLONIAL FARMERS

Very little archaeology has been done in Atlantic Highlands, and accidental in-ground discoveries during excavation and construction have been few and small. As a result, it is not possible to know the precise building patterns for houses, barns, sheds, pathways, etc. used by early settlers in and around Portland Poynt who arrived during its first century between 1667 and the Revolutionary War. Some of the new landowners undoubtedly started, as elsewhere in Monmouth County, by digging a pit six or seven feet deep and perhaps 12 by 20 feet in lateral dimensions; they held back the soil with wooden foundations lined with bark, and gave this cellar a plank floor and sod roof for a first season of occupancy. The next stage was often a one-story, two-room, cabin-like structure with wood walls plastered by clay. The roof was made of either spars insulated by bark and green sod, or reed or straw thatch. Nearer the creeks and their wetlands, instead of a cellar, logs would have been installed some feet below ground level to provide stability for a log superstructure; in excavations in wetlands areas of Atlantic Highlands at three locations in the 1900s and one in 2003, such deep-buried logs were found that were considered "very old," but unfortunately were not dated and their purposes cannot be identified.

At first, cooking was done in brick ovens outside the houses. Soon, however, house chimneys and fireplaces were built to bring ovens and cooking hearths indoors, with metal cranes that suspended kettles and pots over the fire. Chimneys were often wide and inefficient, delivering smoke inside the house and leading to a poetic recognition of the problem: "A smokey chimney and scolding wife/Are two of the greatest ills of life." Winter food supplies were laid in and stored in large quantities, including salted and smoked meat and fish, dried fruit, sacks of beans, and nuts. Sometimes an entire shed contained the household's catch of clams, oysters, crabs, and scallops from the bay; smoked fish could be stockpiled, because it lasted about a year.

Houses eventually grew in size and sophistication, using rough-hewn oak beams, wide-plank floors, and wooden partitions. The norm in the area was one-and-a-half story houses with English-style architecture. Exterior walls and roofs were usually covered in cedar shingles and in-filled with mud and straw. The few windows were small and had small panes; use of glass was minimized because it was a scarce and expensive import and a poor insulator against the cold. Furnishings at first tended to be simple, including homemade seating of wood and rush, beds of straw, and dishes of wood and pewter. But eventually families graduated to goose feathers for bedding, silver for dining, and upholstered seating. The houses of Richard Richardson and Randall Huet Sr. in Portland Poynt may have been of such a high standard, since they hosted meetings of New Jersey's first representative Assembly and Court beginning in 1667.

For the first several decades, major efforts naturally had to be focused on achieving subsistence and self-sufficiency. Much time and labor went into planting, weeding, reaping, and processing such typical food crops as cabbage, pumpkin, beans, potatoes, corn, and grains; grazing, tending, and butchering cattle, sheep, and pigs; catching game birds and animals; and making clothing, candles, soap, and other basics of living. For a while, the Lenape Indians remaining in the area sold some food provisions to the local colonists; Richard Hartshorne wrote a "Dear Friend" letter back to England in 1675 describing the bargain prices he paid them in powder, lead, or English pence for large quantities of fish, venison, and strawberries they brought to him.

Trails and paths that Native Americans had walked were instead now carrying the colonists' horses, carts, and carriages. Today's Avenue D, which was the dividing line between the lots of the first ten colonists, led to a landing on the bay that became "Wallings' Landing" in the early 1800s. At its southern end, that road connected with Kings Highway on its route between Middletown village on the west and the ocean on the east. Other paths, used for driving cattle in from the fields and known as driftways, had less fixed and formal existence.

Sloops continued making runs across the bay to Gravesend, Long Island, and through Long Island Sound to Rhode Island, where the colonists' former homes and some remaining relatives were located. Sometimes the boats brought back new settlers and their furnishings. From 1665 to 1690, Christopher Allmey did that from the mouth of Many Mind Creek, Rumson cove, and Wakake landing (Keansburg). Other boats eventually carried local products—mostly vegetables, fruit, and timber—to be sold in Manhattan, a round trip that could be done in a day.

"Greater" Portland Poynt

Several historians claim that the Portland Poynt settlement was short-lived. They write that it "for some reason did not thrive" and "did not last long." However, research done for this book has now produced a different, more dynamic picture, erasing the previous image of a mysteriously failed town.

The Second Wave of Landowners

Lot 2 of James Bowne passed to his eldest son, James Jr.

Lot 3 of Richard Richardson, who moved to Barbados, and the house he had built on it were left in the hands of his partner George Brown (Hornor 186, 250).]

Lot 4 of Randall Huet Sr. was bought by Cornelis Steenwyck in 1675.

Lot 5 of Henry Percy was deeded to Christopher Almey in 1672.

Lot 7 of Randall Huet Jr. passed to Derick Tunison in 1672, then to John Crawford in 1695.

Lot 8 of William Bowne, who died in 1677, was inherited by his sons John and James.

Lot 9 of William Shackerly was sold to John Jay in 1672.

What actually occurred was a transformation from its origin as a lonely, narrow outpost confined between two creeks, into the core of a growing homeland territory. Its ten home lots had been laid directly next to these sources of fresh water, with close-in boat access from the bay. Its houses were set in a cluster of rectangular lots, making a strategic nuclear settlement for purposes of self defense, as officially mandated in the Monmouth Patent. At the same time, it had been very quickly recognized that the settlers needed additional acreage if farming and grazing were to be conducted on a scale that offered not only family and community subsistence, but also the promise of individual enrichment and local economic growth. The village's first residents were not pampered gentlemen, idealistic dreamers, or sleepy layabouts, they were very practical and ambitious people who knew (or found out) how to thrive and prosper. And the land, far from being left idle, neglected, or abused, was turned into a productive asset.

Land acquisition was obviously the first requirement, and seven of the first ten landowners at Portland Poynt acted on it. They did not limit themselves to their little village—80 acres of "house lotts." They also obtained extensive lands in other areas of the bayshore, mostly in the largely flat meadows west of the original village. Soon, their total holdings came to over 4,600 acres; the brothers John and James Bowne accounted for 1,400 and 1,360 acres respectively.

Moreover, as shown by new research into property deeds for the territory westward from the village core, at least 35 families, including the ever-present Bownes, took up lands along this bayshore "frontier" during the century of the 1670s to 1770s (see "Western lands" below). This is clearly noteworthy expansion, not decline or stagnation.

By 1700, the first ten settlers within the original village parameters itself were gone. Six of them died, three moved away, and one had never come to live in the village. The village was fully into its second wave of landowners, including Bowne descendants, on seven of the original ten lots.

By the time a third wave was occurring, John and James Bowne began acquiring additional town lots, as well as outlying lots, until a major portion of the original village land was consolidated in their possession. In one expansion of the village footprint, John Bowne took ownership of the adjoining meadow land and lower hill-slope lands east of Many Mind Creek.

Another expansion of the settled village area was in 1743, when Jacob DeBowe arrived and acquired 80 acres of adjoining land along the bay west of Many Mind Creek, apparently including lot number 10, originally held by the Howard family. His farm was bounded by the 100-acre farm to the south that the first Leonard family member in the bayshore had taken over in 1700, by Bowne lands on the west, and eventually by the Carhart farm of about 20 acres on the northwest. DeBowes were in this location at least until the Revolutionary War, when their house is shown on the 1776 map by Colonel Elisha Lawrence.

During all this time, the Bownes in many ways were the "first citizens" and steadiest landholders in the Portland Poynt catchment area. Beginning in the 1700s and lasting into the mid- and late-1800s, their tracts accounted for a significant share of its territory. James Bowne's lot number 2 in the original village was the family homestead and main base. In the first century, the chain of its ownership and occupancy goes from him to his son James, his grandson Samuel (known as "Sam the Sailor"), his great-grandson Joseph, Joseph's cousin Safety Bowne, and Safety's son Daniel. In fact all occupants of this land were Bownes from before 1667 until the 1930s. The "Bowne House" that still stands there includes a 19- by 25- foot portion whose construction has been dated by colonial historians and architectural analysts to before the Revolutionary War, and a 19- by 20-foot addition built thereafter. The structure is listed on the Federal and New Jersey Registers of Historic Places, and is one of the three oldest remaining houses in and bordering on Atlantic Highlands.

It is true that, for various reasons, the name Portland Poynt gradually fell into disuse. Demographically, it became less concentrated as lot ownership became more consolidated in the core village and settlement dispersed over a "greater Portland Poynt" territory. From the beginning, Middletown was conceived as a larger population center; it started with 36 town lots and 36 outlots in the "Poplar feild" and "mountany feild," and its "further inlargement" was to be pursued "westward" of the town (as ordered on December 28, 1669 by the Assembly meeting at Portland Poynt).

In geographic and economic terms, the footprint and agricultural potential of Portland Poynt village and its extended Shoal Harbor zone were always limited by rocky hills on the east, southeast, and southwest and by the wide, marshy edges of the bay. Middletown had a far larger area and contained more level, less rocky, and less marshy land.

Politically, the prominence of Portland Poynt as a regional center was soon reduced. After 1672 there were no more meetings of the local three-town Assembly and general court, which held most sessions in the houses of Randall Huet Sr. and Richard Richardson in Portland Poynt. Even their personal influence was lost when Huet died in 1670 and Richardson left for Barbados by 1685.

As is always the case with larger population centers, Middletown soon overshadowed and absorbed Portland Poynt and its adjacent territory. The settlements along the so-called Shoal Harbor bayshore had close connections to Middletown on the south, in addition to those from Portland Poynt village to the east. At least 12 of the landowning families there also had Middletown village roots. A Lenape Indian trail that connected the village with today's Port Monmouth on the bay coast turned into an important link for the colonists as well. Middletown also received more attention from mapmakers who typically charted this more visible town with its church spires and fair numbers of close-spaced houses, rather than outlying farm spreads with sparse population.

In 1683, when the county of Monmouth was established, it was divided into two townships. The name Middletown Township was applied to the entire peninsula from Matawan and Holmdel on the west, to Sandy Hook in the east, and from the bay on the north to the Navesink River on the south, including what had been Portland Poynt. From that date until 1887, when Atlantic Highlands was incorporated as a borough separate from Middletown Township, it is often difficult to sort out the people living and the events occurring in these respective territories. The distinction has always been particularly blurred when it comes to the immediately adjoining sections that today are called Leonardo, Chapel Hill, Navesink, and Locust, which have longstanding family, geographic, and economic links with the Atlantic Highlands area. The boundaries between Middletown, Atlantic Highlands, and Highlands borough are arbitrary and artificial lines with municipal administrative roles, but little historical meaning in a real-life sense.

Western lands—Shoal Harbor

Four factors—Indian peace, the arrival of more settlers, the westward extension of bayshore lots, and rising economic prosperity—led to dispersal from the original central village of Portland Poynt with its cluster of ten lots. Indian peace, or more accurately, Indian removal and the disempowerment of those remaining, reduced the need for compact, easily defended housing clusters. New settlers were continually attracted, mainly from Long Island and Rhode Island, because large land areas were available under the 1675 Grants and Concessions, and because of the promise of greater political and religious freedom in Monmouth County than they had in their original colonies. The grants of acreage were per head, so there was motivation for each settler to bring in additional people such as cousins, in-laws, servants, slaves, etc. New arrivals often set themselves up in the second division of lands that the Portland Poynt leaders had made in 1669, starting with 36 outlots and salt meadow lots along the bayshore heading west from the village. Rising prosperity also contributed to this dispersion. Farmers with more cattle wanted more land for grazing, as well as for tilling, and the outlots were substantially larger than the town lots; some were as large as 2,000 acres.

The lands along the bayshore included even larger areas of salt marsh than exist now, after centuries of infill and drainage. A 1683–1685 map notes "Sunken Marsh" both offshore and on the land along the bay coast from west of Atlantic Highlands as far as Keansburg; because of these shallow waters or shoals, the colonists called most of the area "Shoal Harbor," encompassing at least today's Leonardo, Belford, and Port Monmouth. A later map from the Revolutionary War period contains the notation, "A Fine Foraging County both for Cattle & Hay."

Unlike today, salt marshes had direct uses and importance for subsistence in the early days. With few open meadows, and given the difficulty of clearing forest to make pasture, many colonists kept their cows where salt hay grew on the high marshes, safe from becoming prey to widespread wolves. Later, the farmers cut as much as a ton of salt hay per acre (yields as good as a seeded upland meadow) and carted it to the animals. The settlers also used salt hay to make paper and rope, and they even cut some of the coarse cordgrass, which they called thatch hay, for roofs, mattresses, animal bedding, packing, basket-making, etc. Coastal farms that included some salt marsh had higher value than those without it—even in the 1870s, when the bayshore area had over 1,200 acres of saltmarsh.

The band of bayside land marked for outlots and salt meadow lots was all suitable for grazing or farming and largely level but with gentle slopes along the south side that rise toward Garrett's Hill and High Point (today's Chapel Hill section). During the 100 years following the founding of Portland Poynt, deed documents show that at least 35 families took up these lands beyond the village's western limit at Bowne Creek and today's Wagner Creek (see box next page). Some of these landowners built houses on the land and physically settled there, using the land for crops and livestock, and fishing in the bay. Some others only fenced their fields and meadows, grazed livestock, and harvested salt hay while continuing to live elsewhere in the area. Still others were apparently land investors, coming on the scene to stay for a while and then resell their properties. Thomas Whitlock, a carpenter, settled in the Shoal Harbor area and bought and sold property there as a speculator, acquiring 11 parcels totaling 929 acres between 1675 and 1696.

Prominent among the settlers of these western lands was Nathaniel Leonard, whose father had helped found New Jersey's first significant industry, and whose descendants were economic entrepreneurs and town founders in what later became the borough of Atlantic Highlands. Nathaniel's father Henry and uncle James were descendants of the Leonard family in an iron-working district in Monmouthshire, England. In 1652 the brothers went to Massachusetts, where they helped build and run America's first iron mills in a number of towns. Henry Leonard and his wife Mary had eight children, and they all went to New Jersey after 1674 when Henry came to assist James Grover in starting a new iron works at Tinton Falls. Grover had three partners with Portland Poynt connections. John Bowne and Richard Hartshorne joined him in buying 6,000 acres of land where he found iron ore in the bogs and set up the works powered by the falls. An equal financial partner with Grover in the project was Cornelis Steenwyck, a wealthy New York merchant who had bought lot number 4 in Portland Poynt in 1675. But Grover quickly sold his half-interest in the mill to Colonel Lewis Morris, a recent arrival from Barbados.

With Henry Leonard as the ironmaster and Morris as owner, the industrial complex grew to include a furnace, forge, chafery, two corn or grist mills, a carpentry shop, a stable, and separate houses for black slaves (as many as 70) and white workers or indentured servants. The products of the furnace were carted to Rumson, where the Navesink River opened to the ocean, and were shipped from there to customers.

On his own account, Henry Leonard built himself a mansion house near the iron works and acquired over 1,000 acres in the surrounding region. Henry's five sons also bought a total of 5,116 acres in Shrewsbury and Colts Neck. The family members were wise to invest in real estate, because the iron works went out of business around 1714. In 1700, Henry's third son, Nathaniel (born 1662) made a strategic geographic move that laid the groundwork for the founding of Atlantic Highlands almost two centuries later. He swapped his Colts Neck lands for a tract on the bayshore west of today's Atlantic Highlands. He took up residence on a large farm that had belonged to his sister Sarah's husband, Job Throckmorton; Job had inherited it from his father John, whose residence had been at Garrett's Hill in today's Leonardo, with 100 acres adjoining and 20 acres of meadow.

Transplanted to the bayshore, Nathaniel Leonard and his wife Hannah Grover had three children. This branch of the Leonards soon named the area Leonardsville, today called Leonardo. Their son Nathaniel Jr. (1712–1763) was commissioned as Lieutenant of "Middletown Middle Company" in the British colonial militia of New Jersey in 1739. He married Deliverance Lippet in 1737, had four sons, and remained on the bayshore lands.

Families in the Western Lands, 1670s–1770s

Thomas Applegate	Samuel Legg
James Ashton*	Nathaniel Leonard
James Bowne	George*, John, Mathias and Thomas Mount
John Bowne*	John Pearce
Daniel Brown	Sarah Reape*
David and Benjamin Burdge	Christopher Roop
Thomas Carhart	Daniel and James Seabrook
William Compton*	John and Thomas Stillwell
Thomas Cox*	John* and David Stout
John and George Crawford (aka Crafford)*	Edward Taylor
Samuel Culver	Job Throckmorton*
Richard Davis	John Throckmorton*
Daniel Estell*	Edward Tilton
Peter Farrah	Henry Tunis
Richard Gardner	Garret (or Jarret) Wall*
Charles Haynes	Thomas Walling
Daniel and Thomas Herbert	Thomas* and William Whitlock
John and George Jobs	

Family that also had Middletown village roots as of 1667

During the Revolutionary War, two of these sons were active on the English side; their lands were confiscated by the revolutionary patriots, and one of them left the country. It is not known what lands were involved, but if the family was set back by the loss, it did not last long. Through the youngest son, Thomas, the Leonard family line continued its presence, added to its properties, and kept on expanding its influence in the bayshore area for more than two centuries (see chapters 6 and 7).

An earlier settler than Nathaniel Leonard was his immediate neighbor to the west, Thomas Applegate. Thomas arrived from Long Island about 1674 and by 1677 settled on 140 acres in Leonardo west of today's state marina. He became a prosperous farmer, helped by his six sons. Before he died in 1699, he established a boat dock known as Applegate's Landing. His great-grandson and namesake eventually donated a half acre of this land as a public landing in 1808, next to the area's first general store that he owned and ran.

His son Richard became the next big family landowner, and Richard's son William (1726–1776) inherited his "considerable estate." In the 1750s, William went on a buying spree that expanded this domain even farther. He acquired 100 acres from Thomas Herbert, a small parcel of bayshore meadowland from the heirs of Samuel Culver, an adjoining swamp-and-upland lot from John DeBowe, and an unknown amount and type of land from Samuel Legg that adjoined DeBowe and Herbert properties.

John Jobs, whose place of origin is not known, was present on the bayshore by 1667. By 1678 he had acquired at least 256 acres of land, and so had George Jobs, probably his brother. Despite his wealth in real estate, John was at first something of a scofflaw. In 1670 he was fined by the court at Portland Poynt for refusing an order from the town constable to help arrest drunken Native Americans at night and for cursing at him ("What a divell have I to do with you or his majesty either?") and his aides ("A plague confound you all"). Ironically, Jobs himself was appointed constable in 1675. In 1679, George Jobs was also taken to court for failure to pay Derick Tunisson for building him a house. John Jobs's holdings included land west of Portland Poynt village that he bought in 1676 from Thomas Huet, son of an original Portland Poynt settler. In 1685 John Jobs was wealthy enough to import three servants. A public road was laid out in 1706 across a corner of his fenced field and through his neighbors' lands; this probably is today's Leonardville Road. One of John's five sons, William, was still in the area in 1721.

Among the people from Portland Poynt village who also acquired land in the Shoal Harbor area were John and James Bowne, sons of original settlers. In 1697 they became owners of a "sedge island" seven acres in size located at the mouth of Compton's Creek. When John Bowne died in 1684, his holdings passed to his son John Jr. Known as "Captain John Bowne," the son resided in today's Holmdel, though he retained his Portland Poynt property at least until 1706, when a road was laid out along a path connecting his land to that of his neighbors John Jobs and Samuel Culver. By 1715, John had expanded his holdings in the county to over 3,500 acres, of which 2,400 acres were in the Portland Poynt/Middletown area.

As for James Bowne, when he died in 1695, his son James Jr. inherited his extensive lands and his five slaves. James's attachment to the Portland Poynt settlement is shown by the fact that he acquired his brother's half of the Shoal Harbor tract and held on to it, and that he lived in the house on Portland Poynt lot number 2. It is further underlined by his shedding lands of his father in other locations, which he conveyed to his four brothers.

During the course of its first century, the greater Portland Poynt area was a "small world" with close connections among the several dozen families living there. There was a chain of inter-marriages involving at least 17 of the families, led by the many offspring of the original Bownes. Among seven local Bowne males, one each married women from the Applegate, Seabrook, and Stout families, two married DeBowe women, and two married Grover sisters. Two Bowne women became the wives of Stillwells, and others wed a Compton, a Hartshorne, and a Wall. Other local families linked in marriage included Applegate-Stillwell, Applegate-Wall, Whitlock-Seabrook, Tilton-DeBowe, and Carhart-Walling. Large families were the norm, and available records show that five children or even five sons plus an unnumbered quantity of daughters were not unusual.

Eastern meadows and slopes

There was also eastward expansion from the original village, though it was less intensive and less extensive than in the westerly direction. Only a few landowners acquired property on the east bank of Many Mind Creek and the forested hill slopes east of today's First Avenue. Some of the creek-side lands, low-lying with a high water table, were bog or swamp, and part was meadow. Farther east, soils were rockier and less suitable for farming and grazing than those west of the village, and the land's main value was for wood supply.

The landowner with the largest acreage and longest sustained involvement in the entire eastern area was Richard Hartshorne. After arriving from England and making his first acquisition in Wakake (today's Keansburg) in 1669, he bought the rights and interests of William Goulding, an original patentee. This gave Hartshorne the zone topographically labeled Navesink Highlands, which stretches from the bay to the Navesink River, takes in all of the Borough of the Highlands, and includes the eastern hills section of what is now Atlantic Highlands. He expanded these holdings by purchasing Sandy Hook as well as lands in other parts of Monmouth County, until eventually he held about 4,000 acres in all.

In 1703 he moved from his homestead on the Navesink River to a new house on lot number 25 in Middletown village. Around this time he transferred the Navesink Highlands and Sandy Hook properties to his son William, who kept them intact until he died in 1748. William's sons Robert and Esek then divided the properties, with Esek obtaining the northern half. Esek's portion was 750 acres that parallel the bay, and it included the eastern 270 acres of today's Atlantic Highlands—an area called "Navesink Park" when it was annexed to the borough in 1915.

Also located east of Portland Poynt village was Benjamin Devill, an early arrival from Newport, Rhode Island. Beginning in 1667, he obtained extensive lands in the bayshore area, including 250 acres in Portland Poynt in 1676. This land was located along the bay and the east bank of Many Mind Creek, bounded by Richard Hartshorne on the east. It included the sandy beach now covered by today's marina parking lot, and a large area along today's lower Ocean Boulevard and Mount Avenue. Another local connection for Devill was that, in 1689, he married Judith Compton, granddaughter of original settler William Bowne and daughter of early English settler William Compton, the namesake of Compton's Creek in Belford. In 1693 he sold all his land to William Davies of New York City and moved to Gloucester County. Five years later, Davies resold it to John Evans, Commander of H.M. Ship *Richmond*. No information is available on Davies and Evans from their times as owners of this land.

Around the mid-1700s two houses were built up in the eastern hills, completely isolated from the core settlement in the flatlands around Many Mind and Wagner Creeks. The nearest one was a small farmhouse at "Point Lookout"—a wide bluff above steep bayside cliffs, with a view toward Sandy Hook, the ocean and the bay, the Verrazzano Narrows, and Manhattan. This house had a small role in the Revolutionary War and War of 1812 (see chapters 5 and 6) and still stands as a section of a larger house. Made of stone, it was supported by "tree beams" that can still be seen. A frame structure was added in the early 1800s. When part of the north-facing wall was removed in the 1990s, it was discovered to be packed with clay and straw wattle, a method dating to about 1800–1810. After that a third floor was added, and later still east and west wings.

Trades and occupations

The main occupations among the early landowners in Portland Poynt village and outlots were farmers and watermen. In the farming category were grain and vegetable crops, fruit trees, and animal husbandry. The watermen engaged in fishing and clamming, and running boats for freight and passenger traffic. Other trades represented included such basic occupations as blacksmithing (Percy), trading (Huet), weaving (Thomas Carhart), and shoemaking, leather working, and tailoring (several Bownes in the 1740s–1770s).

The variety and value of the available lands and livelihoods is well represented in an advertisement, published April 26, 1770, in the *New York Journal of General Advertiser*. It offers for sale "A Plantation . . . whereupon is the noted Watering Place, on the Highlands of Navesinks," today known as the Spout House above Henry Hudson Springs (illustration no. 12):

> It contains about One Hundred Acres, the greatest Part Wood Land; There is on said Plantation, a good Dwelling House, with a good Stone Cellar under the same, a good Kitchen, and an Out-House, a young bearing Orchard of good Fruit, likewise a considerable Number of other Fruit Trees, such as Peaches, Plumbs and Cherries; the Land is tolerably good for Grain, and Plenty of Fish and Clams, to be had in the Season, within a small Distance from the Door. it is commodiously situated for a Tavern, as a great Number of Watermen resort there in the Summer Season. Whoever inclines to purchase, for further Particulars, may apply to John Stout, living on the Premises, by whom a good Title will be given to any Purchaser.

As more land was bought and developed, the size and wealth of some farms was becoming noteworthy. For example, by the 1770s John Stillwell had 200 acres on Garret Hill, as well as three horses, 13 cattle, one slave, and a riding chair. Another diversified local landowner was Richard Hartshorne. In the late 1600s he possessed and managed large tracts of land in many parts of Monmouth County, was a partner in the Manasquan Beach Company with 2,500 acres of land near Barnegat Bay, was apparently a real estate speculator, had 30 to 40 head of cows and seven or eight horses, worked as an attorney in private practice, and had local and provincial governmental roles, including repeatedly-elected speaker of the East Jersey Assembly.

Other occupations and commodity trading of significance during the first century of bayshore settlement included the peltries trade, whaling, livestock, water trades, and logging.

Peltries. For some decades after English colonists arrived, commerce in the bayshore included a trade in furs and pelts that depended on Native-American hunters. Up to the early 1700s they were still catching bears, wolves, and foxes, as well as raccoons, otters, muskrats, skunk, deer, and some beaver. They brought the skins and furs to sell to the English in exchange for duffle coats or cloth, kettles, axes, and other iron goods, guns, and rum or brandy. One buyer of peltries was Christopher Allmey, who purchased lot number 5 in Portland Poynt in 1672 and who during summer months up to 1690 carried passengers and peltries to Rhode Island ports for shipment overseas. In a kind of export-import business, on the return trips he loaded up goods from the New England colonies that were in demand by bayshore buyers.

Livestock. Salted pork was another export product from the area. This is evident from an order received by merchant John Bowne in October 1697. Andrew Belcher, a Boston businessman, paid him £112, 10 shillings to supply 40 barrels of "well salted" pork (cured with salt from the ocean) and two "barills of mackrill." He wanted the barrels delivered to a hired sloop in New York that would carry them to New London, Connecticut, there to be boarded on a vessel headed for Barbados.

Tax records of the 1770s list livestock holdings of many local farmers, and it was not unusual for one farmer to own six pigs and a dozen cattle. A few farmers had a dozen or even two dozen pigs and herds with 20 or even 30 head of cattle. Higher numbers suggest a farmer had a large family or, more likely, was in the business of selling milk, meat, or hides.

Whaling. Soon after they set foot in the area, some early settlers in and around Portland Poynt got into the whaling business. Their interest may first have been aroused by the mention of whales in the 1664 land sale deed for the Navesink Highlands region. In that document, the Lenape chief Popamora reserved for "my own proper Use and Benefit the one half of all Such whale Fish that Shall by Winds and Storms be cast up upon the Sea Coast." The Lenape used these washed-up "drift whales," but they had neither boats nor weapons suited to subduing and capturing huge live whales out in the ocean. One point where a whale was captured in 1668 was Sandy Hook, which explains the naming of Spermaceti Cove.

The English settlers did not wait for half-shares of the occasional beached whale and went out in the ocean to catch them. At first, they ignored English law that assigned ownership of all whales to the king and required paying royalties to the king's East Jersey Proprietors for any whale caught (one-sixteenth of the oil and bone). For example, Christopher Allmey, who bought lot number 5 in Portland Poynt in 1672, was ordered to be arrested in 1677 for taking a whale off the New Jersey coast ("one boatload of blubber") and "converting it to his own use" (not paying tax on it).

Finally, hewing to the law, 12 local men established a whale fishing company on February 9, 1679, under a charter and proclamation from the East Jersey Proprietors. The founders included three Huet brothers, Randall Jr., Joseph, and Thomas, who were original settlers at Portland Poynt; John Whitlock and Thomas Applegate from the Leonardo/Belford area; two Leonards from Tinton Falls, Henry and Samuel; and five others. Randall Huet Jr. may have engaged in whaling before that, using the "boat or sloope" he owned as of April 1674.

The attraction of whaling was that, during the largely unproductive winters and in autumn harvest and spring planting, it offered a harvest of another sort. In winter, smaller whale species migrated from the Arctic Ocean to the warmer Atlantic bight between the coasts of New Jersey and Long Island. In this region the most common species was the Atlantic right whale, known as the "whalebone whale," which yields more oil than other types. Some new

56

settlers quickly exploited this opportunity to bring in extra income, probably even organizing regular "whale watches" as had been done on Long Island where they had previously lived.

Whaling was part of the attraction for settlers to come to East Jersey. This is clear in a 1683 report to the absentee proprietors in England by their surveyor general, Samuel Groome. He wrote: "Many both of New England, New York, and some parts of this Province stand ready to sit down" along the Atlantic as far south as Barnegat. There they could take advantage of not only the "good Upland and Meadows but also the Whale Trade," which he believed was likely to continue developing. On July 20, 1683, the proprietors instructed their resident governor, Gawen Lawrie, to take steps to promote fishing, and "especially the whale fishery, which we desire may be encouraged."

In 1685 "Whale Oyl and Whale Fins" from this coast were being exported to England, in addition to "Beaver, Mink, Racoon, and Martine-skins," as reported by John Reid. He said the coast was "exceedingly well furnished with safe, convenient Harbours for shipping."

Water trades. From early times, fishing and clamming, and travel and commerce by the watermen were central to the economic life of Portland Poynt and the neighboring bayshore. The watermen who were boaters sailed packets to the growing New York market, carrying the produce of local farmers (fruit and vegetables, and such livestock products as cheese, beef, and pork), the catches of local fishermen, and the logs of local wood choppers.

At first the packets anchored offshore. They were loaded from small boats rowed out into the bay from three places: the foot of today's First Avenue next to the mouth of Many Mind Creek, the foot of today's Avenue D, and from the Applegate farm at the foot of today's Appleton Avenue in Leonardo. Eventually docks were built at these points for greater convenience of loading and to reduce dependence on tides. The first dock was built of stone at the foot of today's First Avenue, probably in the 1750s; it was the watering place for shipping during the French and Indian War (1754–1763) when New Jersey law required all able men from 16 to 60 to arm themselves. The stone used in this first dock later became the basis for the pier of stone and timber that hosted the first steamboats and then the railroad trains in the late 1800s.

Logging. In eastern Atlantic Highlands, the wooded slopes and toplands of the Navesink Highlands had been targeted for logging as early as Hudson's 1609 visit, and had actually been harvested for timber by Dutch ships heading back across the Atlantic to relatively treeless Holland. But following the arrival of permanent English settlers in the late 1600s and early 1700s, this occasional tree cutting was succeeded by more sustained logging for the multiple needs of the new residents. Steep, rocky places and indifferent soils—like the Navesink Highlands—were favored for the location of woodlots because they were not prime farming areas.

The main wood uses were domestic: lumber for building houses, fuel for cooking and winter warming, and fencing of crop lands and livestock pastures. White oak was especially good as sawn lumber for houses. Hickory and other nut trees were favored as firewood, because they gave the most heat for their bulk. Fencing, which was usually post-and-rail style in the bayshore region, mostly used chestnut and red cedar because of their greater resistance to rot, as well as oak. Other domestic wood uses were for shingles, barrel staves, and furniture.

Gradually, local forestry developed a commercial side. Businesses were started for logging, woodcutting, lumbering, and producing such products as charcoal and tar, and transporting them to sell in local and more distant markets. In 1677 Christopher Allmey seized a

A Rowdy Lot

The people who colonized the bayshore area were not all virtuous, genteel, and hard-working. Early visitors write that the men as well as the women drank, that the whole population was interested in betting, rolling nine pins, horse racing, cock fighting, dog fighting, dicing, and card and cudgel playing. Lewis Morris, nephew of the iron-mill owner of the same name, described them in a 1700 letter to the Bishop of London as "perhaps the most ignorant and wicked people in the world. Their meetings on Sundays are at the Public House, where they get their fill of rum, and go to fighting and running of races..." The winner's prize in the horse racing was an intoxicating gallon of applejack.

Morris also accused the people of the area of being abettors of piracy and political rebels. There may be truth in the first label as Sandy Hook Bay and its many coastal inlets were well suited for harboring the ill-gotten gains of hijacking on the water; and in 1699 pirates were known to work from Bray's Landing just west of Pews Creek and Port Monmouth. The second label was indisputably correct, especially when people were rebelling against the hated Lewis Morris.

wrecked boat "laden with log wood and other goods," and was taken to court for transporting the logs out of state without paying customs. Carrying cordwood to New York from the bayshore and other areas of northeastern New Jersey within a day's sail of Manhattan was common at least up to the Revolutionary War.

A property being advertised for sale in 1758 on the bayshore was described as being well-wooded with oak and hickory and having "a convenient Wharf lately built, sufficient to stow 500 Cord of Wood, from which Place a ten Cord Boat at any common Tide, may go loaded, and with a fair Wind may be at New-York Market in three Hours from said Wharf." A decade later, an advertisement offered for sale a farm in the Middletown area bounded by a creek "where it is very convenient for carrying Logs or Cordwood" and near to a landing "from which a Boat may go all Winter, and not freeze up" and would thus be "very convenient to carry Wood to New-York." One of the earliest docks in the Portland Poynt area, Applegate's Landing, was a site for shipping cordwood.

According to a 1674 document, Portland Poynt hosted a tar-making business. The document created a partnership with equal profit-sharing between Randell Huet Jr. of lot 7 and Charles Haynes in "getting pine wood and making tar." Suggesting that they were waterborne in marketing their products, Haynes also bought a one-third share in Huet's sloop with rights to one third of the profits.

Resistance, Riot, and Rebellion

The dispute over the Monmouth Patent, which the early settlers prized and the proprietors rejected, had eased in 1675 (see chapter 3), but not for long. In the villages of the Navesink region, and in other East Jersey towns as well, there was still opposition to paying quit rent (land tax) to the proprietors. Many landowners refused to turn in warrants of survey for the lands they held, and thus avoided having their names appear on the quit rent rolls. Among those in arrears was original settler John Bowne, who in 1683 owed quit rent going back to 1678 for 940 acres at "ye Navesinks." The Navesink towns repudiated the proprietors' claim of the right of soil and of government, and upheld their privileges of self-government from the Monmouth Patent. Governor Lawrie, the agent of the proprietors, was instructed to combat this position. In 1684 he began negotiating with the objecting towns to make landowners take out proprietary Patents and pay quit rent arrears.

Led by Richard Hartshorne, representatives from the Navesink region villages met with Governor Lawrie in July 1684. Hartshorne asserted that the inhabitants were entitled to make their own "prudentiall Laws" and elect their own officers, and were exempted from contributing to support of a minister; he also made several demands regarding land use. If the governor accepted these points, Hartshorne offered that the towns would pay half the proprietary rate of quit rent and make up for one-third of the arrears within two years. Governor Lawrie's reply was a yes-and-no mixture, but his refusal to accept the proposed reduction of quit rent put matters at a standstill.

Six months later, after more fruitless exchanges, Governor Lawrie ordered the sheriff to take actions of distraint, meaning forced confiscation, against the delinquents in the Navesink villages. But these attempts were unsuccessful, and so Lawrie obtained a show-cause order against them in April 1685, demanding an explanation for their nonpayment of quit rents. This led to a compromise settlement in July 1685 under which the original patentees would pay half the quit rent rate set by the proprietors.

In April 1686 Governor Lawrie convened the East Jersey Assembly. A first order of business was to elect a replacement for John Bowne, the assembly speaker for the previous four sessions, who had died in 1684. The vote went to Richard Hartshorne, who held the post for 10 of the next 13 years. Having lost the confidence of the proprietors, Lawrie was removed from office in October 1686. Despite his strenuous efforts, collection of quit rents remained seriously deficient. In 1686, the payment rate was 51 percent for the 47 names on the quit rent rolls for the Middletown area, which included only a portion of the actual landholders. As assembly speaker, Hartshorne continuously resisted successive governors' attempts at taxation as a matter of principle.

Disgruntled elements in the bayshore area continued to resist rule by governors appointed by the proprietors until that system was replaced in 1702 and New Jersey became a royal colony. Resistance against proprietary government reached a peak and broke into outright rebellion in 1700 and 1701.

It started when 250 East New Jersey inhabitants, including James Bowne of Portland Poynt, signed a petition of "Grand Remonstrance" to King William in London in 1700. The petitioners refused to accept the new governor, Andrew Hamilton, who was appointed and instructed by the proprietors and beholden to them. Instead, they wanted a governor who would be "an indifferent judge" in the controversy between the proprietors and inhabitants. However, such peaceful protest by petition was not enough for some people, and mob outbreaks flamed in several areas.

In July 1700 a mob broke into the jail in Middletown village to free a dissident who had been arrested by the sheriff appointed by the governor. A few days later, Governor Hamilton actually led a band of 40 to 50 armed men to Middletown village to reassert his rule. He was met by the most violent and revolutionary opposition so far experienced—170 men from the Middletown area armed with clubs and staves. They forced him to return to Burlington. This rebellion was described in a letter written by Richard Hartshorne and Andrew Bowne, a nephew of the deceased John Bowne. They reported how Lewis Morris had threatened that the people must submit to Hamilton or he would embroil the province in bloodshed. Morris, nephew of the deceased iron-mill owner also named Lewis Morris, was a hot-headed supporter of the governor; he had been appointed by him to subdue the opposition to his government, and his threat was upheld by the governor. This attitude, accompanied by harassing and jailing dissidents and staging arbitrary proceedings against them, only stimulated further popular opposition and strengthened the desire to have a governor appointed by the king, not the proprietors. Hamilton, for his part, believed the inhabitants were deluding themselves that, if proprietary government was ended, they could tear up existing government land Patents and avoid new ones, acquire land by Native-American purchase alone, and stop paying any quit rent.

The biggest open revolt by Middletown and bayshore inhabitants occurred on March 25, 1701. It took place in Middletown village at a court presided over by Governor Hamilton, with the hated Lewis Morris sharing the bench. According to locals, the court consisted of a usurping governor and his bogus justices convened to examine a put-up case against a supposed smuggler and co-pirate of Captain Kidd, Moses Butterworth. Some observers then and historians since maintain the rebellious anti-Hamilton scenario that then unrolled in the courtroom was pre-planned by Hartshorne and several colleagues. A local innkeeper loudly declared that the governor had no authority to hold court. Outside, a local militia company was drilling by prearrangement, and the persistent beating of its drum drowned out the court proceedings. Then the company drummer, Thomas Johnson from the Portland Poynt area, led 40 militiamen into the already full courtroom. They were joined by a mob 100 strong, which broke up the session, shredded the court papers, released the prisoner, and seized the justices and the court staff, who fought back with swords. Believing that a rioter named Borden might die of sword wounds, the locals imprisoned the governor, Morris, and their cohorts in the jail portion of the court house, implying that a high official might be executed if Borden died. Four days later when he had recovered, the prisoners were released.

It took another year, further acts of dissent and disruption across the province, and a fear in London that the colony would destroy itself before the proprietors offered to surrender the right of government to the king, on condition that their personal land ownership was preserved. The King's Council approved the surrender, which was signed by Queen Anne in April 1702. The bayshore rebels saw it as a big victory. It was a landmark event for this new breed of independent-thinking, independent-acting people, who increasingly saw themselves as Americans rather than transplanted English colonists. In some ways its was a precursor of the Revolutionary War that broke out in 1776.

Slavery as Wealth

From the late 1600s until the early 1800s, many owners of extensive farming and grazing acreage in the area, like the Bownes, Hartshornes, and Stillwells, used slaves to work the land, process its products, and run their households. The Long Island area from where some of the early English settlers came had depended on slave labor during decades of Dutch rule. In February 1665, soon after the English took over all of New Netherland including New Jersey, official legal encouragement was given to slavery. This permissive stance turned into a virtual requirement a few months later, when the Monmouth Patent was granted in April to early settlers along the bayshore. It called on settlers to keep "an able Man servant or two such weaker Servants" and offered more land to masters with more servants; 150 acres for every full-grown, able-bodied male slave, and 75 acres for non-adults. The Barbados people who came to the area in the 1660s and 1670s were also used to having slaves. Only about 12 miles up the bay, the port of Perth Amboy received slave shipments from the West Indies and Africa for much of the 1700s, and Monmouth County farmers were known buyers.

Slave labor was crucial for new settlers getting started. Richard Hartshorne told potential settlers it was important to have "three or four sons or servants" to cut timber and plant corn quickly. There were at least four slaves in Middletown village in 1691. Slaveowners could generate more wealth than non-slaveowners because of larger land grants and the extra labor that produced extra income. Slaveholders in the Middletown area between 1784 and 1808 owned more than five times the average amount of land, four times the number of cattle, and five times the number of horses as freeholders without bondspeople. One author described enslaved blacks as "the species of property that best insured prosperity."

More than one out of five inhabitants were slaves in the 1790 census for the full territory of Middletown, which then covered the entire peninsula from Sandy Hook to Matawan; there were 491 slaves among 2,225 inhabitants, or 22 percent. Over the years, the biggest slaveowning families were van Maters, Crawfords, Hendricksons, Holmes, and Stillwells.

Available historical documents make clear that slaves in this area, like others, were simply regarded as property, like a plow or furniture, with a value calculated in hard currency. The 1715 inventory of Elizabeth Bowne's Middletown estate listed five child slaves aged 8 to 16, valued at £20 for the youngest to £40 for the oldest. However, the "Negro Boy Sextus about 10 years old with fitts" had a price of only £10. When James Bowne of Portland Poynt lot number 2 died in 1750, the estate inventory placed his five slaves near the end of a 26-item list, between an entry for "an old Chest Bowls knives and a Pole" and "2 loads of hay And a Pair of Boots." As evidence of slaves' property value, owners offered rewards for runaways in newspaper notices. For example, in 1756 Richard Stillwell of Middletown (probably from the Garret Hill area) advertised for the return of a slave with the name Cato, identifying him as "a sly, artful fellow" who "pretends to be free, speaks English as if country born, and plays on the fiddle."

In the late 1700s and early 1800s, there were moves toward the freeing of slaves. Some owners released slaves as a moral stance against human servitude, and some were simply saving on the costs of maintaining slaves in service; in later years, owners were complying with laws abolishing slavery. In other cases, a manumission fee was paid by the slave or a free black relative. The result was that by 1830 there were 37 times more free blacks in the Middletown area than in 1784 (see table). In 1849 the township still had at least one slave, whose owner sold his remaining six years of service.

It is believed that local ex-slaves may have been among the earliest free blacks to settle in the Navesink and Hillside sections directly south of Atlantic Highlands. Its long-time black population included the founders in 1855 of one of the first African Methodist Episcopal churches in the county, Quinn Chapel, which is still an active congregation. Prominent in the section and the chapel have been black people named Stillwell, originally coming from the lands of the white slave-owning Stillwells less than a mile to the west.

The table below lists a sample of 38 slaves and 18 slaveowners who were present in the greater Portland Poynt area during the period 1699–1825. The data comes from the 1784 local tax list, the 1790 population census, wills and inventories of deceased slaveowners, the freedom papers for slaves known as deeds of manumission (literally, to let go from the hand), and the

African-American Population		
Year	No. of free blacks	No. of slaves
1784	16	n.a.
1790	62	491
1820	389	261
1830	591	76

A Sampling of Area Slaves and Slaveowners, 1699–1825

Owner	Slave name (age)	Year and activity
Richard Applegate	Unnamed slaves	1775: Richard, aged 13, inherited slaves
	Jane and son York	1815: York born
Joseph S. Applegate	Jane and son Jacob	1808: Jacob born
John Bowne	Whan Deara	1699: bought from Richard Hartshorne
		1716: John Bowne's negro Jack to serve
		Frances Bowne for 2 years "commencing
		when Richard Hartshorne starts the term."
Andrew Bowne	Robin and Jack	1701: Andrew died as Middletown resident;
		his will freed Robin after 6 years, Jack after 7.
Elizabeth Bowne	5 slaves – 3 boys, 2 girls	1715: died at Middletown; inventory
(Andrew's widow)	(aged 8, 10, 13, 15, 16)	valued slaves at £ 125
James Bowne	Peter, Phillis, 3 children:	1750: James died at Middletown; estate
	Parvis, Pompey, unnamed	included slaves
Daniel Brown	Belfame (21-40)	1808: freed
Robert Carhart	Lot and daughter Lette	1806: Lette born
John Compton	Clarissa and son Harry	1813: Harry born
John Edgar	"The wench Phillis"	1787: John bought her from William Bowne
Richard Hartshorne	Whan Deara	1699: sold to "Capt Jno Bowne"
Esek Hartshorne	One slave	1778: listed in Middletown tax rateables
	Robin (21)	1792: freed
	Aaron (21-35)	1794: freed
Richard Hartshorne	One slave	1778: listed in Middletown tax rateables
Thomas Seabrook	Amy	1786: Thomas sold her
Stephen Seabrook	Hager and daughter Poll	1809: Poll born
John Stillwell	Phillis (21-40)	1805: freed
	Prince (21-40)	1815: freed
	Hester Hampton (28)	1825: freed
Thomas Walling	Cate	1816: sold her to Nimrod Woodward
Nimrod Woodward	Cate and son Cezar	1816: bought Cate from Thomas Walling;
		Cezar born
	Phebe and son John	1804: John born

so-called "Black Birth Books." These last two documents were tools for monitoring and enforcing compliance with the 1804 law for the Gradual Abolition of Slavery passed by the New Jersey Legislature. It provided that children born of slaves after July 4 that year would be free after serving their owners up to 25 years of age if male, and 22 if female. So that children could document eventual claims to freedom, slaveowners were required to register in the Books the birth date, gender, and name of each child, the mother's name, and their own names and places of residence.

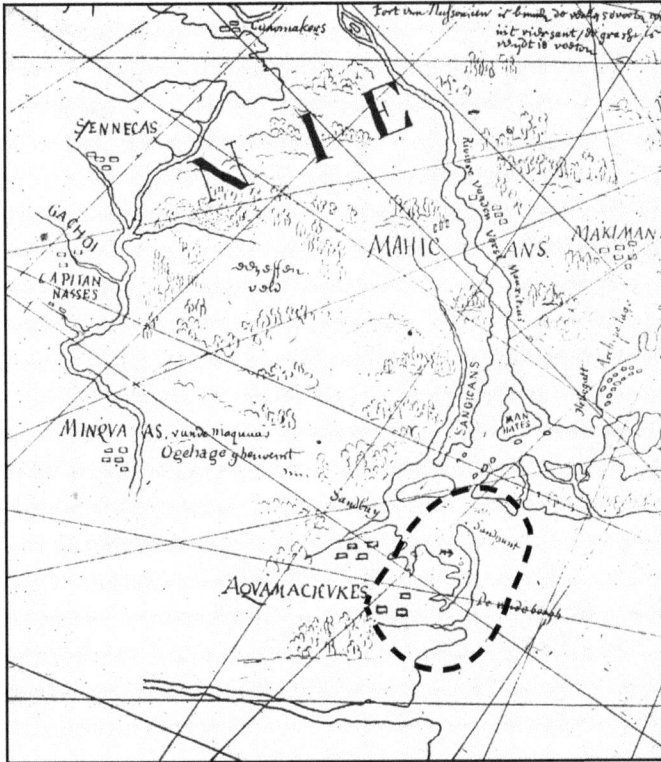

1. Indian villages. *This 1614 map was made by Dutch explorer and fur trader Adriaen Block. On the Navesink peninsula (inside dotted circle) he drew three rectangles representing Lenape villages located between the bayshore and the Navesink River. To the right of Sandpunt (Sandy Hook) is an anchor, showing that Block landed on the bayshore just about where Hudson did five years before. Above the circle, note the island labeled Manhates (Manhattan).*

2. Giovanni de Verrazzano, 1523. *He was one of the earliest European visitors to Sandy Hook Bay. He had a good impression but did not stay, noticing the land was already occupied by many people wearing bright feathers. If he had settled here, would we speak Italian (his nationality), French (his employer), or Lenape (his hosts)?*

3. Lenape lands. *Today's New Jersey was part of New Netherland until 1664. So this section of a 1635 map has some Dutch place names, such as Sant Punt (Sandy Hook). It also has the names of 16 Lenape Indian groups, including the "Neve Sincks," (Navesinks) along the bayshore.*

4. Lappawinsoe. *One of the few Lenape whose image has survived the centuries, he was a chiefly figure with a medicine pouch around his neck and tattoos on his forehead. This painting by Gustavus Hesselius is from 1735, when Lenape from New Jersey sought refuge in his eastern Pennsylvania territory.*

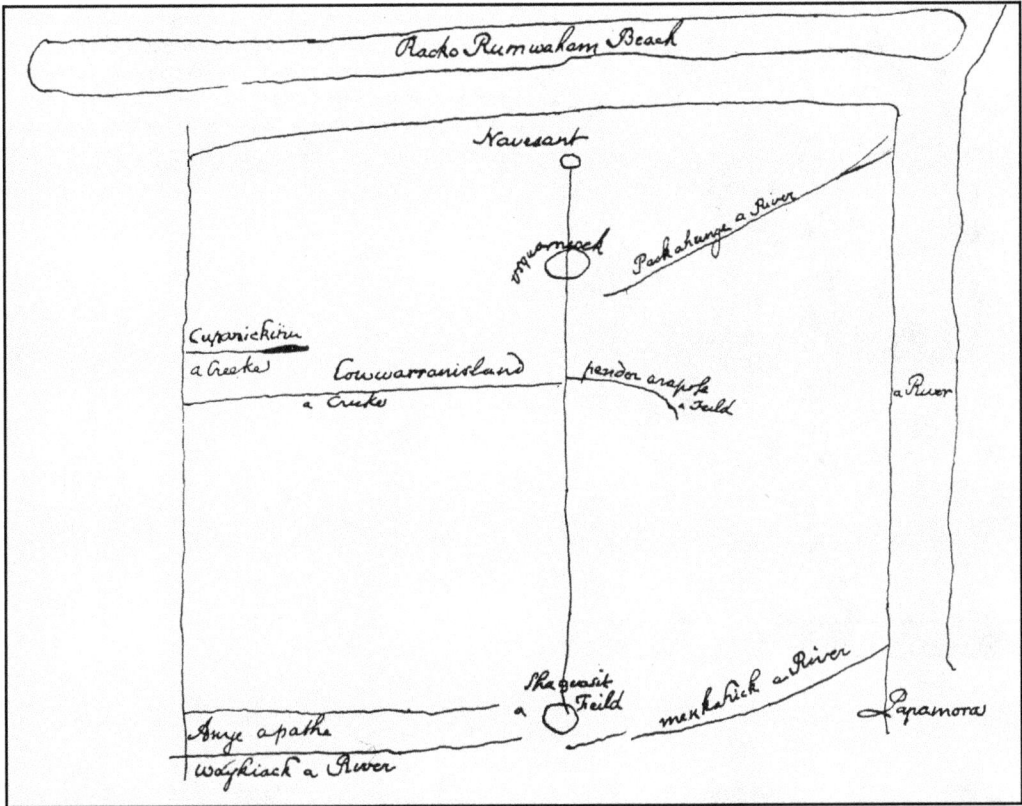

5. 1664 deed map. *East of the Navesink peninsula (north is to the left), "Racko Rumwaham Beach" is Sandy Hook—a Lenape place name followed by an English explanation, like all other markings on this 1664 map. Note the name "Popamora" in the lower right; he's the Lenape chief who signed the sale deed for all this land.*

6. Indian artifact collector. *Godfrey Horn holds a bushel basket with some of his many finds from Lenape times on the Navesink peninsula. He searched for arrowheads, axes, chisels, cooking pots, and other Indian relics during free time from his job as a house painter in Atlantic Highlands and after retirement in the 1960s.*

7. Real estate dealer, *c.* **1651.** *A surveyor and businessman in New Amsterdam, Augustine Herrman negotiated several land-sale deeds with Lenape chiefs along the bayshore, but the Dutch governor invalidated his purchases. Was this because they looked like land speculation or because he had publicly complained about the governor?*

"Henry Hudson's "Half Moon"

8. View from the wigwam, 1609. *Watching that boat pull into the bay had to be a big surprise for the people in the wooded hills. Their ancestors had been on this land for thousands of years. Hudson's ship rested at anchor only six days, but after him came the Dutch, the English, and gradual eviction of the Lenape.*

9. English settlements emerge. The
Navesink Patent *covered the entire northeastern
coastal corner of New Jersey, from the Raritan
River to Barnegat Bay. It was the third New
Jersey tract authorized for English colonial
settlement and soon contained Portland Poynt
(today's Atlantic Highlands), the second town laid
out in the state—Elizabethtown being the first
such tract and town.*

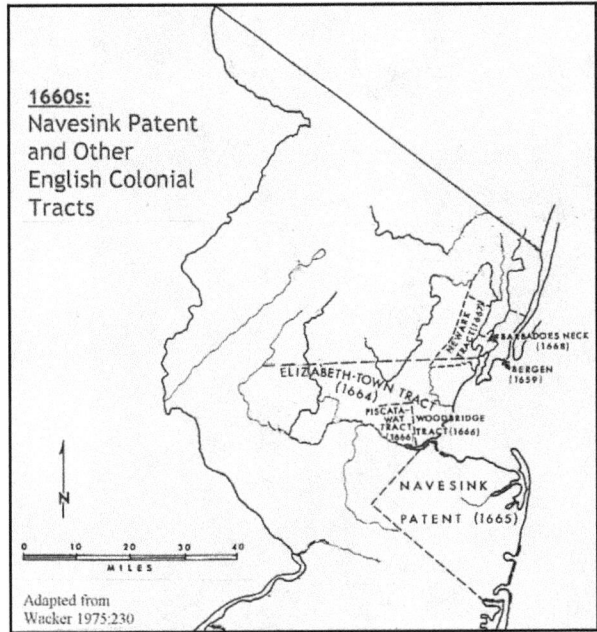

**1660s:
Navesink Patent
and Other
English Colonial
Tracts**

Adapted from
Wacker 1975:230

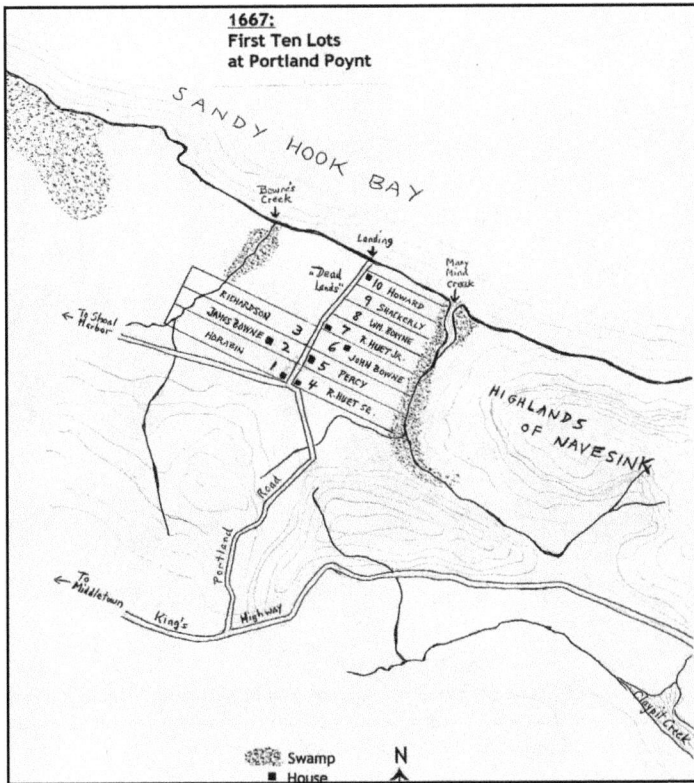

**1667:
First Ten Lots
at Portland Poynt**

**10. First ten lots at Portland
Poynt**. *In December 1667 the
boundaries were drawn for these
long home lots. Five owners came
from Long Island and the others
were from Rhode Island and
Barbados—all English. The location
of seven houses is known from later
maps. The road in the middle is
today's Avenue D.*

11. The mayor of New York lived here? *Cornelis Steenwyck, Dutch trader and storekeeper, peered over his silk-tasseled high collar and signed a deed for lot 4 in Portland Poynt from the original owner's widow in 1673. For three years before and two years after, he was the mayor of Manhattan during English colonial rule—and the second wealthiest New Yorker.*

12. Spout House. *The name was given because its lands contain the natural spring where local Lenape drank for millennia, and where many sailing ships later filled their water casks before heading out across the ocean. This postcard shows the house at its original size, as built before the Revolutionary War. It still stands, though expanded, at Belvidere and Prospect Roads.*

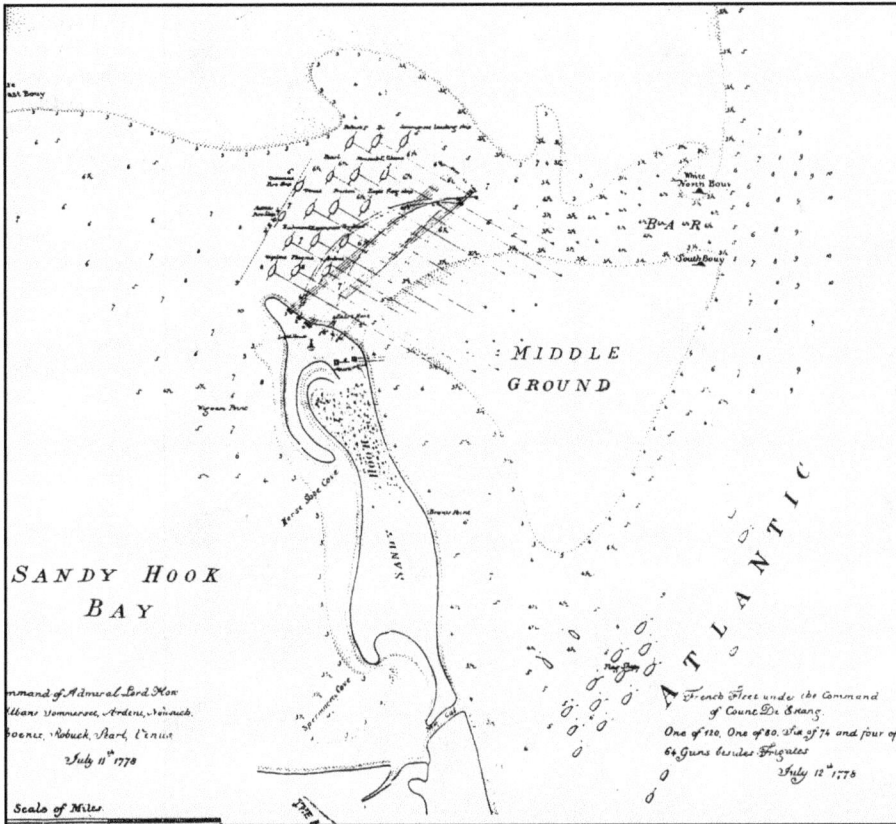

13. Standoff of British and French fleets at Sandy Hook, July 12, 1778. *Seventeen British ships (top) with 614 guns lined up to fire east-southeast, as shown by diagonal lines. Opposite the "new cut" that made Sandy Hook an island (lower right) are 16 French ships with 1,000 guns and four frigates.*

14. Bucolic scene. *This panoramic view from the mid-1800s shows farms in the meadows west of Many Mind Creek (foreground) and woods in the hills to the east (background). A few farmsteads are scattered around the lowlands. Watercress, asparagus, and watermelons were among the crops.*

15. Farms, woods, and bay mud. *Eleven farmhouses are within the boundaries of today's Atlantic Highlands in this 1844 map by the U.S. Coastal Survey Office. Probably half the land is forested. Avenue D has one intersection, where it meets Leonardville Road; from there, Portland Road continues south to King's Highway. Note that the bay has mud, black mud, and "S. Mud" (for soft or sandy?).*

16. **Hooper farmhouse**. *From its position atop the bluffs at today's Scenic Court north of Ocean Boulevard, the Hooper homestead had a sweeping view, as shown in this painting from the mid-1800s. It was on the bay side of today's Ocean Boulevard opposite Grand Avenue.*

17. Point Lookout. *From the panorama over the bay, Sandy Hook, and the ocean, as well as toward New York and Staten Island in the distance, it's easy to see why this high point in Atlantic Highlands became a strategic observation and guard post in the Revolutionary War and War of 1812—and a tourist attraction up to today. Little changed by 1880 when this drawing was made, except for the many fishing and clamming boats.*

18. The big picture. *Looking from Hillside Avenue down to the bay, this 1879 panorama painting was a real-estate promotional tool. The new building lots in the foreground were for sale, the curving "lake" in mid-picture was actually swamp land around today's Foodtown mall, and the Methodist church located along First Avenue on the right had not yet been built.*

19. Developers arrived rapidly. *By 1883 home-building lots were offered for sale on seven large tracts. The largest one was the Atlantic Highlands Association, a church-dominated group that also held camp meetings in the Auditorium (lower left). This map was published by Reverend John C. Nobles—minister, real-estate agent, and publisher of the* Atlantic Highlands Herald *newspaper.*

20. Plenty of patriotism. *All surviving old soldiers who were veterans of the Civil War (1862–1865) still had places of honor more than 50 years later with backing from a float full of flag-waving youngsters. The scene is from the June 15, 1917 Loyalty Parade that promoted registration for military service in World War I.*

21. A founder and first mayor. *This portrait of Thomas Henry Leonard (1843–1930) gives hints of his steely determination and buttoned-up mind that concentrated on promoting the new town of Atlantic Highlands beginning in the 1870s. He was a big dreamer, a practical capitalist, a committed Baptist and temperance man, and had a yen for history—both to write it and be in it.*

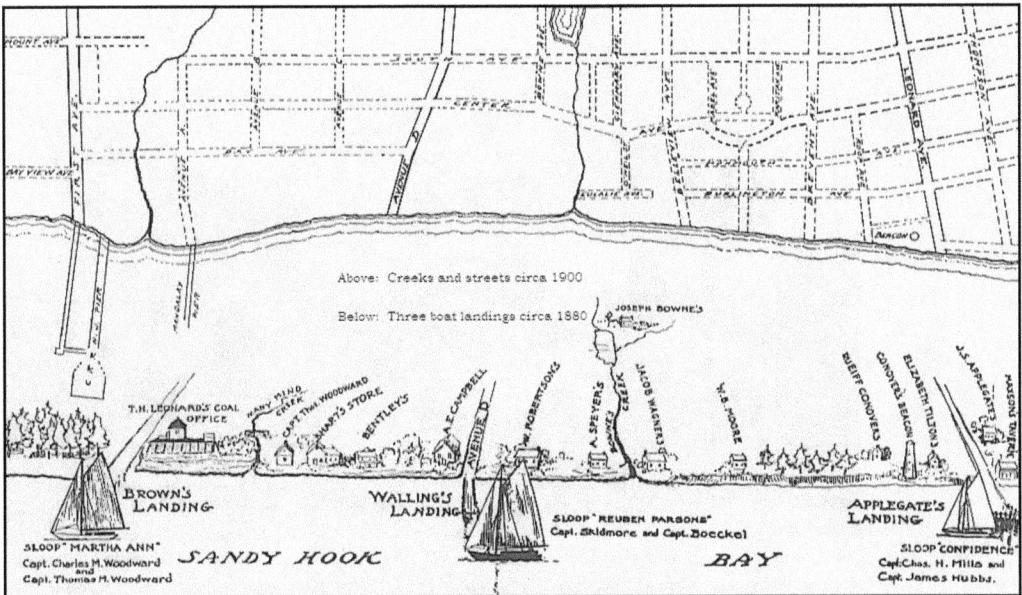

Above: Creeks and streets circa 1900

Below: Three boat landings circa 1880

JOSEPH BOWNE'S

T.H. LEONARD'S COAL OFFICE

MARY MIND CREEK

Capt. Thos. WOODWARD

SHARP'S STORE

BENTLEY'S

A.E.CAMPBELL

AVENUE D

M. ROBERTSON'S

J.A.SPEVENS

JACOB WAGNER'S

W.B. MOORE

SHERIFF CONOVER'S

CONOVER'S BEACON

ELIZABETH TILTON'S

J.S.APPLEGATE'S

PARSON'S DEPOT

BROWN'S LANDING

WALLING'S LANDING

SLOOP "REUBEN PARSONS"
Capt. Skidmore and Capt. Boeckel

APPLEGATE'S LANDING

SLOOP "MARTHA ANN"
Capt. Charles M. Woodward
and
Capt. Thomas M. Woodward

SANDY HOOK

BAY

SLOOP "CONFIDENCE"
Capt. Chas. H. Mills and
Capt. James Hubbs.

22. Water transport was always important for Atlantic Highlands and the bayshore. *In the 1870s, small packet boats worked from three nearby landings to carry local fish and vegetables to the New York market. When Brown's Landing got a 1,450-foot long dock in 1879, it started dominating the maritime scene for commerce and added tourism and commuters to the mix.*

73

23. Foster's Pavilion was on First Avenue at the end of the steamer dock. *One of the first buildings in the emerging town (1880), it had bath houses, a restaurant, a few rooms to rent, and a pavilion and a pier for enjoyment by "the moral, temperate and religious elements from the cities." Owner William Foster (inset) was active in the 1880s promotion of the new town.*

24. Travelers stop and sip. *The Columbus Hotel's 25 guests were not vacationers but commercial people. It received one of the earliest liquor licenses in town in 1893, over strong opposition by temperance people. The photo shows proprietor Edward Oakes, wife Katherine, some of their five children, a 1915 Packard (left), and a Model T Ford of 1912–1915 (right). Later renamed Lenox Hotel and Tavern, then no longer a hotel by 1923, it burned down in April 2004.*

25. Posh places. *The classy hotels of the Victorian era were on Bay View Avenue (today's Ocean Boulevard). The 125 guests at Sea View House, the porched hilltop building (upper left), paid the most: $30 a week in 1917. Other big, stylish spots were the Lockwood (60 guests), Windsor (80 guests) and the massive Grand View (400 guests), known for Sunday concerts and horse riding. The long arch-roofed building (lower right) is the Bay View station of the railroad.*

26. Regaled at the resort. *After daytime outdoors sporting, vacationers headed to the Casino, located on a high bluff on the bay side of today's Ocean Boulevard. Built in 1896 as the social and entertainment center of the resort, it hosted dances, shows, assemblies, card games, billiards, etc., every night of the week from Memorial Day to Labor Day.*

27. Hotel Normandie. *Still standing at the southwest corner of Bay Avenue and Avenue A, the building that housed the hotel until 1920 was built in 1881. Most hotels and boarding houses were on the east side of town and catered to the summer resort crowd, but the Normandie was on the west side and stayed open year-round. It had beds for 25 guests.*

28. Auditorium. *In 1881 the Atlantic Highlands Association began holding summer camp meetings in a hillside bowl called the Auditorium (today's Auditorium Drive) and running a tenting ground called Camp Hilton (along today's Bayside Drive). The Auditorium had a small stage and plank seats for 4,000 people.*

29. Tenting. *Named for Judge Henry Hilton, who owned the land, the camp grounds extended from Henry Hudson Spring a quarter mile down the road. Tents were set up each summer on wooden platforms and 20 to 25 families would vacation there. The grocer and other merchants hauled provisions to campers by horse and wagon.*

Camp Hilton, Atlantic Highlands, N. J.

30. Tents, boats, trains. *Next to the tent camp was a dock for recreational boating and swimming in the bay. Along the water's edge ran the railroad line between Atlantic Highlands and Highlands, which delivered campers to a stop called Hilton Station (see train at right).*

31. Graceful rustic-style span. *Known as the "Stone Bridge," it was built in 1896. It carried Mount Avenue from the high hills, then called Navesink Park, down steep "Breakneck Hill," where carriage riders risked life and limb, over Grand Avenue, to the Victorian homes district. The bridge was restored to its original condition in the 1990s.*

32. Protestant row. *Built in 1894, the Central Baptist Church at Third and Mount Avenues is unusual for its Romanesque Revival architecture. It is still one of the largest wood-shingle structures in Monmouth County. Some called Third Avenue "church street" because Baptist, Presbyterian, and Methodist congregations were (and are) all there, within a couple of blocks.*

33. Seven slate roofs. *That's how many top sections were on the fancy railroad terminal in Atlantic Highlands. This photo shows a waiting stagecoach and sulky and, in the foreground, the drinking fountain with one side for people and one for horses.*

34. Just like they had out West. *A local stagecoach line ran in the 1890s from the railroad terminal and the steamboat-railroad dock in Atlantic Highlands to Navesink village. The owner-driver since 1867 was Charles Green, shown here with his horse, coach, and passenger in front of the Atlantic Highlands National Bank, still standing at First and Bay Avenues.*

35. Train jobs. *Transport and employment both improved in town when the railroad was built in 1892. The Levering-Oliver lumber shed is in the background. Did local cattle herds require train cow-catchers?*

36. Railroad-steamboat pier. *The set-up from 1892 onwards is clear in this early 1930s aerial view. First Avenue is the white diagonal heading up the hill, and the railroad tracks are the other diagonal. Passengers reached the pier by the narrow L-shaped boardwalk at left. The track toward Highlands goes off to the left. The short pier on the right leads into the small boat-harbor lagoon next to Many Mind Creek.*

View of Atlantic Highlands from the Pier

37. Shore cottages. *Coming off the railroad-steamer pier, the train heading for the Highlands swung around to the east and passed in front of the row of grand Victorian houses lining the bayfront—and they still do. The arc of water beside the railroad trestle is where landfill in the 1940s created today's harbor.*

38. Porches and gables. *Owned by a town grocer, George Brooks, this Queen Anne cottage on Third Avenue also had gingerbread, diamond ,and scalloped shingles, and the gracious air that verandahs offer. Its size, style, and hilly location are fairly typical of many houses built before and after the turn from the nineteenth to twentieth centuries.*

39. The ice man cometh. *Before electric refrigerators, food was preserved in ice boxes. Thomas Dowd made a business of keeping them filled, via home deliveries with his horses and wagons. His team is resting at First and Center Avenues in this photo, which, judging by the utility pole, dates from after 1896 when electricity arrived in town.*

40. Horse-drawn carriage road. *Looking north from near Center Avenue, First Avenue was a dirt road at the turn of the century. The first flagstone sidewalks were laid in 1890. The traffic jam consists of four wagons and a bike in a single block. Striped awnings were "in" as front dressing for stores and the Columbus Hotel, the hipped-roof building second from right.*

41. Buggy street. *Looking south from Bay Avenue a few years later, First Avenue has many parked cars, a bicycle, and a child mid-street staring at the photographer. Rows of second-floor porch balconies line both sides of the street. Varied architecture adds to the picturesque appearance. The Atlantic Highlands National Bank with its unique window arches is at far right.*

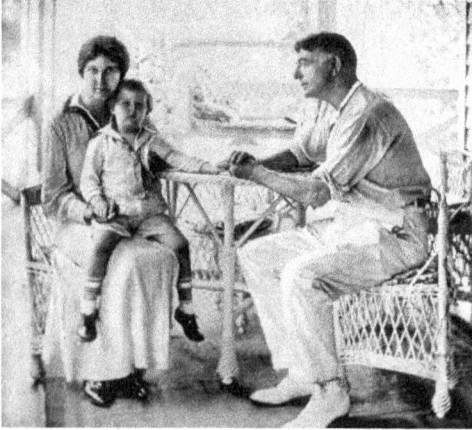

42. Theatricals. *Robert B. Mantell, a famous actor and director at the peak of his 50-year career, is shown with his wife and leading lady, Genevieve Hamper, and their son Robert Bruce Jr., after 1907. That year he bought the elegant house, which he named Brucewood (today St. Agnes Thrift Shop). During the summers, members of his Mantell Theatrical Company lived in the third floor and rehearsed plays in a converted barn.*

43. Teddy was here. *Arriving by boat from the north, leaving by train for the south, President Theodore Roosevelt came ashore in July 1902, proving that Atlantic Highlands was a key transport terminal and turnaround point—and a celebrity magnet. Left of TR is New Jersey Governor Franklin Murphy.*

44. Strauss and house. *The most privileged ferry riders had reserved staterooms, including the three Strauss brothers, who were partners in a Manhattan import and notions business. In 1893 Adolph (in profile) built the 21-room Queen Anne-style mansion atop Mount Avenue, now owned by the Atlantic Highlands Historical Society and known as the Strauss Mansion Museum.*

45. Steamers to the Shore. *On summer weekdays, three commuter ferries with many wealthy commuters aboard made 70-minute runs across the bay from Cedar Street in Manhattan to Atlantic Highlands. The queen of the fleet was the 297-foot* Asbury Park *(1903–1918), shown with flag, pennants, and populated decks. The other two were* Monmouth *and* Sandy Hook.

46. Atlantic Beach Amusement Park (1915–1941). *Never before published, this aerial view shows the whole layout. The midway ("S" shaped path in the photo) had games of skill and chance. To the right is the undulating roller coaster. The merry-go-round is the large circular building. Swimmers' bathhouses are in the rectangular building above the "A" in "Atlantic." The photo is from Dorn's Photography Unlimited Classics Collection, Red Bank.*

STEAMER
Mandalay
MUSIC · DANCING

TO ATLANTIC HIGHLANDS, FOR
ALL JERSEY COAST RESORTS
SCHEDULE
WEEK DAYS AND SUNDAYS
Leave New York   Leave Atlantic Highlands
9.45 A. M. · 1.45 P. M. · 8.00 P. M.   11.45 A. M. · 5.30 P. M. · 9.45 P. M.
TRAINS AND TROLLEYS TO ALL POINTS

47. Fun sailing to fun. *The Mandalay brought thousands of excursionists daily on three round trips from Manhattan to the amusement park. The trip featured many flags flying, live music and dancing, and joyful crowds before and after the rides, games, and beach antics at Atlantic Highlands. The Mandalay first docked at Avenue A, then moved to a new pier at Avenue D.*

48. Trolley times. *From 1908 to 1921, Atlantic Highlands was connected to Highlands, Belford, Red Bank, and Keyport by trolley lines. In town, trolleys went north on First Avenue, west on Center, south on Railroad Avenue, back to First. In the photo, passengers are at the Water Witch stop in the Highlands. Fare from Atlantic Highlands: 5¢.*

49. White's Grocery Store, 1912. *On the northeast corner of Ocean Boulevard and First Avenue, White's stocked fancy groceries for its summer clientele from New York. The photo shows Eddy's Fruit Jellies, Sunshine Biscuits Bon Bon, Crystal Sugar, Borden's Eagle Milk, and bananas. Daily orders from mansions and camp tents were personally delivered. Left to right, here stands Charles Mount, Maynard Card, unidentified, and Ashley Roop.*

50. Building with three lives. *On First Avenue between Mount and Center Avenues, this building was a livery stable until automobiles came on the scene. Around 1904 William N. Snedeker turned it into a garage and car showroom, seen here through its front door. In 1921 it was remodeled as the Atlantic Cinema, 25 years later got a new facade, and is still a movie theater.*

51. Dress-up time. *School play? Halloween costumes? Fashion show? For some reason elementary students were all costumed in 1915, already showing a lot of character.*

52. "Snyder's Bathtub."
Under Mayor Charles Snyder (1916-1920), a lagoon was dredged and bulkheaded to provide a boat basin on the west bank of Many Mind Creek next to the bay. Sometimes, a dozen large sloops and a schooner or two were based there, as well as numerous power launches. The Atlantic Highlands railroad pier can be seen at the far right.

53. Sign up for war. *These women carrying the flag were part of a large parade on First Avenue, held June 15, 1917, to promote millitary registration for World War I. There were floats, 69 decorated autos, fire company rigs, bands playing Sousa marches, Red Cross volunteers and 1,000 children stepping out, and 8,000 people at the ceremonies.*

54. Off for training. *The volunteer spirit was exemplified by two local enlistees in uniform, Private Ashley Roop and Major Brayton E. Failing, M.D. They rode in an open-top buggy draped with a large sign reading "We Went, We Were Not Sent."*

55. Back from battle. *A major Welcome Home Celebration was held for returning troops August 21, 1919. Officers and men, soldiers and sailors marched between lines of spectators and parked buggies. In official ceremonies that day veterans received a special medal and framed testimonial from General William Barclay Parsons of the famous fighting engineers.*

56. Homefront service. *Led by two horses, three soldiers in uniform and six nurses in white rode on this float. The banner on the side reads: "The girls behind the men behind the guns." Soldiers were offered dinner and an entertainment festival at the bayfront amusement park with patriotic tableaux, dancing, a band concert, and fireworks.*

57. Not coming home. *118 young men and women from Atlantic Highlands served in the Great War. One of them, Paul Montanye Brunig, led a platoon in the 27th Division of the American Expeditionary Forces in France. Breaking through the German army's forbidding Hindenburg Line, Paul was in the vanguard and was killed. He was the only mortality from town.*

58. On the beat. *Is he signaling "halt!" to a scofflaw, saying "hello" to a friend, or doing swing-arm exercises? It's Police Chief Snedeker on storefront sidewalk duty in the 1920s, on the west side of First Avenue near Center Avenue.*

59. Top secret research. *During World War II, this house had a line-up of strange machines on its porch, all pointed at the waters of New York harbor. Secluded behind barbed wire at the bay edge off Bayside Drive, it was a testing lab for the development of radar, which helped detect German planes and submarines and win the war.*

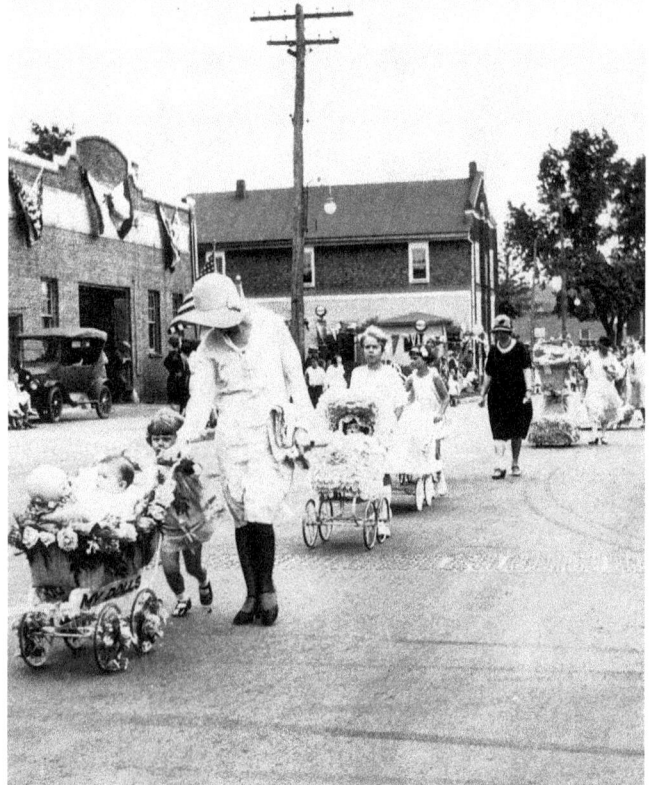

60. Dimpled babies. *200 of them competed for 37 winners' cups at the second annual Baby Parade, August 24, 1927. There were flags flying, music in the air, 5,000 watchers, and a wee toddler dressed as "Boob McNutt."*

Chapter Five

REVOLUTIONARIES AND LOYALISTS

At the famous "Boston tea party" in December 1773, colonists dumped chests full of tea from British ships into the harbor to protest the tea tax imposed by the parliament in London. This and earlier examples of "taxation without representation" had also angered people in Monmouth County and elsewhere in the American colonies. They were further enraged when the British retaliated for the tea dumping by closing Boston port and clamping down on the liberties of people in Massachusetts. In response, Monmouth County farmers donated aid to relieve the needy city in 1774. They sent a sloop loaded with 1,140 bushels of rye and 50 barrels of rye flour, together with a message urging Bostonians not to yield and promising more food when needed.

In June 1774 Monmouth County representatives also took action locally. They ordered the "entire stoppage of importation and exportation from and to Great Britain and the West Indies." In September the Continental Congress expanded the ban to the whole eastern seaboard, effective December 1774. Overlooked from Atlantic Highlands, Sandy Hook Bay was a key location for enforcing this stoppage since its waters provide the navigation channels between the ocean and the ship harbor of Manhattan. To spot violators, Monmouth County formed a "Committee of Safety," which instructed that British ships arriving in Sandy Hook Bay should be detained and prohibited from going on to Manhattan.

Sandy Hook Bay Tea Party

The bay was even the site of an anti-British "tea party" in 1775 after the harbor pilots took on the main responsibility for the local ban on British imports. The job of the pilots, who worked from Sandy Hook but lived where Atlantic Highlands now stands, was to guide ships northward through the channel to New York harbor. But now they switched to checking cargoes on British ships. In February 1775 the harbor pilots turned back the British ship *James* and seized the cargo of the *Beulah*. In April they refused to take the *Nancy* up the bay, and even kept its captain from leaving the ship to get supplies in New York. The Committee of Safety assigned some bayshore people with a sloop to keep a watch on the ship.

When the next ship, the *London*, arrived from England, inspection by pilots revealed 18 chests of contraband tea were aboard. This led to the Sandy Hook Bay "tea party," which was visible from Atlantic Highlands. A raiding party boarded the ship, threw the tea in the bay, and forced the captain to put out to sea again. Such actions led a pro-British New York paper to describe the Monmouth Committee of Safety as "a snarling, pediculous litter of raccoons" (pediculous meaning "infested with lice").

However, the pilots and boatmen could not stop all British ships. In June 1775 colonists watched from the bayshore, massively outgunned and outnumbered, as three men-of-war and 25 transport ships carrying 10 or more regiments of British soldiers swarmed into Sandy Hook

Bay and anchored there briefly before sailing up to suppress rebels in Boston. In October the British war ship HMS *Viper* stayed long enough in the bay to capture three small trading vessels that arrived from the West Indies carrying imported salt and other cargoes belonging to local merchants. The seizure of one sloop involved two bayshore men from families with a long history in the Atlantic Highlands area—a Bowne who was co-owner of the *Polly*, and William Curry who owned its load of sugar and molasses. Loss of the salt, needed to preserve local fish and meat, would have been crucial since the British parliament had banned all salt production by the colonies. Fortunately, the stolen cargoes were recovered and delivered to their rightful owners when the Committee of Safety ordered seizure of the *Viper*.

Raiders' Target: the Bayshore

From these first local rebellious and war-like acts against the British, until the king's troops and cooperating local Loyalists were defeated by the American colonists six years later, Sandy Hook Bay and its shores were the scene of many engagements, skirmishes, raids, and counter-raids between the opposing sides. In July 1776, after the Declaration of Independence was issued, the British brought 430 ships and 45,000 soldiers and sailors from New England and Canada to the bay under the command of Admiral William Howe, outnumbering by three to one the American militia that had been raised by then. Throughout the war, the Sandy Hook peninsula, the bay, Staten Island, and New York City were in British hands, and the occupation of Sandy Hook lasted longer than any other piece of the 13 colonies. As seen from the rebel guardhouse at Point Lookout off today's Ocean Boulevard in Atlantic Highlands, the bay usually swarmed with British warships and large troop transport ships at anchor, as well as cargo ships, supply boats, tenders, and schooners bringing rum, salt, and sugar from the West Indies. Also moving among them were as many as 150 small sloops and numberless barges and whaleboats belonging to Tory traders of New Jersey, Staten Island, and Long Island who sold local products to the British forces.

The effects of the war were not limited to the waters of the bay. Lands along its shore were peculiarly liable to incursions by British troops, Hessian mercenaries, Loyalist militia, and refugee bands. During all the years of the war, these raiders came ashore to obtain supplies by forage, to punish, capture, or kill rebel leaders, and to deplete the resources and undermine the support available for the revolutionary cause. Plundering Tories made off with crop harvests, beat men, women, and children who resisted, ransacked houses for valuables, and smashed unwanted items with muskets or ripped them with bayonets. Clothing, bedding, and papers were piled up and set afire. They also burned mills and churches. With robbery, arson, and murder rampant, not to mention numerous local traitors trading with the enemy, there was widespread economic disruption, social unrest, and political insecurity in the area. Sometimes bayshore people moved inland for refuge from the marauders, like the Applegates, who lived next to Atlantic Highlands; the widowed mother and her seven daughters often went to stay with a relative in Holmdel, leaving their 14-year-old brother Richard hiding in the barn or the swamps with a gun to protect the family property and livestock.

Geographically the closest coastal targets for raiders from Sandy Hook seeking food supplies were the farm lands in the western and southern parts of today's Atlantic Highlands, as well as in the neighboring Leonardo and Navesink sections of Middletown. Also, the forested hills of the eastern part held valuable wood resources and fresh-water springs—both being very scarce on the Sandy Hook peninsula. A main water source was the bayside spout that had been used by the Lenape, Henry Hudson's crew, and other ocean-going ships and fishing boat fleets since 1609. It was marked "Watering Place" on the Monmouth County map made by Lieutenant Colonel Elisha Lawrence, who commanded the First Battalion of New Jersey Volunteers. This was a provincial corps of the British army made up of Loyalist refugees; based on Staten Island, they made frequent raids along the bayshore for supplies and revenge.

The raids were so memorable that some local residents told tales about them two centuries later when the Atlantic Highlands Historical Society was collecting oral histories in preparation for the 1976 bicentennial of American independence. William Burdge Mount told a story, handed down in his family for about seven generations, about his ancestor known as Grandmother Burdge. When she was warned that Hessians were arriving to steal food, she took some hams she had smoked for later consumption and hid them at the bottom of a barrel of feathers she was saving for bedding. "The Hessians came, searched the house, and checked the barrels," Mr. Mount explained. "They bent over and swished their hands in the barrel of feathers and were tickled, but never reached the bottom and the smoked hams were saved."

Another local resident, Ashley Roop, reported that Hessians also raided his old family homestead near the bay, which had been built in the early 1770s. In the 1970s when Mr. Roop was interviewed, still in the house was a desk that the foraging Hessians tried to open and still visible were the marks left where they tried to wedge open the drawers.

Other raids that swept the countryside were more bloody and warlike. Numerous homes were razed near the Bowne House in the area laid out as Portland Poynt village. So many residents were killed, wounded, kidnapped, captured, and imprisoned that William Hornor, a local historian who loved purple prose and alliteration, called the British and all their cohorts "murderous Tory scum," accused them of "the red ruthlessness of rabid revenge," and described the Loyalists and Refugees as "pestilential outlawry" and the raiders coming from Sandy Hook as ""putrid packs."

The raids from the British side were numerous and unending. The effects were so widely felt that some inhabitants who favored the American cause felt obliged to show allegiance to the crown lest they lose their property. Other inhabitants, who were awed into submission to the British side or saw an opportunity to enrich themselves by despoiling others, even took up arms against their neighbors. Outright Tories in the county were emboldened to challenge local authority directly in November and December of 1776, when the British army had advanced well into New Jersey. By Christmas localized Tory insurrections had gained control of much of Monmouth County, including Middletown and most of the Sandy Hook and Raritan bayshore. However, the next month the Tory groups were successfully scattered by a detachment of Continental soldiers from Pennsylvania.

As the war continued, defensive actions and counter-attacks by the revolutionaries became more and more frequent along the bay coastal lands, including today's Atlantic Highlands. The patriot militia patrolled the shoreline, unexpectedly encountering and clashing with Tory local partisans or royal troops and supporters landing from Sandy Hook. The character of the conflict was that of long, drawn-out civil war and guerrilla warfare. Only one battle in the county—the battle of Monmouth near Freehold in 1778—was of the type seen in classic military campaigns, with infantry, artillery, and cavalry soldiers of opposing armies lined up in formations and aiming to conquer defined territories.

The Navesink Massacre

The first engagement between British and American troops in Monmouth County took place February 13, 1777, north of the Hartshorne Woods and east of today's Atlantic Highlands. Esek Hartshorne had a house on a hill near today's Highway 36 and overlooking the bay. In early 1777 his house was used as the garrison of the First Monmouth militia regiment, of which his uncle Richard Hartshorne was probably the quartermaster. In the regiment were 125 to 135 soldiers, chiefly from the bayshore area, Holmdel, and Shrewsbury. They were commanded by Colonel Nathaniel Scudder, some of whose family descendants, like those of Hartshorne, still live on the Navesink peninsula. The troops were assigned to keep watch on Sandy Hook and its adjacent waters, where numerous British ships had been present since mid-1776.

On February 10 a British invading force of 170 soldiers sailed from Staten Island aboard the ship *Syren*, commanded by Major Andrew Gordon. They were to be joined by about 100 Loyalist men from the 1st New Jersey Volunteers in attacking the Hartshorne house. On the chilly morning of February 13, the invaders waded ashore and divided in two. One group went uphill toward the garrison. The other group headed west along the beach to today's Atlantic Highlands, turned inland and uphill over the ridge, probably descended via Sears Avenue, and went to seal off the rear of the Hartshorne house. The attackers were within 200 yards of the garrison by the time an alarm was sounded, and the surprised defenders faced a barrage of fire.

A few dozen militiamen, including some wounded, left the house by a back door, headed west, and at Many Mind Creek took whaleboats to row downstream to the bayfront at Atlantic Highlands. Their escape may have been a deliberate withdrawal decided by Colonel Scudder, who saw no chance of defeating the invaders' superior force.

The fight was over almost before it started, and 25 militiamen were dead and 72 were taken prisoner. Historians call it the Battle of Navesink Hills, but a more appropriate label would be "The Navesink Massacre." The captured men were marched to Sandy Hook and later went by boat to New York's infamous Sugar House on Liberty Street, a former warehouse converted into a British prison. Others were jailed on a former British warship, the *New Jersey*, which sat on mud flats in Brooklyn and flooded at high tide, forcing prisoners to cling to ceiling beams. In these primitive jails, fever and disease, poor medical care and sanitation, and starvation from lack of food killed still more of the militiamen. Conditions and treatment were so bad that three-quarters of the prisoners never came out alive.

Soldiers from local families involved in the Navesink battle whose fate is known include Second Lieutenant John Whitlock, who was killed in battle; Lambert Johnson, Joseph Goodenough, Obadiah Stillwell, and James Winter, who died in prison; William Johnson and James Morris were imprisoned and survived; and Captain Samuel Carhart survived the battle, escaped, and was still in the militia in 1781.

British Forces On the Move

Reports of naval raids, skirmishes, and battles on Sandy Hook Bay and on the neighboring ocean are often based on observations by spectators on the heights of the Navesink Highlands, which offered a perfect vantage point. Their view reached over the bay and the Hook, and farther north and east to the upper bay and the ocean. Watching from on high were ordinary residents, concerned patriots, rebel activists, and designated American spies. Farmers and watermen along the lower elevations and shorelines could also clearly see activities on the bay. Engagements between rival armed ships off the Hook could be long, spectacular, and loud, like the four-hour, 50-cannon battle in January 1780 between an American privateer brig and an English brig, the *Admiral Rodney*. Many captures of rival ships were made by both sides just off Sandy Hook in the channels approaching the bay and the route into New York harbor.

A more than usually large audience would have gathered for two historic deployments of the British fleet departing from Sandy Hook Bay in 1777 and returning in 1778. A huge armada of 211 sails was in the bay on July 23, 1777, and took on loads of British troops, who then sailed south to Chesapeake Bay. There they disembarked and fought their way to Philadelphia, which they occupied by late September for the winter.

In spring 1778, under General Sir Henry Clinton, those troops evacuated Philadelphia and headed through New Jersey to join other British forces in New York. Near Freehold on June 27, they fought a major engagement with General George Washington's forces at Monmouth battlefield. This was the area's only traditional set-piece battle, which has been extensively chronicled in numerous accounts. When the battle ended, the British started marching toward Sandy Hook, a distance of 15 miles. En route, they camped in High Point (today's Chapel Hill) and elsewhere in the Navesink Highlands. The baggage, coaches, horses, mistresses, and plunder of the rich British officers stretched out 12 miles behind them.

One camping place was the farmhouse at Point Lookout off today's Ocean Boulevard, where excavation of its dirt-floor half-cellar in the 1980s yielded brass buttons from British Revolutionary War uniforms. Logically, the troops staying at this house were from the 14th and 15th Regiments under Colonel O'Hare, having followed the shoreline when they "marched from Belford to be embarked for Sandy Hook" at its southern end, as reported in an officer's journal. When he arrived on the Hook, O'Hare took command of all British forces there.

At their campsites, the British soldiers had to wait a week for their fleet to reach Sandy Hook Bay in order to carry them to New York. Also, they could not move until a pontoon bridge was built over the breach (called "the gut") carved out by the ocean the previous winter near the base of Sandy Hook, turning it into an island. Beginning July 5, about 12,000 British and Hessian troops marched across the inlet and boarded ships anchored in the bay. The colorful embarkation was watched by local citizens on surrounding hills as scows, barges, longboats, and yawls ferried troops, artillery, baggage, and equipment out to the waiting transports for the trip to New York.

By July 11, having landed its military passengers and cargo, the British fleet sailed back to Sandy Hook Bay. The commander immediately lined up 17 of his ships to block the entry channel from the ocean and defend against a rival French fleet of 14 ships that had dropped anchor southeast of Sandy Hook, intending to battle the British (illustration no. 13). On board were 4,000 soldiers sent by France, which had officially entered the war on the American side in March 1778. The map shows the positions of the British and French fleets, whose 1,614 guns aboard 33 ships could have fought a thundering naval battle offshore.

Instead, weeks passed and the British warships stood their ground while the French fleet and American ground forces tried to arrange a joint attack on the British in New York. One story is that, during these weeks, the French sent teams on shore and across the Navesink Highlands (so as to avoid likely British attacks from Sandy Hook) to collect fresh water at the spout, which appears on maps of the period. The French-American attack was cancelled when it was discovered that the great French ships could not pass through the shallow Sandy Hook channel.

Insurrection, Suffering, and Cow pens

Right after the Battle of Monmouth there was an alarming increase in murders, robberies, house-breaking, house-burning, horse-stealing, pillaging of stores, and sniping at travelers. This violence was mainly perpetrated by Tory sympathizers who mounted insurrections under the protection of the British forces still remaining at Sandy Hook and on ships in the bay. In reaction to this, in 1778 the local revolutionary government decided to try to restore a measure of peace in the countryside by charging the Tory rebels with treason and banishing them. More than 1,200 were condemned and many of their properties were confiscated and sold.

But this action did not end the violence. The toll was particularly heavy in the bayshore area of Monmouth County, located at the edge of the British-dominated zone of the bay and its northern and eastern shores. All historical sources agree that the area suffered severely during the entire six years of conflict. One authority, Michael Adelberg, thinks it "probable that no county anywhere in the Thirteen Colonies hosted either the same quantity or variety of violent incidents during the American Revolution as Monmouth County." Other areas experienced one or two types of violence, but Monmouth faced all four: civil war between local factions of patriots and Tories, British and refugee raids against the countryside, increased crime caused by economic troubles and disaffection with the new government, and confrontation between opposing armies at the 1778 Battle of Monmouth.

Dates and locations are known for at least 68 skirmishes and engagements between 1776 and late 1782 in the bayshore area. Of these, 11 engagements were on land, another 11 were naval actions in Sandy Hook bay, and 28 were boat captures or gun battles at sea near Sandy Hook. In addition, the American rebels made 17 attacks on Sandy Hook itself, hitting British encampments and the tent city called "Refugees' Town" and trying to recapture the 1762 lighthouse. Examples of some engagements are in the box at right.

In addition to onshore raids, the British also had other methods of squeezing supplies out of local sources. Along the southern coast of Sandy Hook Bay/Raritan Bay, they organized a systematic traffic of local food, cattle, and mill products for delivery to British and Loyalist troops. This traffic moved on roads leading to designated creek mouths that emptied into the bay.

At least three such collection areas, called "cow pens" or penfolds, were officially established by the British. One location was "on the shore near Sandy Hook," which may mean the flat bayside lowlands around Many Mind Creek or Wagner Creek in western Atlantic Highlands, where farms lay directly inland from the shore. Goods delivered here were mostly for use by British ships anchored in Sandy Hook Bay and by troops and Loyalist refugees on Sandy Hook. A second location, occasionally used, was at Port Monmouth where boats were loaded to carry supplies to New York City. The largest and best known cow pen was at Keyport. It had many small enclosures for individual farmers and shippers, as well as sheds devoted to storage of butter, cheese, and other farm products. Supplies from this depot mostly went to enemy troops on Staten Island, ferried overnight in large flat-bottomed scows.

Providing produce to these depots was not exactly voluntary for the farmers along the bay. They were told the items to deliver in specific quantities. If they failed to meet their quotas,

Loyalist foraging parties raided their farms and drove off their livestock, with no payment to the farmers. This prospect led many farmers, even those favoring the revolution, to take British "protection." However, some farmers did double duty by furnishing supplies to the British while also providing intelligence to rebel leaders about how the British deployed and supplied their forces. Reportedly spies were even planted along the shore to watch and obtain information about the enemy to feed to American military commanders.

Of course, some local traders, just to make money and survive or to support their chosen side, made stealthy trips from coastal inlets of the bay and ocean in small boats carrying goods

Land Attacks and Naval Maneuvers

•**April 26, 1779**: British soldiers and Loyalists burned and looted the houses of leading civil and military officials in Middletown before being driven back to their boats.

•**September 1779**: Over three days, 800 British men plundered properties and captured locals all the way from Shrewsbury to the bayshore. At Shoal Harbor, whaleboats with 72 militiamen drove the invaders into the bay and sunk three of their boats.

•**December 1779**: A fleet of 140 British merchant ships maneuvered into the bay, bringing supplies for royalist forces at Sandy Hook and then sailed out with protection by a convoy of men-of-war, heading back to Britain. Later that month, 100 British ships passed the Hook carrying troop reinforcements to British armies in the southern states. Both fleets were too big for rebel forces to attack.

•**January 1780**: Freak Arctic-like weather trapped the British fleet in the bay and cut it off from food and fuel sources. Its crews were hungry, cold, and stuck on board like sitting ducks. Militamen from bayshore villages ventured over the ice by night to attack the immobile ships. In one attack 40 militiamen traveled in sleighs from Freehold, secured their rigs at the shore of Atlantic Highlands near Many Mind Creek, walked over the thick ice on the bay, boarded three ships in Spermaceti Cove before daybreak, captured surprised and sleepy crew members, took such portable equipment as weapons, compasses, and telescopes, and burned the ships.

•**Late January 1780**: Desperate for supplies, the British sent a small force around chest-high snow and ice slabs to pilfer food, fuel, and blankets from farms and shops on shore. Journeying from Highlands and Atlantic Highlands to Middletown and Matawan, the scavengers raided farms and homes but found little food. After capturing five militiamen, they retreated to Garrett's Hill next to Atlantic Highlands and confined them in Loyalist barns. The next day, militiamen from nearby towns converged on the hill and released their compatriots. The British returned to their ships with a few stolen blankets, clothing, and a load of firewood, but no food.

•**June 21,1780**: A 100-man party landed on the Middletown bayshore, consisting of British regulars, Loyalists, and 30 blacks under Colonel Tye. A former slave, Tye had become a forceful raider based at Sandy Hook, commanding up to 800 men, both black and white. The party plundered several houses, captured 10 prominent citizens, several blacks, and a lot of livestock. Local militia fought back, but the raiders still made off with their 10 prisoners.

•**June 1781**: 1,000 British from Staten Island went foraging for meat in the Middletown area. Local militia forced them to retreat to Garrett's Hill and rescued some stolen sheep, but the the British burned two houses and took off with 40 cattle and 60 sheep.

and wares to market among British and Loyalist consumers in New York City. Some were captured, sunk, and killed in the bay by patriot boatsmen trying to cut off British supplies.

Whaleboat Wars and Bayside Spies

No American naval operations were possible in the Sandy Hook Bay region. But a small fleet of light, fast whaleboats was "able to wage successful warfare for five long years against the overwhelming odds of British force and power," wrote a local historian. The wooden boats of this mini-navy were designed for the tricky shallow water of the area from Sandy Hook along the bayshore to Matawan. They were usually no longer than 30 feet, broad of beam and shallow of draught, and pointed at both ends so that oarsmen could quickly reverse direction when necessary.

Fishermen and craftsmen from bayshore communities rowed the boats out from hidden coves and creek mouths at night and harassed enemy ships. Each boat crew had 14 to 24 men who were drilled and disciplined for silent, powerful navigation and precise, sudden strikes. Sometimes they were joined by 10 to 15 local militiamen picked for their guerrilla-war prowess. These commandos boarded British vessels and stole guns, powder, rum, and other provisions. Often they set ships afire, enraging British officers who watched from Sandy Hook or Battery Point outlooks in Manhattan. Among the whaleboat and militiamen were such well-known local names as Bennett, Carhart, Conover, Schenck, Stillwell, and Walling.

Eventually, working with the local intelligence network for General George Washington's Continental Army, the bay raiders often targeted ships to capture British officers or prominent Tory civilians. These captives were then offered as pawns in exchange for Americans from the Middletown and Shrewsbury areas who had been taken prisoner during British raids. The ships were selected from lists they received from John Stillwell, a designated American spy. Stillwell watched ship and troop movements on the bay from his Garrett Hill house next to Atlantic Highlands and issued messages headed "These Ships Are For Sinking" (see box).

A revenge movement began in 1780, when 436 Monmouth County residents signed "Articles of Association." They pledged to strike against British ships in the bay and make tit-for-tat response to British and Loyalist raids on land. The "retaliators" (as they were called) signing the pledge included men from at least 23 families with long histories in the Middletown/Atlantic Highlands area. A number of men bore the names Bennett, Bowne, Brown, Conover, Covenhoven, Herbert, Lane, Mount, Posten, Quackenbush, Seabrook, Schenck, Smock, Stillwell, and Van Pelt, and there were individuals named Antonides, Carhart, Goodenough, Johnston, Roberts, Stryker, Thorn, and van Mater.

A deep hollow in Atlantic Highlands also played a role in the revolution, probably related to the intelligence gathered locally and fed to General Washington. Now a section of the Lenape Woods Nature Preserve, this deeply forested hollow is a U-shaped valley above the eastern end of Washington Avenue. Its slope rises steeply to the north through 150 feet of elevation to a ridge line overlooking Sandy Hook Bay. Here "some of the horses of the Revolution were wintered," according to Thomas Henry Leonard. Located in the hollow, the horses were hidden from the British forces in the bay and on Sandy Hook. Likewise, the hollow is obscured from the Navesink River to the south by intervening hills. Fresh drinking water for horses was at hand in the headwaters of Many Mind Creek, which begin to flow through the hollow. Logically, horses quartered in the hollow would have been part of George Washington's spy system. Relay horses were posted at 20-mile intervals to carry intelligence reports from Stillwell's Garrett Hill watching post above the bay to the Continental Army commander wherever he was camped.

Near the hollow is "the historical spot where the guard-house was situated, at Point Lookout," according to Leonard (illustration no. 17). This high point is located over the ridge north of the hollow and below today's Ocean Boulevard. It has a broad view over the bay and ocean and along the curving bayshore to both east and west. It was a strategic place to post guards to spot enemy landings and incursions and then move to stop them. A small pre-revolutionary farm house served as the guardhouse and remains a central part of the much expanded residence still located there; it still has original "tree beams" supporting stone walls of the late 1700s stone house.

> ## 65 British Ships in the Bay
>
> "Yesterday Afternoon three Frigates arrived within Sandy Hook. In the Evening a fourth Ship of War run in....
>
> This Afternoon a Large Fleet appeared Standing for Sandy Hook. The air my intelligence says was too Foggy for good observation But that before Sundown he counted Sixty five Sail of Ships of War and Transports distinctly—and saw a Number more in the offing—That Immediately they run within the Hook as they Arrive.
>
> From there Running Immediately into the Hook as they arrive it will not I feel sure admit of a doubt of there not being British and I think it is very likely from Carolina."
>
> Saturday Night Elevin O Clock
> 17th June, 80."
>
> Extract of report from Stillwell conveyed by David Forman to General Washington.
>
> Stillwell's Diary 1780–1782, contained in George Washington papers in Library of Congress

Taking Sides

Before the Declaration of Independence, people who had wealth and power in the bayshore area and wider Monmouth County tended to hold off at first from joining the swelling resistance to British rule. If they opposed the tyrannies from London, they looked for reform from within rather than an insurrection, which was likely to be quickly put down—and in which they had much to lose.

When war actually began, local residents split in no less than four ways. Some became revolutionaries or patriots, in spirit or also in action. People in the bayshore area, particularly its poorer class, were predominantly in favor of the revolution. According to available records, 70 percent of the adult males in the Middletown/Atlantic Highlands area whose loyalties were known in 1776 were Whigs or patriots, with the remainder being Tories or neutral. Of the patriots, 41 percent were landless and 16 percent had 25 acres or less land. Also especially militant were members of the Baptist and Dutch Reformed churches. The Baptists met in 1777 in Middletown and pledged to act "to the Utmost of Our Power, in Defence of Our Rights and Previliges Both Sivil and Religious, Against Our Cruel Enimies." Many patriots who lived within a mile or two of the shore line had to abandon their farms, shops, and homes and move into the interior where pressure from the British, Loyalists, and refugees was less constant, and where their neighbors felt more free to retaliate.

Others took a neutral stance. Perhaps they disliked contention, were friendly with or afraid of both sides, or wanted to continue free trading and money making with any parties who needed the supplies or services they provided. Still others remained passive Tories while still being good neighbors or feigning loyalty to the Crown in order to gain protection from British military commanders. Called Loyalists, this group accounted for most of the military action in the bayshore region, but had very limited organizational or political strength.

A fourth group turned into traitors and left the area. They went as refugees to New York or Canada, joined the military forces of the Loyalist New Jersey Volunteers, or became guerrilla raiders based at Sandy Hook or Staten Island. As described by one historian, the refugees who took up arms were "malignants who joined the enemy marauding bands and warred against their former friends and neighbors—robbing, burning, and sometimes slaying."

Some families were split among two or more of these tendencies. Some even deliberately divided their sons between the two sides so that, whichever side prevailed, at least part of the family would get to keep their property as a reward for their loyalty. During the early war years, the "disinterested and uncommitted" outnumbered the Loyalists and revolutionaries combined, but the incursions by British forces in late 1776 and early 1777 turned the tide, and many more people supported the goal of independence.

How the sides shaped up becomes relatively clear in the records of several kinds from the Revolutionary War period. Listed there are over 580 residents of Middletown Township, including residents of the lands now included in Atlantic Highlands. Assembled in Michael Adelberg's "Roster of the People of Revolutionary Monmouth County," these records show who lined up with the American revolutionaries, who were British Loyalists or at least sympathizers, and which families split their allegiance between the opposing forces. There are dangers in such labeling, unless a collection of corroborating facts can be put together for an individual or family. In general, however, the range of political positions can be seen by looking at three local families with numerous members for whom good data are available—the revolutionary Stillwells, the Loyalist Stouts, and the divided Van Maters and Bownes—and a few other families with clear loyalties.

Revolutionary Patriots

Fourteen Stillwells of the Middletown area, including some in Leonardo next to Atlantic Highlands, were apparently all Revolutionary patriots. Nine were in the military, including a captain, a lieutenant, a quartermaster, and six privates. Two others paid substitutes to perform military service in their stead. Two Stillwells sold produce to the Continental Army in 1780. However, even with this much revolutionary fervor in the family, a fifteenth Stillwell was apparently a "bad apple in the barrel" since the property of James Stillwell was confiscated by the revolutionary government in 1779 because of his Loyalist activities.

The very first military company to be organized by colonists in the county, in September 1775, was led by Captain John Holmes of Middletown and included representatives of such local families as Bennett, Bowne, Burdge, Covenhoven, Hendrickson, Roberts, Schenck, Snyder, Stillwell, Stout, Van Pelt, and Wall. Other local families favoring the rebel side later sent their men into the militia, including as many as 10 Wallings, six Carharts, and six Smocks, as well as a few each from the Seabrook, Stryker, van Cleaf, and Whitlock families. The commanders of Monmouth County's cavalry and artillery companies were Captain Jacob Covenhoven and Captain Barnes Smock, each of whom was captured twice by the British during the war.

Loyalists

The record for the Loyalist Stout family presents almost exactly the opposite picture from the revolutionary Stillwells. No less than seven Stouts in the Middletown area were accused of disloyalty to the American cause and were stripped of their property—an act called "forfeiture" and "confiscation." The charges against Peter Stout were for stealing horses, David was convicted of high treason in 1782, and Abram's mistake was soldiering in the Loyalist militia known as the New Jersey Volunteers. Even two slaves of the Stouts, who escaped from their masters, joined the Loyalist "Black Brigade" based on British promises of official emancipation after the war. As with the Stillwells, a minority of two Stouts were on the opposite side from the rest of their family and took up arms in the rebel militia, including an enlistee in the earliest militia.

Leonards, Lufburrows, Mounts, and Wilsons—all local families in the Atlantic Highlands/ Middletown area—were also Loyalists. John and Joseph Leonard forfeited their estates in 1777, and Joseph was also arrested for "disaffection." Lufburrows were confirmed, notorious Tories; one was arrested for "disaffection," and the estates of the other two were confiscated. Four Mounts of the area were on the British side in the war. George Mount was "savagely murdered by the rebels" in 1779. His son George Jr. was arrested for conspiracy. John Mount was placed under house arrest for refusing militia service and fled to New York, resulting in confiscation of his property. And Timothy Mount was a sergeant in the Loyalist New Jersey Volunteers. As for Wilsons, Benjamin was accused of being active in a "Tory rebellion" in 1776, while James was indicted in 1782 for "Contraband Trading, Seditious Words, Petty Larceny, and Boarding an Enemy Vessel."

Other Loyalists in the Middletown area included three Stevensons, eight Taylors, and three Thornes. Altogether, the estates of 46 Loyalists in the area were "inquisitioned for forfeiture" and then confiscated by the local government authorities.

Split Loyalties
It was not uncommon for family allegiances to be split between the opposing sides. As one historian described it, there were "fathers and brothers taking different sides, and mingling in savage conflict in murderous opposition to each other." This was the case for the Compton, DeBow, Hartshorne, Hendrickson, and McClease families in the Middletown area.

The van Mater family exhibited a notorious split. Chrineyonce van Mater was apparently a completely pro-British renegade. His estate was confiscated in 1777, he was fined and jailed in 1778, indicted for high treason in 1779, and became a refugee in British-held New York in 1782. John van Mater, also an active Loyalist, refused to take a loyalty oath to the Continental government, was jailed in 1776, and was later accused of being active in the Tory rebellions in December of the same year. Clarence van Mater's anti-revolutionary stance led to his estate being confiscated. Looking at the other side, however, at the same time six other van Mater men were members of the rebel militia. In 1896, John H. van Mater, a revered family doctor in Atlantic Highlands, still kept in his office the old gun that his grandfather carried in the Battle of Monmouth—not saying for what side it was used.

There was a three-way division among the 12 Bownes in the Atlantic Highlands-Middletown area and 16 others in Monmouth County; they splintered into patriot, Tory, and neutral factions. Some Bowne patriots suffered greatly at the hands of the British and Loyalists. The area around the Atlantic Highlands-Middletown border, where a number of Bownes lived, was hotly contested, with many nighttime raids and daytime skirmishes; it was also a center of contraband trade between opportunistic locals and the British. Samuel Bowne and family then resided at the homestead farm on Portland Poynt lot number 2 where his forbear James Bowne had settled in 1667. Marauding refugee Loyalists attacked the house, captured his cousin Safety Bowne and Safety's son Worden, and took them to the

Old Sugar House prison in New York, where, a report says, "they died from cruel treatment and want of the necessities of life." David, another son of Safety, "was bayonetted to death by the British." The family was robbed of all its possessions. A third son, Daniel, still a boy, was forced to carry some of the plunder and then released.

Bownes who were revolutionary activists included William, Elias, and a second Samuel Bowne from the Middletown area who were privates in the militia. William was a soldier in the Battle of Monmouth in 1778. Later, he and his brother Joseph supported the vigilante patriot gangs formed by the Association for Retaliation in Monmouth County. James Bowne, also from the Middletown area, put four of his horse teams to work hauling baggage for the Revolutionary army and himself served as a soldier. After the war, James took part in the funeral of Ham Johnson, a local man who had helped the Tories forage in the neighborhood and who even took raiders to his employer's house to get feather beds and other furniture. The burial complete, James stuck a shovel in Ham's grave and said "Lay there, you old Tory, you will never take any more feather beds."

On the Loyalist side at least three Bownes had their properties confiscated "for joining the army of the King of Great Britain," as charged in official records. One of them was Andrew Bowne of the Middletown area, who was convicted of high treason in 1782. Among Bownes elsewhere in the county, one joined the Loyalist New Jersey Volunteers, two had their estates confiscated, and two became refugees in New York.

Still others of the Bownes seemed to live out the war as opportunistic neutrals, simultaneously serving in the local militia and illegally trading with the British. Because they had access to transport by water and were more vulnerable to British pressure, a larger proportion of people living along the shores of the bay and ocean were given to trading with the enemy than was the case with people living farther inland.

War's End and Aftermath

After British General Lord Charles Cornwallis surrendered to General George Washington at Yorktown in October 1781, the hostilities continued in the bayshore area while the terms of peace were being negotiated and long after.

Between the surrender and December 1782, more than a year later, there were nine more British-American skirmishes, including one on land at Rocky Point on the eastern end of the Navesink peninsula in May 1782, two at the Tory camp on Sandy Hook, three naval actions inside Sandy Hook, and three at sea east of the Hook. Privateer ships and enemy vessels still plied their trade for many months. Monmouth farmsteads continued to be harried by raids, fires, and plundering carried out by furious, embittered Tories who ventured from their base at Sandy Hook

Dislike of the disaffected—one term for the refugees—was still ingrained in December 1783. A state law was passed to deny the vote to anyone who had joined the enemy, been convicted of treason, had their property confiscated, or been fined or imprisoned for refusing to take the state loyalty oath. In the same month, 200 Monmouth County residents signed a petition against the "numerous intestine enemies who still remain amongst us" (Tories and Loyalists) and against the return of "every former inhabitant, who hath at any time since the revolution gone off or joined the enemy."

Chapter Six

MEN OF THE LAND, BUSINESS,

AND WAR

In the century between the Revolutionary War and the late 1870s when the modern town of Atlantic Highlands was conceived, the predominant rhythm of the area was the peaceful, routine pace of hardworking farmers and watermen. The land, infrastructure, and economy of the area were developing gradually, mainly along existing lines. There was still no division of the bayshore into separate villages, and the continuity of large farm tracts paralleling the coast remained unbroken from the original Portland Poynt lots west of Many Mind Creek all the way to the eastern edge of Waycake (today's Keansburg). In fact, a map issued around 1810 still labeled this entire area "Shoal Harbour."

There was a rising curve in population, as shown by tax and census information for the wider Atlantic Highlands area, including parts of neighboring Navesink and the Leonardo-Port Monmouth bayshore corridor. Looking at two sample years, around 100 adult males can be identified in this area in the 1794 tax list. A similar search in the 1850 census yields a count of 148 heads of household, all of them male except two. These figures suggest that the full population, including women and children, may have increased by 50 percent in a half century, from 300 to 400 in 1794, to perhaps 450 to 600 in 1850 (or more, since three, four, or more children per family was not uncommon).

In 1790 the total population in Middletown Township as a whole, including the Atlantic Highlands area, was 2,225. The total included 491 slaves, or 22 percent of the township's population. This shows that slavery was very significant in the area, not just in the South, and that the area had a sizeable black population long before any migration of ex-slaves from the South after the 1861 Emancipation Proclamation.

The Atlantic Highlands area had ten households of free blacks in the 1850 census. Almost all were in the Navesink section, and five were families named Stillwell. It seems likely they were from slave families who had previously lived and worked about a mile west of there and had taken on the family name of their master, John Stillwell. His family long owned a large farm on the gentle slopes of Garrett Hill facing the bay, in the area of today's Stillwell Road in Leonardo/Chapel Hill. John Stillwell was among the largest slaveowners in the area. He had 10 slaves and freed three between 1805 and 1825. While it was not yet the age of significant immigration, in 1850 a few of the wealthier households in the area had laborers or servant girls from Ireland (12), Germany (2), or Canada (1).

Family businesses for the growing and selling of basic farm produce still predominated in 1850; about one out of three men were farm owners or farm workers. Fishing and boating were the second most common business, occupying one out of ten men; masons, carpenters, merchants, and shoemakers each numbered a handful or less. Other trades with one each in the 1850 census were jeweler, harness maker, hotel owner, engineer, painter, lighthouse keeper, telegraph operator, and surveyor. In addition, a few entrepreneurs branched out into other lines, such as docks and shipping, a bark mill, piped spring water, marl fertilizer, bunker oil and fish meal, specialized market crops of watercress, asparagus, and watermelon, and the brewing of cider and "Jersey Lightning" until it was wiped out by angry temperance campaigners. The only jarring events were two wars—the War of 1812 against the British, and the Civil War in 1861–1865—and the collapse of a large cliffside block of land along the bay in April 1782.

The 1782 collapse was not a landslide, but the slumping of an entire block of land some 40 acres in size above the bay. It sunk directly down to a considerable depth, "forming a cavity equal in circumference at bottom to the void space above," according to a published account of the time. The noise was heard for a distance of several miles. The location was described as "Greenland bank, the highest point of the highlands" about two miles northwest of "Beacon Hill" (today's "Twin Lights"). The slumped land made a new flat-topped bluff at a lower elevation than the original cliff it left behind. Today it's the eastern Bayside Drive neighborhood in Atlantic Highlands. This phenomenon, which later occurred at other sites along the highland ridge, was defined as "slump blocking" in a 1974 scientific study by the U.S. Geological Survey.

Land

The eastern and western parts of the territory making up today's Atlantic Highlands have always had different characteristics. In the west, land that's nearly flat, soil that's generally easy to work, and the presence of two fresh water creeks all combined to favor farming. Also, direct access from land to the bay made fishing and shipping attractive there. Similar geography prevailed farther west in Leonardo and over to Port Monmouth—the Shoal Harbor plantations of early European settlers. In contrast, in the east, rocky geology, hilly topography, wooded slopes, the absence of creeks, and the high bayside bluffs made it less attractive for agriculture, fishing, and early settlement.

The distinction is clear in the 1844 map of the area made by the U.S. Coastal Survey Office (illustration no. 15). In the west between Many Mind and Wagner Creeks, the land is divided into farm fields and dotted with nine farm houses. However, the land east of Many Mind Creek is covered with trees and very little is subdivided, and shows only two houses. Today still, the pattern is larger lots, less dense housing, and greater afforestation in the eastern lands.

Interestingly, the area of the highlands in the eastern part of today's Atlantic Highlands remained largely unsettled for about 275 years after the first Europeans arrived. Soils, geology, and topography were not the only reasons. A principal explanation was ownership by the Hartshorne family, which happily retained most of the eastern end of the Navesink peninsula for a very long time. In 1672 Richard Hartshorne had acquired all the land east of a line running from Point Lookout on the bay to Claypit Creek along the Navesink River, plus Sandy Hook. His son William inherited this estate, kept it intact until his death in 1748, and left it to his sons Robert and Esek. In 1762 they drew an east-west line through the peninsula, more or less on the watershed divide, with Robert taking the half on the south or river side of the peninsula and Esek the half on the north or bay side, each tract containing about 740 acres.

When Esek died, this northern share of the peninsula finally passed out of Hartshorne hands after 135 years and was sold by his executors to Tylee Williams on June 8, 1797. Parts of the tract were divided off in the next three sales. About 1812 Nimrod Woodward obtained the northeastern area that became the Borough of the Highlands in 1900. West of that, in about

1830, James Patterson acquired the area south of today's Ocean Boulevard called Lenape Woods East, as well as land on the western side of Buttermilk Valley. And Andrew Mount about 1830 bought around 260 acres of woodland, including Mount Mitchill, the spout, and the bayside flank of the highland hilltop. After Mount lost a large amount of money in the South at the time of the Civil War, he was unable to retain the property for long. In 1879, a group of wealthy men from New York came into possession of these 260 acres and established the Navesink Park Company with the aim of developing home properties and waterfront facilities for millionaires. Following several unsuccessful marketing attempts (see chapter 7), the scheme was abandoned. In 1915 the area was incorporated into the Borough of Atlantic Highlands. However, extensive residential construction did not begin until after World War II.

Moving from the highland hilltop to the western slope of the highlands, the next landowners along the bayside in the early 1800s were the Hoopers, starting with Joseph in 1800. His son Samuel worked the farm there after 1812. The Hooper farmhouse was on the bay side of today's Ocean Boulevard opposite Grand Avenue (illustration no. 16). Around mid-century, Samuel Hooper sold all but 85 acres of the estate, which he passed to his son, Judge Edward Hooper. The southernmost 100 acres were bought by Nathaniel Roberts, who used it until 1879 for growing watercress and asparagus as a business, while the 50 easternmost acres went to Charles Sears, who successively ran two small businesses there (see below).

West of Hooper's lands, during the 1700s, the descendants of the original Bowne settlers in Portland Poynt had come into possession of much of the land—the gentle lower slope and meadow leading to Many Mind Creek, and considerable farmland west of the creek (illustration no. 14). On November 25, 1768, about 100 acres of this were bequeathed by John Bowne to Daniel Brown, who passed ownership through succeeding members of his family (Mary, William, and Wainwright Brown). William Brown is the one who established Brown's landing in 1834 at the bay edge of this tract and around the same time built the family homestead along the path that later became First Avenue. In 1867 the Brown house and land were sold to Thomas Leonard, adding to the family's already extensive holdings.

In the century following the Revolutionary War, the Leonard family progressively acquired more and more land in the Atlantic Highlands area. Their holdings and influence were so extensive in the district just beyond today's western boundary that it became known as Leonardsville when the first post office was established there after 1850. The large farm that Nathaniel Leonard had obtained by a swap in 1700 remained with his son Nathaniel Jr. and his grandson Thomas. Up to 1786 Thomas was captain of a vessel that sailed between New York and the bayshore and sometimes as far south as Virginia. Around 1786 he ended his transient existence as a sailor, got married, and bought a 40-acre farm in Leonardville.

In the next generation, his son William J. Leonard (1798–1873) built a house in Leonardville center in 1808 and had three lines of work:

- Merchant. In 1812 after brief service in the War of 1812, he founded a family business, the "village store" at Leonardville center. Today this structure still remains, somewhat remodeled, at the northwest corner of Leonardville Road and Avenue D. There was also a second store in the family, at Riceville (today's Navesink), that was operated by William's nephews Thomas and Joseph as of 1837.
- Shipping. William was also involved in packet boats for shipping

produce from the area, first as captain of the *Friendship* and then as owner of the *Patriot*, another packet boat.

• Farming. Starting with the old family farm he owned in 1808, William acquired four more farms nearby between 1810 and 1836. they were the Thompson farm, which later became the Mardean section of Leonardo; an Applegate farm, which became its Ocean View section; his father's old farm; and the Walling farm at Avenue D and the bay in today's Atlantic Highlands. This made him one of the biggest landowners in Monmouth County. As of 1832 he was growing watermelons on 20 acres for sale in New York City. His son Thomas and grandson Edward continued the business, but Thomas, who had injured his arms and back in 10 years of farm labor, switched to running the family store.

Active in church life like all Leonards, William also took part in efforts to build the chapel on Chapel Hill that gave the area its name. He had four sons and two daughters with his first wife, Elizabeth Applegate; his second wife was Elizabeth Conover.

William's second son, Thomas Leonard (1815–1897), lived on the 50-acre homestead farm all 82 years of his life and died there. An enterprising farmer, he expanded his holdings to incorporate the Debowe and John Brown farms and most of the Bowne farm south of today's Highway 36.

For a period in the 1830s, Thomas took charge of shipping the watermelon crop to New York, staying there from Monday through Saturday. Later, he pioneered in getting the Hopping Station rail depot established where Leonardville Road meets Chapel Hill Road. He helped keep the old stage route running from this point to Leonardville, Navesink, and Highlands until a new railroad company extended the line to Sandy Hook, and he then was a director of that company for some years. He was also one of the principal organizers and then treasurer and director of the Atlantic Highlands Association, which strongly influenced the creation of the new town (see chapter 7).

Thomas Leonard's four sons kept up the family's active involvement in the area. James H. (1841–1894) farmed on the 60 acres of Debowe lands his father had bought, led in creating steamboat service between Atlantic Highlands and New York, and captained the first boat. Edward, born 1853, carried on the general store at Leonardville center and was postmaster for a time. John J., born 1856, was a principal organizer and director of the Atlantic Highlands Association, like his father.

Thomas Henry Leonard (1843–1930), the second son, made his mark as a modern entrepreneur and town booster (illustration no. 21). He started out as a farmer and coal dealer and ended up as a main founding father of Atlantic Highlands. In 1871, he obtained the John Brown farm and homestead that his father had bought—100 acres on both sides of today's First Avenue, extending to the bay. At once he began dreaming about the creation of a more developed town and taking practical steps in that direction. In 1871 he widened the sandy lane that ran in front of his homestead, in the stretch between the bay and Washington Avenue. Some of his neighbors thought its new width of 50 feet was excessive. Near the bay he built a coal yard and office next to the landing. The next year he laid out Mount Avenue between First Avenue and the top of the hill at Prospect Avenue. And he tried, but failed, to interest farmers in joining together to finance construction of a pier. Partly because of a financial panic and economic downturn in 1873, the pier plan was shelved and not dusted off for reconsideration until

1878. But these first actions and plans by Leonard were a partial forecast of the big boom that would come in the 1880s.

Among the other families in the western area between Many Mind Creek and Port Monmouth during all or part of the 1800s up to the 1870s were Applegate, Bowne, Burdge, Carhart, Compton, Conover, Frost, Hubbard, Lufburrow, Maxson, Mount, Roop, Seabrook, Sharts, Speyers, Stillwell, Swan, Taylor, Tilton, Waymans, and Willett, in addition to those who sold their farms to the Leonards during the period (DeBowe, Thompson, and Walling).

Business

The 1800s saw the early stirrings of a business spirit that went beyond the family farm, fishing and clamming, and such basic trades as carpenter, mason, and blacksmith. None of the new operations were large-scale in their size, production, or earnings, but they represented value-added enterprises of a small-industrial type that built on the existing resource endowments of the area.

The business of shipping, boat landings and docks, and shipbuilding is one example. It had its roots in the fact that, until the railroad came to Atlantic Highlands in 1892, the local connection farmers had to the wider world of commerce was heavily dependent on water. Before that, sailing packets carried the farmer's produce from three main landings. These were located at Applegate's at the foot of Appleton Avenue in Leonardo, Walling's at the foot of Avenue D, and Brown's Landing at the foot of what is now First Avenue (illustration no. 22). In due course, the Applegate and Brown sites became nodes for additional economic growth.

Applegate's landing was established before 1699 by Thomas Applegate, who had arrived from Long Island about 1674. Following great expansions of the family's landholdings in the 1700s, Thomas's descendant, Richard Applegate, by 1800 had an extensive farm and slaves to help run it. In 1802 he established a general store next to his landing. In 1808 he donated a half acre of land next to his store for a general public landing place where all citizens could move the products of their labor to market and receive arriving merchandise for use in their trades and their families.

This donation was public spirited, but it was also a wise business move. A public landing increased the traffic at Applegate's store and at the neighboring tavern owned by Joseph Maxson Sr. It also spurred a small shipbuilding business that mostly made schooners. The space available even made it possible for loggers from the surrounding country to store cord wood there until boats could ship it or until the most favorable price could be obtained. Several "woodchoppers" who worked the eastern highland hills in Atlantic Highlands in the 1800s made this the staging point for their output on the way to market.

One of the first boats leaving from there was a small sailing vessel, the *Sea Flower*, acquired in 1810 by William Leonard (grandfather of Thomas Henry Leonard). His captain, Thomas Bowne, ran it to and from New York City. By 1812 Richard Applegate himself built a packet boat called *Friendship*, which was attacked on its way to New York by a British ship during the War of 1812 (see below). By 1822 another boat working the landing and shipping produce was the *Patriot*, owned by William and Joseph Leonard and James and John Hopping from nearby Belford.

At first, cargo-laden wagons and horses were driven into the water of the bay at the time of low or half-tide. They unloaded their produce or cord wood onto boats waiting on the sand flats. However, sometimes a wagon got caught in a rising tide and floated away while waiting its turn to unload, with a resulting loss of cargo and income. Eventually small piers were built to overcome this problem and allow loading/unloading at any time of day. Later, the piers were lengthened so that bigger boats carrying more cargo could dock in deeper water. The first record of a small pier was the "Mud Dock" that was built at Applegate's in 1850 by the farmers of the community (Applegates, Bownes, Burdges, Conovers, Leonards, Roops, Stillwells, Taylors and others) who incorporated as a company for the purpose.

The second landing in the area was established in 1834 on the low beach at the bay end of First Avenue by William Brown, who owned the adjoining large farm. Brown's Landing mainly served fishermen and clammers, including those from Navesink village who made their way to it via the lane (today's First Avenue) that passed the Brown farm homestead. Also on this road, farmers carried their produce and woodsmen their logs to be shipped out in packet boats to markets, mainly in New York City. In the 1850s there were 40 or 50 fishermen working out of the cove surrounding the landing and the mouth of Many Mind Creek. Their skiffs and bateaux were harbored and secured by stakes either in the mouth of Many Mind Creek, or in the shallows a little offshore, which they reached by a shared small "dinkey" boat.

As had happened at Applegate's, the boat traffic passing Brown's Landing attracted a merchant to build a store there. The first proprietor, Bradford Warren, was succeeded by Walter Murray, William Robertson, and finally John Sharts. In the 1870s, Captain John H. Skidmore owned a packet sailboat that worked out of Brown's Landing. When a bigger dock was built at this landing in 1878–1879, the remains were found of an old stone dock that had projected into the bay. Supposedly it had been the watering place for shipping at the time of the French and Indian War (1754–1763), and the new dock used many of its stones.

At the foot of Avenue D, a third landing had been established, later than Brown's at a date not specified. Known as Walling's Landing, after the landowner, it was the same location that the original English settlers used after 1667 for their boat loadings and unloadings, in addition to likely landing points on their lots that fronted Many Mind Creek. Walling's Landing remained a very low-key, small-scale, basically private access point to the bay. The relative abruptness of the land's edge there made it a less than easy loading and unloading point.

Farther west along the bayshore, the general drive for more outlets and water connections led to other docks and piers being built in the 1850s and after. A 400-foot pier was constructed at Bray's Landing, today known as Ideal Beach, east of Keansburg. In 1855 a new enterprise called Port Monmouth Transportation Company began developing an entire complex of facilities around Compton's Creek: a 2,000-foot pier, a new steamboat to carry freight and passengers to New York, a large barn-stable shed structure for waiting people and goods, a large hotel near the landing, and stagecoach companies to connect to several points. Eventually the company also laid a plank road to eliminate muddy bog-downs en route to Middletown village and dredged a channel to another dock along the sedge banks that accommodated two more steamers. (The hotel, called Foster's Hotel, was owned by the father of William M. Foster who in 1880 built Atlantic Highlands' first hotel, Foster's Pavilion, at Brown's landing.) The enterprise was reshaped with a new steamboat dock more than 6,000 feet long in time for the January 1860 opening of the Port Monmouth terminal of the New Jersey Southern Railroad (also called Raritan and Delaware Bay Railroad). From there, local station stops were made at Hopping Station (intersection of Leonardville and Chapel Hill Roads) and Chapel Hill, and the trains then continued south through Red

Bank, Lakewood, and Bridgeton to Delaware Bay. During the Civil War, the steamers, the Port Monmouth terminal, and the New Jersey Southern were all used to transport Northern troops from New York City toward camps and battlefields in the South.

The bay front within the borders of today's Atlantic Highlands, in addition to its landings, was also the basis for at least four other small business activities in the 1800s: a bark mill, piped spring water, marl fertilizer, and a bunker oil and fish meal factory. Inland areas also sprouted several agriculture-based businesses.

The bark mill was located at the mouth of Many Mind Creek. It ran on the power of the tides and was used to grind bark for use in tanning hides. Its remains were found when the new dock was built in 1878, but its size, shape, output, and life-span are all unknown.

The spring water source was the spout, known the world over for its superior water quality ever since Henry Hudson's ship crew filled their water casks there in 1609. The added value brought to the spout in the 1830s was that its waters were carried by a pipe down to the beach, making it more convenient for ships to collect. At the same time the owner of the spout began charging 5¢ a barrel for the fresh water and making a profit. This practice was started either by Louis Despreaux who owned the property in 1830, or by his successor George Eldridge after 1850. There were two categories of customers: sea-going ships that sailed between New York and all parts of the world, and that had to pass Sandy Hook Bay; and the fleet of the New England fishermen, which at certain times numbered as many as 300 sail. Outgoing ships would beach their dories and dinghies with barrels to fill with water and then idle awhile in the cove, waiting for favorable winds to pursue their course. One author described their departure, "To witness their simultaneous hoisting of sail and leaving the harbor, the scene heightened by the bright morning sun, whitening this vast expanse of sail, produced a scene of remarkable beauty, not easily surpassed." Eldridge, a retired whaler and waterman, in 1863 invented the long-handled hard-clam rake, making it easier to collect clams from the bay bottom.

Marl fertilizer shipping was a business operated in the 1860s by Charles Sears on the bayfront about a half mile west from the spout. Sears had been the president of a famous but failed cooperative-socialist community, the "North American Phalanx," west of today's Phalanx Road in Colts Neck. With several partners, he bought about 50 acres of waterfront property that formerly belonged to the Hooper estate in today's Atlantic Highlands. On its high bluff was the Point Lookout farmhouse of pre-Revolutionary War vintage, which Sears made his home. Just west of the farmhouse a steep roadway ran from the ridgetop at today's East Mount and Highland Avenues down to the bay. It became known as Sears' Landing Road, because it led to a long shipping dock that Sears had built. From that dock his business was to ship large quantities of green sand marl that had been mined for sale and use as an agricultural fertilizer. He exported this material to points on the New Jersey coast, Delaware, and other eastern states. However, because of the high cost of transportation and the loss in a storm of several freight vessels they used, the business did not last long.

Sears then turned his attention to manufacturing other products in a fish factory he established at the same site. The business was a partnership with his son-in-law Seth Chapin, namesake of Chapin Drive above Point Lookout, and Charles P. Dey, who lived on East Washington Avenue (formerly Dey Avenue) near Sears Avenue. The raw material was moss bunkers caught by local fishermen, who delivered up to 500 bushels of bunkers a day to the Sears Landing dock during the 1870s. When processed, this yielded 250 to 275 gallons of bunker oil, a product used to dress leather in tanneries, manufacture paint, rope, and soap, and keep ticks off sheared sheep. The factory also produced around five tons of fish meal a day, with a high nitrogen content that made it especially good as a fertilizer for asparagus (a key crop in area farms). Unfortunately it was also a "stink factory," producing strong, even noxious odors if the bunkers were partly spoiled. As Atlantic Highlands began transforming itself into a resort, there were so many objections to the smells that the bunker factory was shut down by the Board of Health in 1880.

In the 1800s another town product, of gentler smell and taste, was watercress. Atlantic Highlands bears the distinction of being the first point, or at least one of the first, from which watercress was shipped commercially in the United States. When Nathaniel H. Roberts bought farmland in the southern area of town then known as the Valley, he discovered that watercress was growing profusely near Many Mind Creek, whose source was in springs of ice cold water. He hit on the idea of selling watercress to the New York market as a special delicacy. He coddled the crop, increased the acreage, and developed a virtual monopoly. The soil adjacent to the springs was later found to be good for raising asparagus, which Roberts was soon shipping in large quantities, making a nice profit. It needed very little labor, since most asparagus shoots resurfaced and grew on their own every crop season.

Also going beyond the mundane basic crops of potatoes, corn, beans, etc., watermelon had special appeal on the New York market. Like watercress and asparagus, watermelon was a "niche" crop for which the area had an edge and large acreage was devoted to it.

Cider was a value-added agricultural product based on the many apple orchards in the area. The Leonardville district had the distinction of having a cider press and still-house within its territory. Samuel Cooper ran another local still on the Stillwell farm near Chapel Hill village. Cider, in its fermented form called "Jersey Lightning," was often served at such community events as farm-field plowing bees, corn harvest frolics, and house or barn raisings where the drinking sometimes left too few sober men to put up the rafters.

However, a counter-move came in the form of the temperance movement that looked on this drink and other alcoholic beverages as value-lost products. Beginning in the 1830s, several preachers organized temperance meetings at Riceville and other places in the Atlantic Highlands area. Methodists at High Point/Chapel Hill formed a temperance group called "Washingtonians" for some reason, while others dubbed it the "Swill Tub Society." In 1842 the group strictly renamed itself "The High Point Total Abstinence Society" when 225 local people, including several Leonard family members, signed a pledge not to use or traffic in intoxicating liquors. Rally-like temperance camp meetings were held annually in a grove near the Navesink Baptist Church. The local movement became so popular that the number of taverns in the area was reduced from a half dozen to one. In 1850 several local preachers and lay church members bought a great deal of liquor, burned it, or poured it out on the ground. Local production of Jersey Lightning was wiped out when many orchards were dug up and still-houses destroyed. By the time the future Atlantic Highlands was being promoted for tourist excursions in 1879, and then for Christian summer camp meetings in 1881, it was firmly based upon temperance.

War of 1812

Unlike the Revolutionary War, the War of 1812 did not involve major troop movements in the Atlantic Highlands area, raids and destruction by enemy forces on the land, or contending factions among the residents. Its impact in the region came from a few naval skirmishes offshore, measures to guard the area against possible invasion, and the military service of a small number of area residents.s

Declared in June 1812 and sometimes called the "second war of independence," the conflict was mainly sparked by British ships stopping and searching American ships and capturing and impressing seamen into naval service. Commercial and trading competition between England and America was also a factor, and one of the British war moves was a naval blockade that seriously hampered trade along the southern New Jersey coast. There was fear that the blockade would be extended northward, or even that the British navy would attack the key trading center of New York. As a result, an American flotilla was stationed in Sandy Hook Bay during the war to protect the approaches to New York.

The federal government, which had acquired the Sandy Hook lighthouse in 1790 and much of the peninsula in 1806, stationed a large contingent of soldiers there for defense. It consisted mostly of New Jersey militiamen drawn principally from Monmouth County. They built a large log fort about a half mile north of the lighthouse, on what was then the north point of Sandy Hook (since extended by ocean-driven sand).

A year after the war began, there was local naval action. A British man-of-war, the *Pictier*, was in the Sandy Hook area together with its tender sloop *Eagle*. Perhaps the fiery independent spirit of the Fourth of July is what prompted a well-armed party of 33 Americans that night to attack the sloop. Under command of Sailing Master Percival, they sailed out of Many Mind Creek in a fishing smack called *Yankee*. Thirty of them were hidden in the cabin, while on deck were only three men, dressed as fishermen, as well as a calf, a sheep, and a goose they had bought. When the *Eagle*'s crew stopped the *Yankee*, they assumed no threat or danger from its apparently innocent, pastoral passengers. But now the attackers left their hiding place, shot their muskets, quickly jumped aboard the *Eagle*, and drove the 11-man crew and its young midshipman commander into the hold. The Americans killed some of the crew, buried one on Sandy Hook, captured the rest, and sent them as prisoners to New York.

Another Sandy Hook event involved Richard Applegate from Leonardo. His sail packet *Friendship*, which he built, regularly carried fresh fruits and vegetables from bayshore farms to markets in New York. One day during the War of 1812, his boat was passing Sandy Hook, under Captain William J. Leonard. The cannon of a British man-of-war fired at her from behind the Hook and hit the mainsail, piercing the sheet. Despite the damage, Captain Leonard sailed onward out of the cannon's reach and completed the journey.

The hills of Atlantic Highlands and neighboring territory were ideal vantage points for watching the water maneuvers and clashes. In the 1880s John Maxson Brown remembered his boyhood in Navesink and one of his earliest memories—witnessing a naval skirmish of the War of 1812 from the highlands hills. Because of the distant bay and ocean overview from the cliffs, the small plateau at Point Lookout was used for the construction of a block house fort during this war, the same point that had hosted a sentinel post during the Revolutionary War.

A thousand troops from five artillery companies and three rifle companies of the Jersey Blues were stationed on the heights of the highland hills during the war. Regiments doing duty there under Brigadier General Ludlow came from near and far: the Ten Eyck Rifles of Middletown, but also two units from Trenton, two from Newark, and one from Bloomfield, New Jersey. A fort with barracks and blockhouses armed with 32-pounders, built by 280 workmen, was brought in. It was named Fort Gates after a Revolutionary war general, Horatio Gates. The units disbanded and returned to their homes after the war ended with the signature of the Treaty of Ghent on December 14, 1814.

Information on local men who served in the military is scant, with only five names known. Two men reported in a local history as enlistees from "this section" were John Thompson and Samuel Van Schanck, both probably from the Highlands. James Hopping from Belford/Chapel Hill organized a company of militia for service in the war and received his commission as captain in September 1814. Samuel Hooper was a captain in one of the New Jersey regiments. After the war he worked his farm along today's Ocean Boulevard near Grand Avenue. A grandson of the first Leonard who settled on the bayshore, William J. Leonard became a soldier in the war at age 23. There is no information on where these five men were stationed or saw action during the war. Its battles were mainly fought far from the bayshore, in such places as Canada, Ohio, Chesapeake Bay, and Washington D.C. (set on fire by British General Ross), and on the high seas, often involving American privateers.

The Civil War

Andrew Bowne cracked his whip loudly to speed up the horses of his "People's Line" stage. On his route from the steamboat dock in Highlands, he was carrying a mail sack, some packages, and city newspapers to deliver in Riceville, Leonardville, and Chapel Hill. At the corner of today's Avenue D and Leonardville Road, he stopped his coach and went into Thomas Leonard's store. Handing him a few letters and the *Tribune*, Bowne pointed to the headlines. "It's war," he said. "The rebels have attacked Charleston." Bowne took Leonard's outbound mail and watched him scan the front page and shake his head in surprise and disbelief. When Bowne left, Leonard sat down and began reading aloud for the benefit of three customers in the store who were eager for the news:

THE WAR COMMENCED
The First Gun Fired by Fort Moultrie Against Fort Sumter
THE BOMBARDMENT CONTINUED ALL DAY
Spirited Return from Major Anderson's Guns
The Demand for a Surrender and Major Anderson's Refusal.
OUR CHARLESTON DISPATCHES

Leonard told his listeners he was sure the southern rebellion would not amount to much and be over in no time at all. This was April 13, 1861.

The next day, the news of President Abraham Lincoln's reaction came by telegraph to Charles Havens, the marine observer and telegraph operator up at the Twin Lights. The president was calling for 75,000 troops to be raised immediately, to serve for three months, to put down the rebellion, and to preserve the Union. Hearing this, neighborhood men wondered if mobilization orders would be given to the governor's Light Guard unit that trained under Captain William Truex at his blacksmith shop on the King's Highway in Middletown village. Or would they first call out the county militia? All agreed that the rebellion by six southern states wouldn't last beyond the beginning of summer.

In these first days, no one could know that a four-year war had been launched, that five more states would join the Confederate side, and in all 500,000 soldiers would die and 600,000 would be wounded. Slaves would be emancipated and black men would be enlisted into infantry and artillery regiments, just like whites. From the wider Atlantic Highlands area, 33 local men—fathers, husbands, sons and brothers—would go off to war between

1861 and 1865. Three area soldiers would never see the bay and hills of home again and 11 would return with injuries, illnesses, or disabilities.

Within six weeks, half of the 10th Regiment of the New York Volunteers was stationed on Sandy Hook. There was fear that Confederate forces would arrive and try to blockade or capture New York. But the volunteers were quickly moved out to actual battlegrounds in Virginia after the Union defeat of July 21, 1861 at Bull Run.

In the first year of war, the North suffered a series of military setbacks on the battlefields, and economic impact was mounting on the homefront. Many products were in short supply, such as cotton and tobacco that came from the South where ports were now closed by the Union blockade. Steamboat service to Monmouth County was interrupted as the government took over boats for war use. Farmers had to rely on slower, less reliable sailing vessels to meet New York market demands. Profits were suffering. Many wanted peace above all else. "Let the Confederate States alone. No more of this disastrous war!" was one of their proclamations.

In August 1862, posters went up all along the bayshore at docks, post office–general stores, and hotels announcing a "MASS MEETING at Middletown on Thursday, August 29th at 2 o'clock P.M." The broadbills invited attendance by "all who are in favor of adopting some measures for . . . the peace and prosperity of our distracted country and who are opposed to the present State and National administration." The meeting was called by 168 prominent Monmouth County men. Opposing them came more than 1,000 men who considered the meeting treasonous and intended to prevent or break it up. Before uttering a single word, the keynote speaker fled for his life to a boat at Port Monmouth that took him back to New York. The band hired for the event hid in a private house until it could safely return to New York once the protesters had gone home.

There is no record of who protested that day. However, names are known for the 33 men from the Atlantic Highlands area who went off to war six weeks later, as well as the ages and occupations of some of them at enlistment (see box). The men had varying reasons for volunteering: preserve the Union, punish the rebels, experience the honor and gallantry of war, and join friends and family members who were going to war. Some enlisted to avoid the draft, which was set to begin September 3, 1862, if New Jersey state quotas were not reached. Drafted men qualified for no bounty payments to wives and mothers. They could be assigned to units far from home, staffed with strangers, for up to three years of duty. The men who joined the 29th New Jersey Volunteers felt they would not see major combat, being only "nine months men."

Some joined for economic advantages, such as Hendryck Smith of Riceville/Navesink. Smith was 34 years old when he joined the 29th New Jersey Volunteers in Company D, commanded by his neighbor, Charles Lufburrow. For nine months service from September 1862 to June 1863, he was paid $117. For support of his wife Hester and four young sons, she collected $6 a month or a total of $54 at Town Hall. If instead he had been working his trade as a waterman (clammer or fisherman), he would have earned $150 to $185, a sum that included the labor of his wife and older boys. However, military pay was not advantageous for others. Skilled tradesmen, such as blacksmith John Kipp, sailmaker Peter Valleau, carpenter George Smith, or mason Thomas Card, would have made two to three times more in civilian work.

Eleven local men had injuries or illness in the war. For example, Hendryck Smith suffered from dysentery while in the army and was so ill afterwards that he applied for and received in August 1879 a United States pension of $4 monthly for illness caused by his war service. Sergeant Peter Valleau was discharged at Belle Plain, Virginia, in February 1863 due to disability caused by illness.

Local Volunteers in the Civil War

Twenty men enlisted in Company D of the 29th New Jersey Regiment:

John L. Applegate, Sergeant, 22, farmer	John Schofield
William W. Boeckel, 18, carpenter*	Irving C. Schureman, farm laborer
Thomas Card, 42, mason	Hendryck H. Smith, 34, waterman
Richard Carhart, 18, farm laborer	Frederick Snyder, 25, carpenter
Thomas Carhart, 21, farm laborer	John B. Swan, 20, waterman
Edward T. Johnson	Joseph S. Swan
John G. Kipp, 20, blacksmith	James G. Taylor, 25, farm laborer
Edward P. Layton, 24, waterman	Horatio Tilton,18, farm laborer
Charles Lufburrow, 1st Lieutenant, later captain	Benjamin F. Udell
George W. Marks, 30, farm laborer	Peter Valleau, Sergeant, 45, sail maker

The other 13 local enlistees were in a variety of units:

Somers T. Champion, 24, waterman, Captain Co. B 25th NJ

George B. Davis, 30, carpenter, Navy landsman on Mattabessett

Joseph Eldridge, waterman or clammer, Navy

Robert Emery, Sergeant, 33, Methodist minister, Co. F 3rd Regiment, NJ Militia

William M. Foster, 24, waterman, Bartlett's Naval Brigade/Union Coast Guards, merged into 99th
   New York Volunteers

Joseph W. Gardiner, 17, clerk, unit unknown

Robert Allen Johnson, 23, 14th NJ

John M. Layton, 40, Co. B 12th NJ

Steven H. Powell, Co. C 14th NJ

Webster Swan, 25, waterman, Navy on *Ceres*,

Dennis Sweeney, wagoner , Co. I 29th NJ

Joshua E. Van Pelt, 14, farm laborer, Co. B 29th NJ

Jacob Wagoner [Wagner], 27, waterman, Co. F 29th NJ

* After serving in 1st NY Marine Artillery.

Three local men died of typhoid: Edward Burdge, John Tunis, and Benjamin Udell. Caused by poor sanitation, adverse weather, and the spread of communicable diseases, typhoid fever was so prevalent in army units that it was often called "camp fever."

The 29th New Jersey Volunteers Regiment, including Company D where most of the Atlantic Highlands area men served, was fortunate in its war service. The regiment was mustered into United States service by September 20, 1862, at Camp Vredenburgh, near Freehold, in the fields where the Battle of Monmouth had been fought in 1778. After only eight days of drill, the green recruits shipped out by train for construction and guard duty in defense of Washington, D.C. On November 30 they moved to the Fredericksburg area to guard pontoon bridges when Union artillery and troops crossed the river to storm the rebel-held town. Union forces suffered a major defeat and heavy casualties, and retreated back across the river under fierce rebel cannon fire. Local men and comrades in the 29th New Jersey were the last to cross, all safely.

Lincoln's Emancipation Proclamation of January 1, 1863, was not well received by most of the regiment, as reported in the *Monmouth Democrat* (February 12 and April 2, 1863). There was grumbling that "it will prove more disastrous than the camp fever to the soldiers in the field." Partly they feared that black support staff would be freed from "dirty" tasks, which would now fall to white soldiers. By 1864, "United States Colored Troops" (USCT) units were formed for military service by blacks. Some soldiers went into the USCT from the local black population living in the Hillside section immediately west of the future Atlantic Highlands boundary, in Riceville/Navesink, and in eastern Chapel Hill, as well as farther west in Middletown's Red Hill Road area and Leedsville/Lincroft section. At least 19 men from these communities joined. Many USCT units initially were used in non-combat situations, and some that went into combat were replaced at the last minute by white soldiers to avoid the uproar that would have attended black military success. Four local black men—Samuel Allen, Thomas Fisher, John Fry, and Samuel Mellon—were killed in action.

In January 1863 the 29th Regiment joined the First Corps of the Army of the Potomac and suffered the infamous five-day "Mud March" through mud 18 inches deep, winter wet, and icy cold. On January 24 the men got their first pay in four months of service under a new commander, who improved morale with better living conditions in camp and leaves, while drilling the men in preparation for a spring offensive. It was launched April 30, with 120,000 troops. The main army crossed the river above Fredericksburg, while the division with the Atlantic Highlands area men crossed south of town to create a diversion. When General Lee's confederates overran the main army, the southward troops marched north to help but were caught by Confederate cannons at the river. The Atlantic Highlands area men were not among the casualties.

After five weeks of encampment, the 29th New Jersey was ordered on June 12 to march north, following Lee's army that was intent on invading Pennsylvania. However, on June 16 the men got the happy orders to return to New Jersey for release from service. They were mustered out at Camp Vredenburgh on June 28, 1863. A week later, news reached the Atlantic Highlands area telling of the tragic fate of the men in their old First Corps in the Battle of Gettysburg.

After almost two more years of bloody war, finally the "GLORIOUS NEWS!" was proclaimed in newspapers and posters put up throughout the bayshore. The news on April 8, 1865 proclaimed, "Lee's Rebel Army surrendered, and the prospects of peace are most cheering."

Veterans in the Postwar Years

In the postwar years, at least five Civil War veterans and their relatives played significant roles in the new prosperity and development of Bay View (later renamed Atlantic Highlands) and Navesink village (as Riceville was renamed in 1867). Somers T. Champion, who had been a waterman, served nine months between September 1862–June 1863 as captain of Company B, 25th New Jersey Volunteers, seeing action at the battle of Fredericksburg. In the early days of Atlantic Highlands, he owned nine lots on Bay View Avenue (Ocean Boulevard). He was proprietor of the 90-room Champion House hotel on the south side of Bay View near Third Avenue from 1890 to 1895. He was the commander of the local post of the veterans' organization, Grand Army of the Republic, at its founding in 1891. In April 1897 he was one of the local men who took the Central Railroad of New Jersey special excursion to New York for the dedication of the tomb of the Union Army general and later President, Ulysses S. Grant. Champion died in 1921 at age 90.

Robert Emery from Long Branch joined the 3rd Regiment New Jersey Militia in April 1861, two weeks after the first shot of the war was fired. After the war, as a Methodist minister, he was a founder of the Atlantic Highlands Association in 1879 and established the church there and at Highlands. Until his death in 1906, he was involved in real estate and other businesses in town.

William M. Foster had trained with the Governor's Light Guards under Colonel William S. Truex in Middletown village. One of the first volunteers from the area, he joined Bartlett's Naval Brigade on May 16, which sailed south to be mustered in at Fortress Monroe on May 24. His unit was renamed Union Coast Guards, then merged into the 99th Regiment NY Volunteers, and fought 32 skirmishes during three years of war. Foster was wounded in battle three times and came home with a sword he took from the S.S. *Merrimac* when it was burned. Before the war, he was a bayshore waterman of modest means. After, he went into the excursion steamboat business at Port Monmouth where his father had "Foster's Hotel" at the steamboat-railroad terminal, and managed hotels in Red Bank and Manhattan before coming to Bay View in 1880. He built a hotel and excursion pavilion at the foot of the First Avenue pier. One of the major organizers of Atlantic Highlands borough, the Methodist church, and fire department, he was also post master and a founder of the Casino.

Richard Carhart became the Chapel Hill Light keeper in 1869. He was succeeded by his youngest son, Charles, who maintained it until about 1900. Richard, who lived in the Hillside section, was a Civil War fireman in the Navy gunboat *Southfield* for three years, and later was a fireman for many years on the steamboat *Holmdel's* New York-Keyport route.

Joshua E. Van Pelt was a painter and lived in Monmouth House in Atlantic Highlands in 1895. This 16-room boarding house on Highland Avenue near First Avenue was owned and run by Sarah C. Van Pelt, a widow who was probably his sister-in-law. C.W. Van Pelt, probably Joshua's uncle or cousin, had been a builder (he constructed the Everett House hotel in 1881). At age 14, Joshua had been the youngest local enlisted in the Civil War, and in 1926 he was one of the last two surviving local veterans.

On November 25, 1891, local veterans from towns around Atlantic Highlands met at White's Hall on First Avenue and organized post 114 of the Grand Army of the Republic. The GAR, founded in 1866, had units from Massachusetts to California, with more than 490,000 members by 1890. It was so influential that five Presidents were GAR members, as were most northern governors. At one point 20 percent of the national budget went for Union veterans' pensions. GAR Post 114 was created as an alternative to more distant GAR posts in Red Bank, Long Branch, and Asbury Park. Among its officers, in addition to Somers T. Champion, were William M. Foster, Robert Emery as chaplain, and John B. Swan.

Post 114 was named for Clinton B. Fisk from Missouri, a major general at the end of the Civil War, who died in 1890. He was the benefactor of Fisk University for ex-slaves, visited his Rumson country estate in the summers, and gave land and $3,000 to build an African Methodist Episcopal church in Fair Haven—named Fisk Chapel in his honor. After the war, veterans of the USCT formed their own GAR posts in Red Bank and Long Branch.

Another veterans group, the 29th New Jersey Volunteers Veterans Organization, was formed in May, 1889, and held annual meetings for many years. In 1912, an account of the 29th's activities was published in *Fifty Years Ago, A Brief History of the 29th Regiment New Jersey Volunteers in the Civil War*. In 1896, the annual meeting drew 125 veterans to the Central Baptist Church in Atlantic Highlands, New Jersey, where a group photo was taken.

In 1919, Somers Champion and other local veterans took part in the World War I victory parade in Atlantic Highlands. The last surviving veteran of the GAR Clinton B. Fisk Post 114 and the entire 29th NJ Volunteers was John B. Swan of the Atlantic Highlands area, who died in January 1933 at age 91.

Chapter Seven

VICTORIAN RESORT

May 1, 1879, in the forty-second year of the reign of England's Queen Victoria, was the day when Thomas Henry Leonard began realizing the idea of creating a new bayside destination along the Monmouth County coast of New Jersey, at a place later called Atlantic Highlands. On that day, the steamboat *Thomas Collier* made its first departure from a new tidewater wharf and chugged across the bay to pier 6 in lower Manhattan. If England's Victorian age stood for expansion of the royal empire, accelerated economic development, and an outwardly strict moral code, the New Jersey metropolis that Leonard hoped would grow from the little boat's simple freight run had similar foundations and ambitions.

When Leonard launched his town-building scheme, there had been no pier, only a boat-landing place on the raw shoreline at the end of a dirt road. The fact that he owned both the landing and the road had helped to shape his thinking. He was eventually joined by a few other dreamers and boosters of similar ilk—men who were capitalists, Methodists, and Baptists, and believers in temperance. Together they aspired to make a Christian teetotaling resort town between Sandy Hook Bay and the hills of the Navesink Highlands.

"Monmouth City" on the Bayshore

But Leonard's goals were much grander and far-reaching than one steamboat, one pier, and a bucolic vacation spot for Protestants. In his mind's eye, looking to the future, he saw an expanded "port of New York" with ocean-going vessels docked all along the bayshore "from Amboy to the Ocean." Those shores were mostly lined with shallow shoals, as Leonard knew, so he called for dredging them to accommodate the draft of large ships. In his view, another great benefit was that the material dredged up could be spilled on to the land and "used to fill up the shore meadows, above the tides, fitting them for any commercial purposes." Under his plan, in his own words, Monmouth County would "become the gateway of the future, between New York City and the West" and would "some day become Monmouth City."

Leonard offered this sprawling vision as his own "Prophesy." However, never one to ignore God's omniscience, he qualified it by a bow to the Almighty. He wrote that it would be realized "At some time, in some way, and some how. The Great Creator only knows." Significantly, he was not wondering whether his ideas had divine sanction, only when and how they would be implemented as God saw fit.

As an active capitalist, Leonard was looking forward to a commercial boom as his profit and payoff for investments he had already made. He had widened the dirt road to the bayside landing, laid out Mount Avenue to the hilltop, and personally paid $5,000 to a contractor for building the new steamboat pier 400 feet out into the bay. Together with four other men, he and five Leonards (his father Thomas, James, Richard, Charles, and Sarah) had formed the Bay View Dock and Transportation Company, with shares priced at $50 each.

They bought the steamer *Thomas Collier* for $16,000, paid $1,500 to move a grain elevator from pier 6 in Manhattan and give space for their gangway, and took out a costly lease on the dock. Their enterprise raised concern among competing steamboat companies that had long served farmers and merchants of the bayshore from Port Monmouth and those along the Navesink River from four docks between Red Bank and the Highlands.

The May 1 opening of the steamer route was in time for Leonard's next move— attracting summer excursionists to come for day trips. He was determined that his dock and boat should increase its profits by taking on passenger traffic in addition to freight business. To give visitors a picnic spot and nature experience, Edward Hooper cleared out the groves on his bayside bluff between the dock and today's Sixth Avenue. Leonard opened Bay View Avenue (today's Ocean Boulevard) to serve as a path uphill to Hooper's woods and its elevated view of the ocean, Sandy Hook, the bay, and New York City. In the fall of 1879 he invited Reverend Robert Emery and his Methodist Sunday School from Sea Bright for a special day of oyster and clam bakes, as well as bay bathing and walks in the woods. This opened the way for many ministers and church people to learn about the place and spread the word to religious groups looking for summer outings the next year. It also soon led Emery to form a Methodist Church in town.

October 25, 1879, was the second historic day in the unrolling of Leonard's grand plans. He decided to start the physical creation of a new town by splitting off about 20 acres from his 100-acre farm, dividing it into a grid of avenues, and laying out house lots he would sell. His surveyors began the work on that October day. When they finished, 62 building lots climbed the lower part of the hill from First to Third Avenues between Mount Avenue and Bay View Avenue (today's Ocean Boulevard).

Leonard had to do this on his own. He had tried to interest his Bay View Company colleagues in branching out from the steamboat business to develop this land, but the idea met great opposition. So much so that seven of the ten partners had resigned (including three Leonards), leaving only Leonard, his father, and his brother James. Was this because the departed shareholders lacked his visionary outlook and were not "progressive" and "live men of the day," as Leonard implied, using two of his favorite expressions? Or did they think his idea might just be a profit-grabbing technique for himself as the landowner?

After this failure, Leonard's next tactic worked better. He personally visited local residents and collected pledges to buy lots. Then he got the survey done and held a formal sale where 18 buyers acquired 27 of his lots. Was it a success to be left with 35 unsold lots (is the glass half full or half empty)? In any case, Leonard spent the money he gained to extend the boat pier from 400 feet to 1,450 feet long. Is this the act of a selfless public servant, or a clever investment by the capitalist landlord and boat owner? Reaching deeper water, the pier could handle boat arrivals and departures at any time of the day. Laying across the bars at low tide had been harmful to the boat, and being limited to tidewater sailings had been inconvenient to all parties.

Leonard had managed to marry his personal interests and ambitions with broad public goals of his own definition. Start a real estate market that yields the money for a viable boat service, which in turn adds to the town's attraction. This circle of initiatives contributed to his credit, both financial and political (not that there's anything wrong with that). In his 1923 book, *From Indian Trail to Electric Rail*, Leonard was not exactly modest in describing what he accomplished as "the Founder" in 1879 (capitalization by Leonard himself). About himself, he wrote that "it required long and many years of patient toil, energy and perseverance, placing in line all the material most available to the construction of this enterprise."

Next, Leonard enlisted William M. Foster as day-trip promoter, excursion manager, and host for the next summer's visitors. Previously involved in his father's "Foster's Hotel" in Port Monmouth and then manager of a Manhattan hotel, Foster now moved to town and leased from Leonard some bayfront land next to Leonard's new dock at First Avenue. He put up a building called Foster's Pavilion that included a restaurant, erected 100 bathing houses, and arranged for boat rentals and picnic grounds (illustration no. 23). He aimed advertisements at church Sunday Schools, social clubs, and fraternal lodges. The ad text made clear that "the place will be conducted strictly on temperance principles, which will tend to make it more desirable, as a majority of the places usually visited by excursions have become lager beer gardens principally, and are resorts for roughs and pickpockets." The banning of alcoholic beverages was a condition of Leonard's lease to Foster (mentioned twice) and a strong part of Leonard's own tradition and beliefs; his father and other Leonards had been Baptist founders of the local Temperance Society in Chapel Hill back in 1842.

Wanting a hotel for longer guest stays, Leonard convinced Mrs. Harriet E. Martin to give up the boarding house she ran in Asbury Park, buy two lots on Bay View Avenue, and make plans for building a hotel there. It opened in July 1880. Leonard was responsible for the construction of Bay View House and owned it for several years until Mrs. Martin bought it.

Another idea for both promoting the town and making a profit also beckoned Leonard. On First Avenue, next to Foster's Pavilion, he set up a lumber business to generate and meet demand for house building materials. His younger brother John H Leonard was his partner in this "Leonard Brothers" company.

By the summer season of 1880, word had spread and many groups of excursionists arrived from churches, Christian associations, and clubs from Manhattan, Brooklyn, Newark, and other closer New Jersey places. The steamboat *Thomas Collier* made two and three round tips daily to New York, charging 50¢ a ticket. Bay View House was full of boarders all summer long. The first new house was built on the new lots, the cottage of Edward T. Burdge on Third Avenue. People were finally responding to Leonard's dream.

Bay View, as the mini-town was called, was taking off.

The Devout and the Dealers

Another parallel burst of resort town promotion came from a religious group that wanted to create a rival to Ocean Grove. The Methodist summer camp meeting on the Atlantic coast near Asbury Park had become very popular since it began in 1870. Ocean Grove incited either jealousy or inspiration, or both, in Thomas Henry Leonard, who became very active in organizing a similar camp meeting group called the Atlantic Highlands Association (AHA). Again seeing God on his side, he claimed this was "God's opportunity" and that evidence "clearly showed the leadings of a Divine hand" in this enterprise.

In fact, the main earthly hand in addition to Leonard's was that of a Methodist minister from Sea Bright, Reverend James E. Lake. In early 1881 he and Leonard and two other reverends began to hatch the AHA idea. Leonard courted and promoted Lake to become its president. In March 1881 the association was incorporated under New Jersey law with provisions for a capital stock of $250,000, though paid-in capital was only $10,000.

In a marriage of church and capitalism, of the devout and the dealers, the group would both run a Christian resort and sell real estate in the new town. On June 1, it sold 45 lots at auction, with Methodist ministers doing much of the buying. Especially popular were the lots on the hill east of First Avenue, where streets were laid out in circles following natural contours and parallel terraces. Leonard again congratulated himself, saying that he and Lake had spent "months of labor, sacrifice and patience" overcoming obstacles to the enterprise and building its foundations.

Leonard folded his dock and steamboat operation into the new association, and in exchange the three Leonards in the Bay View Transportation Company received one-seventh of the AHA stock. Also taking a major role were no less than 20 Protestant ministers who became officers, directors, and/or stockholders of the AHA. With Leonard conducting the negotiations apparently singlehandedly, the association quickly began to acquire land. The first purchase was 80 acres of Edward Hooper's highland woods where picnickers already went on day trips, in the area around today's Grand Avenue and Ocean Boulevard. In the end, over 300 acres were bought from the Hooper, Patterson, Woodward, Roberts, Dey, and Swan land holdings, and the former Brown farm east of Many Mind Creek owned by Thomas Henry Leonard. The association ended up owning all the land east and north of Many Mind Creek, south of the bay, and west of Sears Landing Road. By 1883, J.C. Nobles produced a map showing exactly that spread of association ownership (illustration no. 19).

The proclaimed objective of the association was "to found a Summer Resort upon Christian and temperance principles, where all the advantages of sea air, sailing, bathing, fishing, etc., can be secured, with freedom from Sabbath-breaking crowds and intoxicating liquors." The founders at once enacted a lot of restrictions on land use and behavior. No dwellings could be located within ten feet of the street or four feet of the side lines. No stables or out-buildings were allowed so near dwellings as to become nuisances. A long list of industrial activities was banned: livery and stable; dye house; bone-boiling or hideskin-dressing; slaughter house, piggery or tannery; and manufacture of soap, candle, glue, starch, lampblack, and fish guano. Carrying cleanliness still further, all cesspools and privies had to conform to strict regulations.

Other prohibitions were social in nature. No-nos included a house of prostitution or house of ill-fame, a dance or gambling house, conducting "business of any kind upon the Lord's Day," and any activity that is "a desecration of said Lord's Day."

The town was closer to New York than any other New Jersey watering place. Predicting that railroads would come to town within a year, the promoters said this would mean less travel time for vacationers from Philadelphia to Atlantic Highlands than to its shore competitor city of Long Branch. Recreationally, the bay offered the best still water bathing, with sandy bottoms and safe for children. Surf-bathing was only a short distance away by boat or carriage. Good calm sailing, abundant fishing, and beautiful drives on land were all close at hand.

During the association's founding months in 1881, its leaders also identified locations for the emerging town's role as a religious camp resort. The two main centers of activity were an auditorium site for outdoor meetings and a location for tenting grounds for people attending summer camp meetings.

The auditorium was located around today's Auditorium Drive off Ocean Boulevard, east of Grand Avenue. This was a natural amphitheater, an oval depression in the wooded hillside that rises from a flat semi-circular bottom. A regional author described "the symmetrical regularity of this cavity which art could not improve" in an 1889 book. "This surpasses anything I have ever seen," said the Reverend Dr. J.M. Reid, missionary secretary of the Methodist Episcopal Church, quotable praise for an auditorium where the meetings had a mainly church and missionary focus. Its steep-sided bowl of land was forested with large oaks and chestnuts 10 to 20 inches in diameter that had no branches up to a considerable height. In summer time, the place seemed to be shaded by a roof of green resting on gray columns. A small stage was built at the lowest level and bench-type plank seats for 4,000 people were placed in ranks climbing the curved hillside (lower left of illustration no. 19 and illustration no. 28). Everyone in the audience had a clear sight line to the stage. Its acoustic properties were remarkable; an ordinary voice could be heard distinctly in every part of the arena. It also had an outlook to the Bay, through a ravine 100 feet wide.

At the dedication service in July 1881, the scene was lit by Chinese lanterns, a choir performed, and the crowd sang "Praise God from Whom All Blessings Flow." Dignitaries attending included the governor of New Jersey, two bishops, and ten ministers. For at least a dozen summers thereafter, the auditorium hosted religious camp meetings, concerts, and political addresses. In 1886 the Chatauqua Association held its annual meeting and lecture series there. Opposite the auditorium, the association in 1881 also built a large tabernacle shaped like, and known as, the Octagon. It housed religious meetings in inclement weather.

Eastward and downhill from the auditorium was the campground, called Camp Hilton (illustration no. 29 and 30). It extended from Henry Hudson Spring a quarter-mile along the road, on bayfront land owned by its namesake, Judge Henry Hilton. Campers could arrive by train to a stop called Hilton Station and go uphill a short distance to the tenting grounds. Some 20 to 25 happy families would vacation at the camp. Some lived in one large tent, and some in three or four smaller tents connected by breezeways. In the evenings they socialized with sing-alongs beside campfires. Tents were located on green lawns, shaded groves, and side hills. There was a dock for recreational boating and swimming in the bay. The grocer and other merchants hauled provisions from town to the campers by horse and wagon. Proof of this natural paradise in the wilds of New Jersey is a comment by an early camper, "Although in the grove with no netting, yet I have not such as a mosquito in the tent." At the end of summer, Charlie Thorne rolled up the tents, inserted them in barrels, and took them in his wagon to the Spout House, which was owned by his family, for winter storage in the barn.

The camp's popularity did not last long. Reports show waning attendance in 1883 and 1885, and remain silent about other years. Its fate was linked to that of the association, which lost money to the point that it owed $100,000 in 1884. Its annual meeting that year unanimously decided to close out the business. In 1884, Reverend Lake was replaced by Reverend Dr. E.C. Curtis, who pushed for land sales to pay off the debt. It took until 1890 to do this, and not until 1895 could the association close down.

Several reasons are given for this collapse. Many non-resident directors had interests in other competing camp meetings. They did not pay in enough capital and gave themselves dividends in the form of lots—dividends that had no foundation in profits. The resident population was not in "full sympathy," because the association apparently did little or nothing to improve town infrastructure.

The Crowds Come

While the camp failed and the association floundered, the town boomed. By 1883 an onrush of real estate speculators had assembled six additional tracts west and southwest of Many Mind Creek, marked them up for house lots, and offered them for sale. These were the Hubbard Tract (135 lots on the former farm of James H. Leonard), Glenoble Park (80 lots), the Joseph Bowne estate (111 lots), Park, Hillside Park (200 lots), and the J. Edgar Bowne estate (illustration no. 19). It took several years for the market to warm up, but between 1880 and 1890 builders put up 154 dwellings, 100 of which were built from 1887–1890. This burst of self-confident growth dated from the town's vote on March 7, 1887, to incorporate itself as a self-standing borough, and then quickly moving to fix its bad roads and street lamps.

A variety of Victorian houses were built. Some, though modestly called "cottages," were sizeable mansions, mainly on the hillside and its bayfront (illustration no. 38). They had towers, turrets, bay windows, one to three floors of wraparound porches, multiple gables, irregular contours, and "gingerbread" and baroque decoration, such as were popular in that era. Architectural styles included Stick, Shingle, Queen Anne, Free Classical, Colonial Revival, and Carpenter Gothic. Also by 1894 there were churches in Gothic Revival and Romanesque Revival styles. Other houses, mainly on the other side of town west of Many Mind Creek, were simpler vernacular Victorian styles. More than 200 structures built before 1900 survive in the borough today.

Also built in the 1880s decade were 23 stores, mostly on First Avenue, including 15 with attached dwellings (illustrations no. 40 and 41). More than 20 other commercial structures put in an appearance, ranging from stables and laundries to a printing office and a railroad depot. During the same period, 29 hotels and boarding houses were established in town for vacationers and other visitors.

To bring in the larger crowds of visitors, as well as new summer resident commuters, a new larger steamboat, the *Marion*, was brought into service in September 1881 under Captain James H. Leonard. It could carry 1,000 passengers on each of three trips daily between New York and the Atlantic Highlands pier. Excursion tickets cost 60¢. By 1882 the wharf was extended another 350 feet to accommodate two new excursion boats. The vessels were provided by the Central Railroad of New Jersey as a stop on their runs between New York and their Sandy Hook terminal at Horseshoe Cove, where they connected to a southbound coastal rail line. The association described the commuter ferries as an inducement:

> To gentlemen whose business requires them to be in the city during the day. They can
> locate their families for the summer on the grounds, and, leaving the city at the close
> of business hours, can spend the night in the refreshing air of Atlantic Highlands, and
> return to the city in the morning by a cool and pleasant trip up the Bay.

By 1884, during the summer, the steamboats made four round trips a day to New York.

After unsuccessful attempts to induce several railroad companies to extend their lines into town, in 1882 a group of local private investors raised the money to do it. At a cost of $40,000, they built a rail connection between Atlantic Highlands and the Red Bank station of the New York–Long Branch line, and the Central Railroad agreed to run the trains under contract. On July 11, 1883, with 5,000 people in attendance, the new route was opened, ending at a new depot at Washington Avenue west of First Avenue. By 1884 there were five outgoing and five incoming trains a day there. Also in that year, the Atlantic Highlands Association sold the steamboat pier to the Central Railroad, which for the first time could run boats on Sundays—a practice the puritans in the association had forbidden as a desecration of the Sabbath.

The big railroad breakthrough came in 1892. It was the year when the Central Railroad had to abandon its Sandy Hook terminal for safety reasons. The departure was ordered by the federal government, which was using the Hook as a weapons proving ground. The company then established Atlantic Highlands as its new terminal, making the town the transfer point between ship and train for tourists coming from New York. The rail company drove 7,000 piles into the bay bottom to hold a pier that was 2,400 feet long—the second longest in the country. On the pier they laid ten tracks and covered platforms, allowing trains to go right out on to the dock (illustration no. 36). (The pier burned down in two stages, with fires taking place May 6 and July 4, 1966. Passenger service was discontinued in November of that year and freight trains stopped in 1972.)

Major construction work was also done in 1892 to create a rail line running from the pier along a trestle curving to the shoreline (illustration no. 37), and then to lay a bayfront roadbed running four miles eastward to Highlands. Up to 200 railroad cars a day brought slag from Pennsylvania to fill in along the narrow shore. Boulders were brought in to build a bulwark to protect the roadbed from wave action. Four stops were provided on this route; flag stops were at Bayview opposite 6th Avenue (illustration no. 25) and at Camp Hilton part way down Bayside Drive, while manned stations were at Water Witch in Highlands and in the main station in Highlands. There, a rail bridge was constructed across the Shrewsbury River to connect with the existing line, which headed south along the ocean coast to Long Branch.

In 1893 a handsome passenger station was built by the Central Railroad of New Jersey where today's Railroad Avenue parking lot is located. It had cedar shingle walls, leaded-glass windows, a long, high slate roof with seven sections, and a porched driveway to shelter horse-and-buggy passengers (illustration no. 33). At the peak 14 trains a day ran from Atlantic Highlands to New York, and as many returned along the tracks on today's West Avenue (the station burned down in 1949).

Becoming the one combined rail and boat terminal of Monmouth County in 1892 was a "great event which is to shape the future destiny of Atlantic Highlands," as a local newspaper described it at the time. Until then, transport planners had bypassed the area. In the 1860s Port Monmouth had been developed first as a boat terminal, and then a train terminal was added for the Raritan-Delaware rail line that eventually ran all the way to Delaware Bay. Yet the enterprise did not thrive, particularly when a rival boat-train terminal was created at Sandy Hook, from which a train line opened in 1865 to carry passengers going for vacations at the shore. In 1892 Atlantic Highlands was on the verge of becoming the "gateway from New York" that Thomas Henry Leonard had envisioned, but a more modest one leading to central New Jersey instead of to the far frontiers of the West.

Growth in transport, housing, and population went hand in hand, and population growth was promoted as more visitors were exposed to the location and its pleasures. In 1882, there were more than 10,000 summer visitors. The decade of the 1890s was the peak for hotels and boarding houses, with 37 operating during the period. In 1895 there were 307 houses in town, sheltering 340 families. In 1880 there had been only 40 residents. Their number was fewer than 200 in 1885, but rose to about 900 by 1890, and 1,715 in 1895—an eight-fold increase in ten years. An 1895 newspaper noted that this number included a "very large proportion of foreign-born residents," totalling 286 inhabitants who came from other countries. The great majority were born in the United States and had English ancestry, as had been the case in the late 1600s; but other European nationalities had now arrived, including roughly equal numbers of Irish, German, and Dutch (about 40 each), and smaller numbers of Scandinavians and Italians. In addition to these year-round residents, the resort town was naturally more heavily populated in the summer, when the number of estimated seasonal visitors ranged from 10,000 in 1882 to as high as 20,000 in later years.

Some old-timers in Atlantic Highlands have long assumed that black people moved to the area from the South after the 1861 Emancipation Proclamation, and/or were attracted by employment opportunities for domestics in the 1880s and 1890s when the big Victorian hotels and cottages were built in town. Earlier chapters have demonstrated that blacks were already present in the area in the late 1600s and 1700s, long before the Civil War. The 1880 census shows 120 black people living in 19 houses in the Hillside section around the southern end of First Avenue and neighboring Navesink, ahead of the boom that created a new resort town. Of those 120 people, 112 of all ages had been born in New Jersey, including three families with 35 members present from three New Jersey–born generations (Reeds, Richardsons, and Thompsons). In short, the old-timers' stories are a myth.

One group of new arrivals, who really did not stay, consisted of millionaire businessmen from New York. In 1879 about 30 of them banded together to purchase 260 acres of woodland east of the association properties. The tract ran from Mount Mitchill—the highest point on the eastern seaboard—to a little west of the spout (today called Henry Hudson Spring). Originally part of the Nimrod Woodward tract, this land was sold around 1830 to Andrew Mount, who lost a vast amount of money in the Civil War. In 1879 he was happy to sell it to the New York investors, including Judge Henry Hilton, Henry Morgan, William Toil, and about 25 others; from Middletown, the surveyor Esra Osborn, who had just done Leonard's first lot layout east of First Avenue, was also a partner.

The investors formed the Navesink Park Association (NPA) and had ambitious plans for an exclusive enclave with stunning water views, a yacht basin, and homes for the wealthy. They got as far as having a community layout done by Egbert L. Viele, the landscape engineer of Central Park in New York, carving out some roads throughout the property, starting foundations for several residences (never finished), and building a wharf 1,000 feet long near the spout (never used). Only Mr. Hilton became memorable, for the 1880s tent camp ground established by the church men along the bayside was called Camp Hilton, and later the railroad stop near the camp was called Hilton Station, and because a Hilton Road is today in the area.

The NPA was later superseded by another upscale development proposal called "Gateway" and marketed as "Manhattan's Riviera," but little progress was made before the start of World War I halted it. In 1915 the tract was annexed to the Borough of Atlantic Highlands, and again several other start-up attempts were made. They got nowhere until the late 1940s when its present development began and was sustained.

A link between Navesink Park and the Victorian homes west of Grand Avenue was created in 1896 when the graceful, rustic-style "Stone Bridge" was built to carry Mount Avenue over Grand Avenue (illustration no. 31). The avenue's steep slope had earned it the label "Breakneck Hill" until the new bridge provided a more level approach between the two areas. The main proponent and financier of the bridge was George F. Lawrie, who was lauded for this public service, though in fact his motive was to increase the value of land he owned east of the bridge. Lawrie named the bridge Oonuehkoi after a Native-American tribe he claimed had lived in the area. But the word means "a valley" and comes from the Natick dialect spoken by Native Americans who lived around 15 miles southwest of Boston—another myth exposed.

Snapshot of Atlantic Highlands People in 1890s

What were the main livelihoods of people in the late 1800s, and what did they do with their leisure time? People's work life can be seen in published directories from the 1890s.

These list occupations and addresses of residents, hotels and boarding houses, and retail and service businesses in Atlantic Highlands and the vicinity. However, women are largely left out of these directories, reflecting their focus on home-making and child raising. There are also sources of information on churches, lodges, musical events, and other entertainment, including alcoholic beverages (or the lack thereof).

In earlier decades and centuries, farming and water trades had been dominant. But by the mid-1890s a growing share of the town's business was in "modern" occupations relating to the railroad, housing development, summer resort life, and retail business.

From Lenape times until today, fishing and boating have been significant activities in the area. In the 1700s and 1800s a significant share of the working population depended on water trades for a livelihood; for example, in only one location, 40 or 50 fishermen had been based in the cove at the foot of First Avenue as of the 1850s. By 1895, however, the directory listed only 32 people in the water trades at all locations, including not only fishermen, but also mariners, dock hands, and six boat captains.

Because fishing generally provided unreliable earnings and a relatively low standard of living, most of the fishermen were housed in less costly areas, mainly on the west side of town and Leonardo. Catches fluctuated and were sometimes scarce, bad weather and bay ice interrupted fishing, prices went down when catches went up, and working harder did not necessarily produce more fish or money. Many kinds of fishing were done during the warm months including pound netting, gill netting, eel potting, purse seining, fyke netting, hard and soft clamming, and lobstering. The winter was limited to blue crabbing, eel spearing, and soft clamming. Such was the demand for clamming that a couple of blacksmiths in town specialized in making clam rakes and dredges for fishermen.

Only nine farms were listed in the 1895 directory. The Leonard Avenue area had farms belonging to the Burdge, Leonard, and Vanderbilt families. Over in Leonardo were the Bowne, Leonard, and Roop farms. It was the end of an era when Thomas Leonard's major farming enterprise in Leonardo was closed following his death. His crops and equipment were auctioned, including 25 tons of clover and Timothy hay, 1,000 corn stalks, asparagus plow and boxes, mower, hay tedder and rake, fertilizer drill, grind stones, cultivator, hoes, forks shovels, ploughs, wagons, carts, and sleighs.

The 1890s were a transitional period for all farms. They were being bought by the Atlantic Highlands Association and other developers, then subdivided and sold for cottagers to build houses. Not surprisingly, there were 29 businesses connected to the building trades. These included nine building contractors, three plumbers, two masons, several painters, a wallpaperer, and suppliers of lumber, granite and marble, sashes and blinds, stoves, and house furnishings, as well as a planing mill.

By 1895 there were about 40 hotels and boarding houses operating during summer. Their construction helped to fuel the construction business, created a seasonal job surge for locals, drew in short-term hires from elsewhere, and swelled the population with vacationing resort-goers. Total guest capacity was at least 1,200 in town.

Horse transport was the main way to get around, and at least 41 people provided services or equipment for this business in 1895. Nine businesses were stables that rented horses and carriages or ran stagecoach routes, with 23 men working as teamsters, hackmen, or drivers. Three of the stables were located at Center Avenue near the railroad to profit from rail traffic, and four others were in the central area of First and Second Avenues. Away from the main business district, George Bartleson's stable on First Avenue near Jackson Bridge did some retail

1890s Occupations

Occupational Category	No. of people listed *
Water trades	32
Farmers	9
Housing development	29
Hotels and boarding houses	37
Stables, horses, and carriages	41
Railroad employees	37
Other retail and service businesses	61

*In 1895 Stout's Directory of Atlantic Highlands

livery business. Beyond that, he also dealt in such building materials as mason sand, stone, brick, and top soil. An advertised offer of horses "for Ladies to Drive" came from the ninth stable, located on East Highland Avenue between Eighth and Grand Avenues and owned by Charles Ravatte; named "Hollywood Stables," it probably served the next-door hotel with the same name and others nearby (like the Grand View and Sea View House) that were known for socialite guests who went trotting and cantering in the hills. Accidents involving runaway or bolting horses, including some that were terrified by train whistles, were the subject of frequent news items in the local newspaper, but nothing was printed about manure in the streets.

The other businesses relating to horses were two carriage-building firms, two harness makers, a horseshoeing blacksmith, a horse trainer, and several stagecoach lines. One of the carriage manufacturers advertised his products as "road wagons, runabouts, grocery and farm wagons made to order."

Horseback riding was a popular pastime among the summer guests staying in resort hotels. Also, horse races were held on the Fourth of July and sometimes on Saturdays or Sundays. These events took place on the Valley Drive course, including its portion east of First Avenue that is now Memorial Parkway/Highway 36. For example, in 1896 the second event of "the spring running season" was held April 11, was attended by 300 people, and ran three races for competition plus a trotting race for sport.

The stagecoach business had roots going back to at least the 1850s, when a line carrying both passengers and mails went through town on its runs between Keyport and the Highlands. Until 1867 Andrew Bowne had a local stage line, which he sold that year to Charles Green. By the 1890s Charlie's route went between Navesink village and the railroad and steamer terminals. Another local stage route had been established by a Mr. Everett as of 1881, running to Middletown.

Kids used to hook rides on the rack at the back of Charlie Green's coach as it went up First Avenue, but he shooed them off for fear they'd get hurt. One of those kids was William Burdge Mount, who at age 90 in 1973 described it as "a regular coach just like they had out West. There was a rack in back for the trunks, a place for people to sit inside, then Charlie was up front on a high seat."

As a major terminus and connecting point for railroads running between New York City and Long Branch, Atlantic Highlands was a logical location for railroad employees to live (illustration no. 35). The 1895 directory lists 37 of them in town. Included were on-board staff (two conductors, five engineers, a brakeman), ground crew members (two flagmen, foreman, yard master, and signal-office section man) and managerial and administrative personnel (trainmaster, seven baggage masters, ticket agent, freight agent, clerk). Thirty of these employees had West Side addresses.

In addition to the 29 businesses that supported the booming construction industry in 1895, there were 61 retail shops, professional services, and business occupations in town that did everything from delivering babies to burying the dead, and from chopping wood to lighting the gas street lamps. An ice man with two horses and a wagon brought blocks of ice to homes to preserve food (illustration no. 39). The taxidermist doubled as a furrier, and the funeral director was also an upholsterer. Six lawyers took on legal requirements, and three doctors and three pharmacies filled medical needs, often with state-of-the-art cures. An exotic "medicine"advertised by one pharmacy, Antonides and Cooper Drug Store, was "Dr. U-TA-WA-UNs Ma-tta Indian Sarsaparilla Queen, a powerful liver, kidney and stomach regulator for rheumatism and all blood diseases."

The main business section, First Avenue between Bay and Highland Avenues, also had stores dealing in such items as ladies' hats, men's clothing, tailoring, fruits/ice cream/ soda, home laundry (Chinese owned), and jewelry and watches. The jeweler also sold silverware, served as the area's "sole agents for the Noiseless, Light Running, Standard Sewing Machine," was the "only graduate optician within 15 miles" and, naturally, sold spectacles. A retailer at the Market-on-Pier at the bay end of First Avenue sold fish, clams, oysters, and lobsters.

Some town boosters thought greater prosperity would be achieved by going beyond retail and service businesses to attract small industries. They partly got their wish when, by 1895, small investors had established a bakery and confectionery at 7th and Asbury Avenues, an ice cream plant, Lehn's bottling works, and, in the Hillside section, a dairy that was marketing "pure milk" and an industrial-scale steam laundry with 20 employees. The laundry reportedly ran about 1,000 gallons of dirty wash water a day into Many Mind Creek. Every day it shipped out more than 400 clean starched shirts and shirt waists, mainly to a Philadelphia wholesaler of men's furnishings. A large greenhouse, Bridle & Latham, had flourished for four years at Bay View and Grand Avenues, but after the neighboring Grand View Hotel burned down in 1894 it moved to Navesink. In 1897 the Atlantic Highlands Knitting Mills began operation on the third floor of a First Avenue building, employing young women to produce sweaters, leggings, and other woolen clothing. The impression was of a town with a varied, thriving small-business sector.

Churches and Lodges

Churches were very important for residents, and the town had no less than six churches by 1900. The Methodists were the first to found a church in 1879 and the first to have a church building in 1882. The other churches included one Presbyterian (founded 1890), one Roman Catholic (1891), and three Baptist congregations.

The Central Baptist Church, built in 1894 at Third and Mount Avenues, is unusual for its Romanesque Revival architecture and is still one of the largest wood shingle structures in Monmouth County (illustration no. 32). A widely visible town landmark is its square tower, four stories high, surmounted by a lighted cupola. On three walls about half the surface consists of stained glass windows, including a large rosette window on each street wall. The Atlantic Highlands Baptist Church, built in 1889 at Avenue D and West Highland Avenue, was physically moved out of town in 1913 to Leonardo. St. Paul Baptist began as an

African-American congregation in 1899 when it separated from the Central Baptist Church, finally putting up its own building in 1905 on Highland Avenue west of First Avenue. Nearby in the Hillside Section on Prospect Avenue was another black congregation, Quinn Chapel of the African Methodist Episcopal denomination, which had been established in 1855.

Next to Godliness was temperance, and the first "secret society" to be formed in town was the Sons of Temperance, a men's group founded in 1885. Next in sequence, and perhaps in popularity as well, was the establishment of a Republican Club the same year.

Of at least equal importance to the six churches were the local chapters of eight fraternal orders for men. In a speech to one of them in 1897, former Mayor Thomas Henry Leonard said he had "a corner in his heart" for them, "clustering as they do around the great central and foremost figure, the church of God." These lodges were, in effect, secular proponents of moral and charitable goals subscribed to by the churches, with an added large dose of male bonding and social fun and, for some, a pinch of flag-waving nationalism. Their pervasive presence in town is shown by the rosters of 1890s members of the local lodges. All powers-that-be—whether political, religious, business, or labor—were in these fraternities. In 1895 at least one lodge met in White's Hall above his grocery store at the corner of Bay View and First Avenues every night of the week except Sunday.

The nomenclature, purposes, and programs of these widespread fraternal and social groups tell us that the local population had time for some high-flown goals beyond pursuit of the grubby dollar, as well as some taste for ritual and historical echoes. For example, the kindly and peaceful ways of the Native Americans were the nominal ideal of the Improved Order of Red Men—all white men. Their eight slogans included "Be merciful to the stranger found astray in the forest" and their supposedly native-style initiation was more spoof than ceremony. Their chapter was called Vowa Vapon Tribe no. 200, after the Lenape chief who agreed in 1678 to vacate Sandy Hook for 13 shillings paid by Richard Hartshorne.

The other seven fraternal lodges were a mixed bag of charity, politics, military, and insurance. The Royal Arcanum, with its local lodge called Monmouth Council no. 1378, went beyond "love of country, home and friends" and charitable help for the less fortunate; it also offered insurance policies that were affordable and attractive in the light of the economic downturns and job losses of the early 1890s. Aiming to "improve and elevate the character of man," the Independent Order of Odd Fellows was called that because, when the order was founded in seventeenth-century England, it was odd for people to organize for the purpose of aiding the needy. The Masons were sited in their own local lodge hall as of 1897. Their credo had an anti-liquor edge, holding that men of high moral character believe in temperance as well as brotherly love, a Supreme Being, and the King James version of the Bible. There were local chapters of both the Order and the Junior Order of United American Mechanics, who were generally known as isolationist, militant Protestant laborers, and supporters of Benjamin Harrison's Republican campaign for President in 1892. The Knights of Pythias, who could afford to construct their own building in town in 1895, had the motto of "Friendship, Charity and Benevolence" and were committed to uphold government, honor the flag, and heal the North-South rift caused by the Civil War. Military memories from the Civil War were the subject for veterans from the Grand Army of the Republic, Clinton B. Fisk Post (see chapter 6). Finally, as of 1898, a fraternity lodge for black men called the Order of True Reformers was meeting at Quinn Chapel in the Hillside section.

A religious and female character infused the "Willing Hands Circle" of the King's Daughters, with members from each of the town's five Protestant churches; in humane style, they also installed a drinking fountain near the railroad station, with one side for use by people and the other by horses. The Women's Christian Temperance Union (WCTU), led by female officers from four Protestant churches, campaigned against drunkenness and alcohol abuse. In 1889 WCTU built a "Temple" on the south side of Mount Avenue, opposite west of Railroad Avenue where "public entertainments of an unobjectionable character" were held in its 400-seat auditorium—so long as the Puritan ladies approved.

Music and Other Amusements

An "amusement hall" was located at Bay Avenue and Avenue A as of 1895, probably referring to the Commercial Hotel at that location, which had a bar and a bowling alley. One of the most popular pastimes was pool or billiards, which could be played in some of the posh hotels and in the casino after 1896, and also in less grand pool rooms on Center, Bay, and First Avenues.

At its peak in the 1880s and 1890s, Atlantic Highlands had a host of musical events and groups. Vocal and instrumental entertainments were frequent, especially in the summer. They were held in an outdoor auditorium, in hotels, in the casino that was founded for "innocent amusements," and in the WCTU Temple. The first record of a public concert comes from 1880, when the bayside resort was beginning to develop. That year the first hotel, Foster's Pavilion, opened with its own beach and boathouses, and also held summer concerts.

During 1881 a group of nine women and four men that called itself "Our Girls," gave many concerts to raise funds for the town's new firefighting Hook and Ladder Company and for a new Methodist Episcopal Church. The fact that the town started as a summer religious resort that banned alcoholic drinks and dance houses tended to stifle rowdy singing and music, but churches hosted many musical activities.

Opened in 1882, the Grand View Hotel gave a big role to music. From its first summer until it burned down in 1894, the Grand View had a hotel orchestra. Its Sunday evening concerts included selections "mainly from sacred music themes both lofty and inspiring" as well as vocal, violin, and other performances by some guests. In later years, there were daily morning and evening concerts and Saturday night hops.

The Portland Hotel's opening in June 1893 was celebrated in a performance by vocalists. In 1894 an orchestra was resident all summer, led by a cornet player. In 1896, "a fine orchestra" provided music at afternoon and evening concerts daily and during the dinner hour, and held weekly hops every Thursday.

Among many musical events in the WCTU Temple in the 1890s: an evening program arranged by firemen with overtures by a cornet-piano-harmonica trio; male and female vocal solos, including a "sweet little love song;" a mixed quartet; and an instrumental duet. The Fiske Jubilee Singers gave "one of their notable entertainments," the Brilliant Quartette of four male singers from New York performed, and the "Atlantic Highlands Glee Club" gave its first concert. In the 1900s, before St. Paul Baptist Church had its own building, members sometimes met in the temple, and one Sunday, their gospel music was so vibrant and loud in the African-American church tradition that they were asked to move.

Another entertainment center was the Octagon. This wooden tabernacle was originally located opposite the auditorium, but had been moved in sections downhill to Bath Avenue. A bandstand built next to it for the 1895 season hosted the town's first daily summer concerts by an eight-piece orchestra under Charles Kaltenborn, sponsored by a group of businessmen. After being moved to Bath Avenue, the Octagon was used during the summer season for cake walks, fairs, and minstrel shows. The latter were variety entertainments, popular in the second half of the 1800s, in which whites wore black faces and outlandish costumes, sang, danced, did dialect patter and jokes, and played instrumental numbers featuring the banjo. This all ended when the Octagon burned down in August 1902.

Probably the most elaborate Victorian-age musical event was staged at the formal opening of the new Central Railroad line on May 30, 1892. Several bands played march music for an "immense parade of horsemen, footmen and carriages." Bands also played while numerous organizations marched, including a brigade of Italians who helped build the new railroad. They played again when special excursion trains pulled in during the morning and "palatial" steamers came to the dock. Next came a sumptuous dinner at Grand View Hotel, accompanied by "the enlivening music of the bands;" during a two-hour banquet of many courses, they played "dreamy and inspiring airs."

Among the musical groups formed by residents was the Atlantic Highlands Musical Association that met Wednesday evenings beginning in 1883. By 1890 the town had a 13-member Cornet band that practiced in the Commercial Hotel at Avenue A and Bay Avenue, sold tickets for "an entertainment" in the temple, and used the proceeds to pay Philadelphia tailors to make band uniforms with gold and black trim and spats at a cost of $200 each.

At least four musical businesses operated in town in the late 1800s. Blanche D. Robertson of Hooper Avenue was a music teacher in 1889. From at least 1883 to 1907, Marguerite Berst gave private lessons in music, piano, and singing (and also languages); classes were at her house, Strasbourg Cottage, located at Bay Avenue near Avenue B, which served as a "select boarding/day school." As of 1895, a piano tuner named Fred Anderson lived on Lincoln Avenue near Third. One business, owned by F.A. Morehouse on First Avenue, seemed to symbolize the central place of music in town life, as shown by his 1895 advertisement. In a single visit to his store, you could not only buy a house and insure it, but also furnish it with a piano or organ for children's music practice and parlor sing-alongs. Another 1895 advertisement said that he also sold "sheet music, violins, guitars, banjos, mandolins, accordions, zithers, drums, harmonicas, symbals, tambourines, fifes, piccols, flutes and ocarinas." In his spare time, Mr. Morehouse also was the borough clerk.

After the Grand View Hotel was reduced to ashes in 1894, a group of Atlantic Highlands town boosters decided something had to take its place to provide high-class entertainment and promote summer tourism. Their thinking as reported in a local newspaper was that to:

> Make the town superlatively attractive to summer people, more innocent amusements seem to be demanded. Current talk in favor of daily concerts during the summer may be an expression of this conviction. . . . The opinion seems to be pretty general that afternoon and evening concerts will be a practical investment and constitute an attraction of no mean order.

In 1895, the group raised nearly $3,000 by public subscription for music and amusements in a rented building during July and August, including Fourth of July fireworks. Events that summer were so successful that the sponsors raised funds to build a permanent social and entertainment center called the Atlantic Highlands Casino (illustration no. 26).

Opening on July 4, 1896, the casino was located on a high bluff on the bay side of today's Ocean Boulevard a little uphill from Grand Avenue. In early years it featured daily summer concerts and weekly dances on Saturday nights. There were hops, costume balls, minstrel shows, cake walks, vaudeville shows, amateur comic operas, fairs, and other indoor entertainments and public assemblies. An August 1897 children's hop drew 200 boys and girls in fancy costumes and 500 others. At the annual Barn Dance, live farm animals were brought in and everyone wore rural costumes. In a season extending from early June to Labor Day, every evening in the week was dedicated to some gathering—dancing on Monday, Wednesday, and Saturday, card games with prizes on Tuesday, a classical concert on Thursday, and an early evening dance for children on Friday. It became a very popular place during the 1897 summer season, when admissions to the casino for all purposes totaled 17,000 people—an average of 300 per day. In 1910 a tennis club was organized with four clay courts next to the casino and membership limited to 100 people. Some school graduations were also held there.

Townspeople also indulged in pets, so much so that by 1898 the borough had 73 licensed dogs and an official dog catcher named Abijah Yetman.

"Whisky Shops" and "Dens of Iniquity"

In the early years, some significant limits were set on certain periods (Sundays) and types of entertainment (liquor). The Atlantic Highlands Association (AHA) had been founded in 1881 on strict puritan concepts and Protestant church control. Its "Christian and temperance principles" included "freedom from sabbath breaking, crowds, and intoxicating liquors." The very first ordinance passed by its board on May 24, 1881, authoritatively and comprehensively banned liquor. Violators were punished by a fine of $20 (serious money in those days) and a possible sentence of 20 days in the county jail. The ordinance made it unlawful:

> for any person to manufacture, sell, or barter any spirituous or fermented liquors, regardless of wine, ale, beer, and malt liquors or intoxicating liquors, preparations, or substances of any kind. They cannot take place within the premises of an association or upon any pier or landing place connected therewith and leading thereto, or for and within the territory embraced within the limit of one mile from any boundary of the premises without a license from the board of directors.

The new newspaper, the *Atlantic Highlands Herald*, was unfailingly loyal to the temperance and other founding principles of the association and was a constant "booster" for the town's growth. Its owner, Reverend J.C. Nobles, was not only an original stockholder in the association, but also the real estate agent for the sale of its lots and its landlord. In June 1887 the *Herald* praised the anti-liquor ordinance and condemned the alcoholic evils of other resorts:

> . . . all the leading fashionable resorts throughout the country are filled with whisky shops of every grade, yet these drinkers are not satisfied, nor are they willing, that Christian temperance people should even have one place to themselves. In their judgment, no resort should be allowed to exist without a bar. Let Christian temperance men invade their dens of iniquity, such as Coney Island, Rockaway, or Long Branch, and then one will hear the uprising of the thousand and one, denouncing them as fanatics and intruders. It's a poor rule that won't work both ways.

Between 1892 and 1895, major battles erupted over applications for licenses to sell liquor in the area between First Avenue and Avenue A, outside the association boundary. In January of 1892 about 225 businessmen, church members, and other residents signed petitions against four applications. A citizen's "indignation meeting" resolved to "emphatically protest" the liquor plans. A special railroad car was added to a morning train to Freehold so that a delegation of businessmen, ladies of the WCTU, and the Baptist Church pastor could speak out at a court hearing. They described two proposed saloons as shabby one-story affairs that would be "destructive to the good name, prosperity and peace" of the town. One was going to be in Lehn's bottling plant that was already "a place of bad reputation," its vicinity a "haunt for tipplers, injurious to the whole town." The second saloon was nearby, and both were near the Commercial Hotel, whose bar they felt was adequate for the needs of casual visitors to town. In addition, the 50 or 60 men who endorsed the applications were considered suspicious because they were not from town, and some were in the liquor business or "politicians seeking the favor of the liquor interest." The applicants were not boarding houses or hotels trying to meet the needs of guests, were ignoring what residents wanted, and simply planned to sell liquor for profit, so said the opponents. The applicants basically said, under law, the liquor ban cannot extend beyond the AHA lots that have restrictive covenants.

Again in 1893, a crowd of townspeople went to court in Freehold to oppose an application for a liquor license for a tavern in the proposed Columbus Hotel on First Avenue (illustration no. 24). Though not on a restricted lot, it was surrounded by properties of the association whose anti-liquor restrictions would be "unavailing, useless and nullified" if the application were granted, the opponents complained. It would affect the equities of hundreds of property owners who purchased lots in full faith that covenants and the courts would protect them from "the persecution of license boomers," and the "inroads" and "obnoxious traffic" of the liquor interests. The opponents' lawyer claimed that "the growth and prosperity of the town had been largely induced" by its immunity from the liquor trade. More than 200 remonstrants signed a protest against this application, including the association president, the mayor, and the town council.

A similar scene was repeated in 1895, when 150 people signed a remonstrance against the transfer of a barroom from a hotel to a saloon site right next to the railroad. Protest petitions were signed by Protestant churchgoers after Sunday services, claiming the plan would "create a tippling resort near the railroad depot;" a location "particularly prejudicial to the business interests and peace and quiet of Atlantic Highlands."

Over the years, the court granted some of the applications and denied others, but gradually the protests were turned away and declined, and inns and taverns were established in the downtown area. They lasted until the Prohibition era of the 1920s, but even then liquor and social drinking continued to be attractive, and illegal rum-running supplied the demand that went underground (see chapter 8).

Celebrity Watching

Another local pastime was celebrity-watching. Among the famous and infamous visitors to town whose presence was especially noted in the 1890s were the Rothschilds, Diamond Jim Brady (who used to visit friends on Observatory Place), and William Randolph Hearst, the newspaper mogul who owned the *New York Journal* and was worth $80 million. In 1897 Hearst rented the Frosts' "How Kola" cottage on Ocean Boulevard, and other times he stayed at the Portland Hotel. His steam schooner yacht, the *Buccaneer*, was sometimes seen at the yacht club anchorage. It is not known whether he visited in 1898 when his newspaper stoked up the Spanish-American

War after the battleship U.S.S. *Maine* blew up in Havana harbor. The New York Yacht Club pier at the bottom of Fourth Avenue was the anchor point on many summer nights for the *Corsair*, the yacht of J.P. Morgan, and the yacht belonging to John Borden of Borden's Milk.

Brief appearances were made by Presidents Ulysses S. Grant, Theodore Roosevelt, and possibly Woodrow Wilson. Grant came in July 1882 and attended the first anniversary celebration of the auditorium, en route to his vacation in the "summer Capitol" in Long Branch. Teddy Roosevelt's pass-through in July 1902 was on the way to a National Guard camp at Sea Girt (illustration no. 43). Because his ship was too big to dock, he came ashore in a smaller boat. In 1982 an eyewitness in her 90s remembered a large crowd of townspeople and dignitaries had gathered to see him, "his top hat, eyeglasses and toothy smile;" they watched as he boarded a train that was heading east to Highlands and south down the coast, and he waved to everyone from the rear platform. An unverified tale is that Woodrow Wilson played a long round of checkers in the back of the Antonides Drug Store on First Avenue during his stay at Croyden Hall on Leonardville Road, where he wrote his acceptance speech for his nomination as President.

From the world of theater, in the early 1900s the town was the summer home of a troupe of actors and a theatrical star who later made the transition to silent movies and talkies. The troupe was directed by Robert B. Mantell, a famous actor at the peak of his 50-year career (illustration no. 42). In 1907 he bought the estate of James H. Leonard, a half-square block bounded by Avenue D and West Highland and South Avenues. He named the main house (now the St. Agnes Thrift Shop) "Brucewood" in honor of the national hero of Scotland, Robert Bruce, and his given names and his son's were Robert Bruce. During summers he housed his actors in the house's third floor and rehearsed them on a stage he installed in a large barn on the property. In 1911 he put on a packed benefit performance—including his wife and leading lady, Genevieve Hamper, starring as Lady MacBeth—that raised money for the town firemen to buy a motorized fire truck. In gratitude, the company changed its name from Grand View Hose Company #2 to the Robert B. Mantell Hose Company #2. When he died destitute on June 27, 1928, the firemen took care of his burial costs in Bay View Cemetery.

Playing MacBeth with a booming voice in that benefit performance was Fritz Leiber, another star and a neighbor of Mantell across Highland Avenue, whose theatrical troupe also summered in town. After starring nationwide in touring classical plays, Leiber began a silent film career in 1917 as Julius Caesar in *Cleopatra*, with the title role played by Theda Bara. He went on to make as many as four films a year, and up to his death in 1949 had leading roles or character roles in a total of 34 films. His roles included Louis XI, King Solomon, Gaspard in *A Tale of Two Cities*, Louis Pasteur, and Franz Liszt.

In the 1890s, and after, there lived in town a water color painter whose works were exhibited in the national portrait gallery in Washington D.C. This was Charles Payne Sears, son of the socialist-capitalist Charles Sears, who also lived in the old Point Lookout house. He offered local painting and drawing lessons, and is known to have made one local painting on commission of the house at 7th and Washington Avenues, owned by the father of World War I hero Paul Brunig (see chapter 8).

The town produced international celebrities in July 1896 when two local fishermen left Atlantic Highlands on an apparently impossible journey that succeeded when they rowed 3,200 miles across the Atlantic Ocean to win a $10,000 prize offered by the *Police Gazette* newspaper. Frank Samuelson and George Harbo, Norwegian immigrants, had a double-ended 18-foot sea skiff especially built and called it *Sea Fox*. They packed a compass, fresh water, canned meat, biscuits, eggs, a little stove, and took ten pairs of oars and 240 oar locks. They survived 62 days of hard rowing, savage storms, and little sleep, arriving in France in August to great acclaim and praise, and returned home on a steamer.

A water trip of another kind was taken by another vessel, an early submarine known as the *Argonaut Jr.* It was developed, built, and tested in Atlantic Highlands by Simon Lake, the nephew of town founder Reverend James E. Lake. While on the bottom, the *Argonaut* was propelled by turning a crank. His first commercial venture, the Lake Submarine Company, was organized in 1895 in Atlantic Highlands. A half-size model of the vessel is displayed in the Atlantic Highlands Marina, whose east-west road is called Simon Lake Drive. Another recognition of his inventiveness was a nuclear-powered submarine repair ship christened the *Simon Lake* in 1964 by the Navy at Puget Sound.

The Spanish-American War in 1898 produced one actual and one intended celebrity among the volunteers from town. In July, 19-year-old Malcolm Barrett of Atlantic Highlands returned home on medical leave from Company M of the New York Volunteers to recover from wounds and an amputated toe, and to visit his father and brother. He had been hit by four bullets in the famous charge of Teddy Roosevelt's Rough Riders on San Juan Hill. In April William M. Foster, the town's original hotel and excursion entrepreneur, offered to the government to raise a company of volunteers to fight against Spain, if given permission. He had served three years in the Civil War, was now in his mid- to late-50s, and apparently received no response from Washington.

Also in April, many were worried that Spanish ships might attack coastal towns, but this was thought unlikely because Spain had no American sources of coal to fuel warships for such expeditions. It was rumored that the Spanish laid minefields off the Sandy Hook coast. Taking no chances, the bay and New York harbor were closed to all ships between sunset and sunrise, and an American warship was assigned to coast duty outside of Sandy Hook. Even entertainment events focused on the war. In April the wreck of the U.S.S. *Maine* and naval squadron maneuvers were shown during an entertainment held by the Royal Arcanum fraternal lodge in the casino; a forerunner of moving pictures, the scenes presented a "colorscopic diorama of dissolving views" using Edison's "projectoscope" machine. On the Fourth of July weekend, a musical night at the casino included a march called "Commodore Dewey's Victory," commemorating the American capture of the Philippines, as well as other patriotic airs.

Locally, the biggest, longest-playing, and most home-grown celebrities in town were the Leonards, particularly Thomas Henry Leonard (1843–1930). In 1887 voters decided to organize the town as a borough and elected him and six others as borough commissioners. In April the commissioners, in turn, chose him to be the first mayor, inextricably linking him with the town and its founding. At the peak of his boosterism, he served as mayor for eight years and tax assessor for 12 years, was a founder of the Atlantic Highlands National Bank and its president for ten years, became a director of the board of trade, and worked as a real estate agent. His prosperity can be judged from the cover photo of this book, showing his homestead on First Avenue near the mid-point between today's Mount and Center Avenues, with his wife and his four daughters.

Nine men in the Leonard family were active in various town affairs as of 1895. They were merchant, farmer, attorney, editor, grocer, postmaster, real estate agent, fraternal lodge officer, coal-wood-charcoal dealer, carpenter, and manufacturer. Not surprisingly, four of the men were Baptist church deacons and two women were into Temperance.

Vacationers and Commuters

No slice of Atlantic Highlands life of the late 1800s and the turn of the century could be complete without telling what life was like in the town's fashionable resort hotels and the steamboats that carried visitors and summer resident commuters between Manhattan and the town.

No less than 69 hotels and boarding houses were operating in town at one time or another between 1880 and 1921 (illustrations no. 24, 25, and 27). And seven additional hotels were in neighboring Navesink, Locust, and Leonardo. After the 1890s peak of 37 hotels and boarding houses, there were still 35 in 1907, but the number declined to 15 between 1910–1920, and eventually to zero. Some say that the increased mobility brought by automobiles undermined the hotels here, and the 1930s Depression knocked them out.

The big wooden hotel buildings were especially vulnerable to fire when they were empty all winter long and even more so when they deteriorated from lack of use. Fourteen have burned down or been severely damaged in Atlantic Highlands and four in neighboring sections. The town's first hotel, Foster's Pavilion, built in 1880 at First Avenue and the bay, was the first to go up in flames only three years later. Another early fire victim was the town's largest ever hotel, the Grand View, with 400 guest spaces, at the southeast corner of Grand Avenue and Bay View Avenue (today's Ocean Boulevard); in 1894 it fed flames so high and furious that the nearby bay "was illuminated as if by the rays of the noon-day sun," according to a local newspaper. The latest to go was in April 2004 when the First Avenue building that housed the Columbus Hotel from the 1890s to the early 1920s burned down.

Activities organized by hotels included concerts, dance hops, beachgoing, boating, swimming, horseback and carriage rides, and staged dramas. There were hundreds of bathhouse-changing cubicles along the bay. Curtis Pavilion also had bowling alleys, salt water baths, and a promenade pier 650 feet long until it all burned down in December 1898. At least three sloop yachts, a schooner, and several other kinds of boats could be chartered in 1894 for sailing, fishing, or parties. Horseback riding was especially popular at the Grand View Hotel as both an active and a spectator sport, reported a local newspaper:

> The clatter of their horses' hoofs and the fluttering riding habits of the belles accompanied by grooms, trainers or more agreeable beaux, have become daily incidents on our avenues. The ladies make the prettiest of street scenes cantering away upon their ponies and chargers.

It was also fashionable to sit on the hotels' multi-story, wraparound porches for the scenery and the breeze, and gossip about people passing by. Indoor hotel facilities, in addition to common parlors and dining rooms, included billiards, bowling alleys, an ice cream saloon, and a dance pavilion.

Since the cool hills and bay waters were the greatest attractions in the hot months, many hotels were built as close to shore or as far up in the heights as possible. These prime locations inspired the names of many establishments, such as Bay View, Grand View, Sea View, Fair View, Bonnie View, Prospect, Ocean, Beach, Atlantic, Shoreland, Highland, Breezy Point, Wave, and Alpine. Other hotels took foreign or exotic place names ranging from Mandalay to Hollywood. But egotism prevailed as the largest number (23) were named after their owners or managers. About half the hotels and boarding houses were run by women at one time or another.

By today's standards, guest charges were a bargain. In 1917 the daily rate ranged from $1.50 to $4 and weekly charges were between $8 and $30. The highest rate was at the Sea View on Highland Place overlooking the bay toward Manhattan. Many of the smaller hotels, lodges, and tourist boarding houses accommodated a handful or less of guests, but the big-ticket hotels held up to 100 (the Hollywood), 125 (Sea View) and 400 (Grand View) tourists each. Also in 1917, a one-way ticket by steamship from Manhattan cost 75¢ and the railroad was $1.10. Carriages met arriving visitors at the train station or the steamboat dock.

On summer afternoons in 1905, three speedy commuter ferries made 70-minute runs across the bay from Cedar Street in Manhattan to Atlantic Highlands. These boats were the *Monmouth*, the *Sandy Hook*, and the *Asbury Park*, but all harbor captains knew them as the "Millionaires' Boats" (illustration no. 45). During the warm months, many men of wealth rode the daily steamboats to get to their country homes along the Jersey bay and ocean shores. A New York newspaper estimated that the aggregate wealth of passengers on one boat heading down the bay each afternoon was a billion dollars (a lot at 1905 rates) and that the capital they represented or controlled was "almost beyond computation." The old ferries had luxuriously fitted staterooms that the well-to-do could rent and reserve for the summer season for $200 to $500, depending on location.

Among those with staterooms were Oscar and Nathan Strauss, the younger brothers and partners of Adolph Strauss in his import, notions, and commission merchant business in Manhattan. The 21-room Queen Anne style mansion that Adolph built in 1893 still stands at Prospect and Mount Avenues in Atlantic Highlands (illustration no. 44). The 1905 newspaper reported that Nathan Strauss was seen getting on board accompanied by a Wall Street tycoon, with Strauss telling him a rollicking story as they "walk forward arm-in-arm, laughing heartily."

During the bay crossing, politicians (including a mayor and a former governor) made important contacts. Heads of finance held business conferences, sometimes by appointment in private staterooms so as to escape inquisitive eyes. Followed by youths carrying letter cases, some very serious looking men got on board, hurried to their staterooms, and began reading letters and dictating replies. Some stenographers kept scribbling during the whole trip and took the next boat back to the city for an evening at their typewriters. Other prominent men sat in deck chairs on the main deck, preferring sun and air to seclusion. They might have a cigar and read a book or a pile of evening newspapers, or swap tales with fellow businessmen, play checkers, and make bets.

Some high-rollers owned steam yachts and only used the ferry when the bay was too rough for the smaller craft. One man had a high-speed racer yacht that was faster than the big commuter boats and sometimes made great sport at the expense of his friends by flashing past the ferry. The captains of the Millionaires' Boats did not give chase lest it risk harming any of their passengers. They knew, the 1905 newspaper claimed, that injury or loss of life for certain passengers "would shake the money centers of the world."

Another form of transportation—but for regular folks, not the rich—began running to and from Atlantic Highlands on August 13, 1908. The arrival of electric trolleys completed the dream of Thomas Henry Leonard to move his community along the spectrum *From Indian Trail to Electric Rail*, the title of his 1923 catch-all history book. The borough had been scouting and negotiating for trolley service since at least 1903, and Leonard claims he cajoled a senior executive of the Jersey Central Traction Company into approving a diversion into Atlantic Highlands of the route that was already being built.

The electrified rail for the trolley cars connected Atlantic Highlands with Highlands in one direction, and Belford and Red Bank in the other (illustration no. 48). Starting near today's bridge in the Highlands, the trolleys followed today's Highway 36 and ran down Buttermilk Valley to the Stone Church in Locust. There they turned to follow the power line corridor of Jersey Central Power and Light Company, which ran (and still does) west of and parallel to Valley Drive and Memorial Parkway over to First Avenue. They then headed north to Center Avenue, made a loop at the railroad station and came up Mount Avenue, returning to First Avenue. From there, the route went to Leonardville Road and Campbell's Junction in Belford, where there were trolley connections south to Red Bank and north to Keyport. The double-truck, double-ended open trolleys seated 70 passengers. They started on their rounds every half-hour during rush hours and once an hour the rest of the day between 7 a.m. and midnight, with additional cars for summer crowds. In 1916 the fare was a mere 5¢ per zone, allowing one to travel from Keyport to Highlands for 15¢.

By 1922, jitney busses and automobiles had become a preferred mode of travel, and the trolley route from Highlands to Red Bank passing through Atlantic Highlands was abandoned. Some unscrupulous and unregulated jitney bus operators helped to kill trolleys by running ahead of them and stealing customers by offering a slightly earlier departure and lower fare. But the trolley company had also branched out into the distribution of electricity, needed for powering its trolleys and also in demand for lighting homes and businesses. Jersey Central Traction led to Jersey Central Power and Light, and the latter survived. A bus company took on the same route the trolleys used, eventually becoming the Boro Bus Company, and then ceding the route to buses from today's New Jersey Transit.

A Victorian Showcase

The Strauss Mansion is a 21-room, 2.5 story house built in 1893 for use as a "summer cottage" by Adolph Strauss, a wealthy New York importer and merchant. He was one of a group of friends who owned brownstone houses on 49th Street in New York City where they spent winter months. They all put up large houses in the rapidly developing town of Atlantic Highlands, on concentric circles of street capping the hill above Sandy Hook Bay. They called themselves the "49ers," an echo of their Manhattan home street and also the Gold Rush.

Architecturally, it's a prime example of an elaborate Queen Anne style summer cottage (illustration no. 44). Originally called "The Towers," it has two on its front corners, one round, and the other six-sided. Two-story porches wrap around three sides. The third story's eccentric roof line has multiple peaks, dormers, gables, gambrels, and intersecting hips. Natural wood shingles cover most of the exterior. Its rooms are in an irregular plan, with seven stained-glass windows.

Geographically, the house sits on a steeply pitched lot near the summit of the old town. It has commanding views over the historic district, Sandy Hook Bay, the shoreline stretching to the west, the Atlantic Ocean, and the New York skyline.

Culturally and historically, it represents the lifestyle of a coastal resort town from Monmouth County's "Golden Age" in the late 1800s—next to the bay and ocean and also within easy reach of the great New York metropolis by steamer boat and train. It reflects not only the house design, but also the home life, social, and community patterns of the Victorian boom era.

Since 1980 it has been the home, museum, and library of the Atlantic Highlands Historical Society. Most of its rooms have been restored, with some furnished in Victorian style and others containing exhibits on local history. It's the only Victorian mansion in Queen Anne style open to the public in Monmouth County.

Chapter Eight

BAYSIDE TOWN

In its transition from an 1800s farming community to a Victorian resort and village, and then to a modern bayside town during the 1900s, Atlantic Highlands saw its population grow more than 25-fold, from 40 people in 1880 to 1,000 residents in the late 1890s, and then to the high 4,000s by the year 2000. The progression was gradual (see box below).

Significantly, after a peak of 5,000-plus people in 1980, the population actually declined, decreasing to 4,771 in 2000. Clearly the 1.2 square mile area of the town was built up to the maximum, as shown by its population density of 3,857 people per square mile in 2000. This was higher than the average density for New Jersey (995), the Netherlands (946), India (685), and China (290).

As the town grew, people from diverse ethnic origins were attracted to come and settle. A house-by-house listing from memory by a woman who lived on the west side in the 1930s and 1940s reveals it was a small "melting pot." There were residents from English, Irish, Dutch, Italian, German, Norwegian and African-American backgrounds, and even a few Russians, living close together within a few square blocks. A man who grew up in town during the same period recalled that if there was segregation it was between the dominant majority of Protestants and the minority of Catholics, not between races or ethnic groups. People developed a sense of comfort and loyalty about their town, as shown by the fact that many families have made it their home over as many as five generations.

Of course there were still large numbers of vacationers and day-trippers who visited town in the early decades of the 1900s. Before cars were invented and became widespread, the lower decks of arriving steamers were often full of bicycles. People would bike to Long Branch or even Asbury Park, have a meal, and then bike back for an evening boat. In 1973 one eyewitness remembered that "First Avenue was so crowded with boat passengers you could hardly get through there." History seems to repeat, since similar remarks can now be heard about streams of ferry passengers driving through downtown on weekday mornings and evenings, and about the parade of boaters' vehicles coming and going to the marina on summer weekends.

In 1907 there were still 19 hotels or inns and 13 boarding houses functioning, and 14 of those hotels were surviving as of 1920. But the handwriting was on the wall, or rather the tire tracks were

Atlantic Highlands Population

How many	When	How fast
First 1,000 people	By late	1890s
Second 1,000 people	By 1930	40+ years
Third 1,000 people	By 1950	20 years
Fourth 1,000 people	Before 1960	10 years
Fifth 1,000 people	By 1970	10 years
Just below 5,000	Since 1980	

on the road: the automobile made it easier for summer tourists from the metropolitan New York area to go to oceanside resorts farther south. By the end of the 1920s, all but three of the Atlantic Highlands hotels had died out. The total guest capacity of those three was not more than 125, compared to 1,200 guest spaces that the numerous hotels of the 1890s had provided.

Joy Rides by the Bay—1915–1940

Starting in 1915 the town became a destination of another sort when a large amusement park was constructed on a 17-acre tract behind the beach of Sandy Hook Bay (illustration no. 46). Between May and September, the park was connected to the Battery in downtown Manhattan by a steamboat called the *Mandalay* (illustration no. 47). On each of three daily round trips, this ship carried 2,000 or more passengers to Atlantic Highlands on a ride that featured music and dancing on board. Other park visitors came to town on land by train and, after 1908, by trolley. The park was billed as New York's and New Jersey's favorite excursion beach and picnic grove, offering delights for hundreds of visiting clubs, lodges, Sunday Schools, and businesses that sponsored excursions. It was first known as Bay View Park, then Joyland Park, and finally Atlantic Beach Amusement Park. Some people called it Mandalay Park, after the steamboat.

Between 1915 and 1940, the park offered sun, sand, rides, games, sports, and fun along the bayfront. It evokes great nostalgia and fond memories from old-time residents, who remember it as a highlight of their childhoods, a place of special delight and multiple attractions. The park was so big a draw for day-trippers that it helped to put Atlantic Highlands "on the map." It covered the equivalent of about six square blocks, stretching from Avenue A to Avenue D and from the bay southward to Bay Avenue.

The park featured a roller coaster that was considered one of the more daring rides on the Jersey coast. The cars, powered by regular car batteries, ran on a long oval layout with tracks that crossed four times at different elevations. Other rides included a carousel imported from Germany with elaborate horses along the rim that went up and down (catch the ring and get a free ride!); a Ferris wheel near Avenue D that was at least 30 feet high and had spectacular views from the top; a bump-'em and dodge-'em car ride known as the "Whip," with an orange and black color scheme; Custer car racers that went around and under a bridge and back; and an airplane ride that swung out farther with each turn.

The Midway had numerous games of skill. At different times these included skeetball, Dunk-um, a Shoot-Until-You-Win shooting gallery, a strength test using a hammer called "Ring the Bell," a booth of balloons with darts to throw at them in order to win a feather-headed doll, a game of turning dials for remote pick-up of a toy, and an archery. Opposite the archery was a miniature golf course run by a southern gentleman, Mr. Winfield. On the same path were various food stands and a tent with gypsy fortune tellers who wore purples, fuchsias, and bangle earrings. In the early 1930s people pressed their faces to the big oval lens of a "movie" machine to watch photographs flip by inside.

By 1920–1921, a building was added for showing motion pictures. In the 1930s it showed a half-hour of cartoons like Betty Boop and Krazy Kat before the main feature. The moviemakers of Biograph Studio used the park as a filming location. The dance pavilion called the "Sea Breeze" was the site of Charleston contests in the 1920s. There was an athletic field and grandstand.

Shows and attractions that ran at different times included a freak and animal show, an Indian village, "Cesar the Great's Magic Show," performed by Cesar Devlin, the "Slide for Life" done several times daily by Al Morton, who was known as the "Great Nervo," and bathing beauty pageants.

Entrances to the park on the town side were from Bay Avenue at Avenues A and B. The path went under a wooden arch of the roller coaster. Nearby was a ladies' restroom maintained by a woman from Hoboken who was called "little fat Antoinette" by local kids, and who sat outside and crocheted. Next on the path came a green, screened-in restaurant for 1,500 diners. The waiters wore white shirts, black vests, and white aprons reaching to their shoes. Some of them were Japanese from New York City with names so difficult for a local Italian man to pronounce that he called them "Murphy and O'Brien." Opposite the park at Avenue B and Bay Avenue was "Natale's" Italian restaurant, the forerunner of the Natale family's long-time White Crystal Diner on Center Avenue near First Avenue (removed in 2002).

At the long sandy beach, it cost a dime to enter. At Avenue D, a wire barrier separated the fee-paying beachgoers from poorer people who swam for free in the waters to the west. Towels and bathing suits were for rent, hundreds of changing booths were available, and a life guard was on duty. There were floats for people to swim to, sunbathe on, or dive off. The sandy beach and calm bay waters were a source of delight to vacationers from the hot city.

In its heyday, the name "Atlantic Beach" was spelled out in large letters made of white stones that were set into the sloping land at the bayfront, and were lighted to be visible from far out on the water. For display purposes, there were also external lights on the structures housing various attractions.

Local people took summer jobs there serving food and running rides. At one time, the "Ring the Bell" was operated by Sverre Sorenson and the airplane ride by Charles Gordon. The team of Charlie Lynch as operator and Rose Grogan as ticket seller for the carousel worked so well that they got married and continued living in town.

An early proprietor of the park, named Fishbein, was a photographer by trade. He was succeeded by partners who ran the park for much of its lifetime: Samuel Van Poznak, who came from Newark, and John Isbister, who was born in Edinburgh, Scotland, in 1868, and lived in Larchmont, New York, during the winters. While the park was open between late spring and early fall, the two families occupied separate living quarters on two sides of a large house on the park property. Mr. Isbister died of a heart attack at the park in June 1932.

In 1987 a lifetime resident of Atlantic Highlands, Helen Marchetti, remembered the former park as "something special" during her childhood. She said, "We had a boat coming in there, the *Mandalay*. The *Mandalay* used to come right in by the park and they had little trains that used to go right out on the pier and pick the passengers up and bring them to the park." This "scenic railway" train ran the length of the park and back and cost 10¢ a ride. Even though times weren't always prosperous, local children could occasionally look forward to a free ride, Mrs. Marchetti said:

> The park used to close right after Labor Day and then it would open up again around the end of April. Many of the kids used to go over there and get free rides on the roller coaster so they could get the rust off the rails. They let you ride forever and ever until they could get the rails shiny.

The *Mandalay* steamship route and its Avenue A pier extending 900 feet into the bay had been established in 1900 before the park. The pier was paid for by public subscription of $25,000 by the people of Atlantic Highlands. Existence of this transport link had encouraged a Red Bank investors' group, the Land and Loan Company, to build the fun park in the first place, on land bought from Anthony J. Campbell. When *Mandalay* passengers arrived there, entertainment awaited them at the land end of the pier in an open-air pavilion building. A short boardwalk led west from the open-air pavilion, and the swimmers' bathhouses were underneath. Later, the *Mandalay* moved to a new dock at Avenue D, which is when the miniature train was installed.

As of 1920 there was a bus line that ran from the Mandalay pier at Avenue D to Red Bank. It brought in visitors from nearby towns who could enjoy the amusement park or take a steamer to New York, and also allowed passengers from the steamboat *Mandalay* to go on further excursions to the south. Owned by Burdge and Russell, the bus line later became the Boro Bus Company.

Extensive fireworks and patriotic events, as well as the park's regular attractions, typically made the Fourth of July one of the biggest days for visitors to town. On that holiday weekend in 1926 an estimated 67,000 people visited Atlantic Highlands, according to the *Atlantic Highlands Journal*. Between May and September of that year, the log of the steamboat *Monmouth* showed that it carried 236,307 passengers between Atlantic Highlands and New York.

The park was plagued by fires from 1936–1939, especially during winter when it was closed and its frame buildings deserted, though sometimes occupied by the homeless of years past. In December 1936 after the restaurant and bar burned, the dance hall was converted into a restaurant. A December 1937 fire destroyed the bump-'em car ride.

In 1938, the *Acadia*, a cruise ship heading for Bermuda, rammed into the *Mandalay* during heavy fog. The *Mandalay* sank, but all 325 passengers were safely evacuated to the *Acadia*. As they began crossing over to it, Freddie Sleckman and his orchestra were in the *Mandalay*'s ballroom and played the ship's own song, a march titled "Dancing on the Mandalay" by Mabel Besthoff. In 1939, 500 feet of the Mandalay pier at Avenue D burned down. The amusement park closed after the 1940 summer season, and the surviving owner, Van Poznak, sold it in December to the Atlantic Investment Company, whose principal was apparently Henry Hauser. The carousel was reportedly sold to the city of Philadelphia. A disastrous fire around 1946 added the final chapter, but the little train kept on carrying passengers—it was moved to the boardwalk along the ocean beach at Point Pleasant.

Today the former park land is covered by single-family residences. Twelve houses along the north side of Bay Avenue were built right after the park was sold in 1940. In February 1942 a developer mapped the rest of the park land into building lots, with five roads leading from Bay Avenue toward the bay, and marketed it as Hauser Park. But World War II intervened and the development was not built. In May 1949 Henry Hauser offered the three-block beachfront between Avenues A and D for sale to the borough, but without success. In 1958 a new plan under the name Harbor Bluffs was well received; along a new road called Harbor View Drive, nine houses were built by 1960 and eight more by 1965, continuing until 27 houses occupied the former park, with 12 of them fronting the former public beach.

Problems and Proposals at Many Mind Creek

The amusement park was west of the mouth of Many Mind Creek where, during the administration of Mayor Charles Snyder (1916–1920), voters approved a $20,000 bond issue for a major project near the bay. Its purpose was to create a small boat harbor that became known as "The Lagoon" and sometimes as "Snyder's bathtub." The project continued, and also encouraged, an already long process of remaking and re-engineering the creek corridor in whatever way would satisfy the lust for more land and higher real estate values. It was also the forerunner of the much bigger municipal harbor that was built east of the creek and began operations in the 1940s.

Over many years there had been complaints about Many Mind Creek. At least since 1882 there had been agitation to do something radical to "improve" it, especially its final stretch leading to the bay. A variety of plans were hatched. They called for it to be either rechanneled and straightened, dredged and diked, excavated to produce a new bed, given a better outlet and current, made into a lagoon and boat harbor, embellished with a park, or extensively reshaped into a "system of lakes," etc.

The town boosters of the 1880s and 1890s didn't like what they saw in the wetland meadows along the creek. In fact they did not identify them as a permanent natural feature called wetlands, swamp, or marsh that has helped protect water quality, control floods, and provide fish and wildlife habitat. Even the official board of health believed that the wetlands were really stagnant pools of water, left behind when the creek overflowed its banks from time to time and causing a menace to health.

An 1879 painting looking toward the bay from the Hillside section envisions a wide "C"-shaped lake several blocks long all along the stretch where the creek changes directions from west to north, extending all the way from today's Jackson bridge to about Washington Avenue (illustration no. 18). Though fictional, it portrays an attractive border for the Hillside lots whose sale the painting was meant to promote. Was this merely a disguise for the arc of swampland existing in that area, or was the painter fantasizing about creating a wholly new lake?

Explicit proposals to make artificial lakes on the creek were first offered in 1882. That year John S. Hubbard, one of the town's major developers, began selling 135 building lots on the west side, using a map showing a huge "Many Mind Lake" up to a half-block wide running from Center Avenue to today's Highway 36. The next year, developer J.C. Nobles produced another map with a proposed two-block long "Hillside Lake" to be made by damming Many Mind Creek near Leonard Avenue; also, along Wagner Creek he drew in two proposed lakes called Glenoble and Water Witch Lakes and sticking out into the bay next to the creek mouth he added a large square tract of landfill with a "proposed hotel" on it. Also in 1883 some town fathers held a meeting to consider not just one lake, but a "system of lakes" along Many Mind Creek between Jackson Bridge and the bay; the proposed lake nearest the bay would have been "a place for boats" but the proposal was not adopted.

Going beyond proposals, shovels went to work actually to change the creek. In December 1896 the Central Railroad put a crew to work to straighten the final 100 feet of the creek west of the railroad line. The aim was to improve its opening into the bay and reduce flooding along the train tracks. This apparently did not have the desired effect because, only four months later, board of health officers noted that water was still backed up from the creek into the meadows. Their solution? Dig a bigger creek. The board ordered all property owners along the creek to deepen its channel to two feet and expand it to four feet wide in upstream portions west of Sears Landing Road and five feet wide from Jackson Bridge to the bay. Only a few years later, in 1900 the Red Bank *Register* printed a big headline:

A NEW LAKE PROJECT
A BIG IMPROVEMENT PROPOSED AT ATLANTIC HIGHLANDS

Many Mind Creek May Be Converted into a Lake or Chain of Lakes
A Public Park Also Contemplated in the Scheme

The plan called for draining the meadows, dredging the creek bed, dumping the dirt on to the creek banks and meadows, building a dike to form a lake, and transforming "considerable land that is now practically valueless" into "a marketable state." Where the creek turns eastward near Jackson Bridge, wooded land would be cleared and laid out as a park with a "miniature lake." As had been done in Asbury Park, the lake would be encircled by a drive, lighted with electric lights, and made available for a "carnival." No lake resulted.

In 1904 Mayor William M. Roberts and the borough council considered how to improve the entire corridor of creek and meadows located between the east and west side of town, running from the bay to the Hillside section. They felt that this conspicuous corridor was in unsightly condition and should give a better impression to visitors. They fastened again on the idea of a system of lakes. They proposed to dig out part of the creek to form lakes and use the soil to create mounds and islands in an artistic manner. They produced a survey and maps, but then abandoned the idea for unknown reasons. Thomas Henry Leonard liked the idea very much and hoped it would be "resurrected at some time in the great future."

In 1910 a plant to produce coal tar gas was built along the creek and stayed in operation until 1949. For decades a polluting by-product from this plant entered the waterway. To decontaminate it, tens of thousands of cubic yards of sediment and bank soils had to be replaced starting in the late 1990s. Expensive and disruptive as it was, this operation offered a once-in-a-lifetime opportunity to restore the creek to natural conditions, including the functions of its wetlands in improving water quality, controlling flooding, and providing fish and wildlife habitat. There were plans to provide a greenway trail along the creek corridor, but as of 2004 it remained unclear how far the plans would be realized.

Under the "bathtub" plan of Mayor Snyder's administration, in 1916 a box-like space was dredged out of the creek's west bank near the bay, and its sides were bulkheaded to make a small boat basin (illustration no. 52). The creek was made perfectly straight from Bay Avenue northwards, and the dredged material was deposited beside the creek. However, the contractor did not excavate to proper depth and put so much heavy mud and clay right on the banks that part of the bulkhead wall collapsed. When the borough sued him, he claimed the work could not be completed because of the lack of laborers during the World War. Before silting eventually filled much of the dredged box and wetlands re-established themselves there, the basin was in constant use for several decades. Sometimes a dozen large sloops and a schooner or two were based there, as well as numerous power launches.

In the 1930s a "drainage project" was carried out on the creek from today's Highway 36 to the bay in order to achieve a typically 14-foot-wide stream bed and uniformly steep banks. A sinuous S-curve stretch of the creek between Center and Bay Avenues was realigned into a ramrod-straight channel. The project map revealed that a boomerang-shaped creek channel that existed south of Center Avenue in 1887 had already been straightened. These adjustments turned squiggly-bordered lots into the perfect rectangles favored by builders, while also reducing the creek's ability to cope with floodwaters.

In 1944, the creek was again labeled a "problem" and a "headache." The November 30 *Atlantic Highlands Journal* reported that during heavy rains, water from the creek "backs up and causes inconvenience all over the West Side. The most serious trouble is at Highland avenue, where the creek is washing out the roadbed and threatens to ruin the pavement." The *Journal* article went on to editorialize about how troublesome and useless the creek was:

> This stream attracts little attention as it meanders through the flats west of the railroad in Atlantic Highlands, but its capacity for causing trouble is not limited by its size. While the creek serves no useful purpose, it is a waterway of a sort, and thus enjoys state protection. Also, it drains some part of the hinterland, which estops borough officials from saving themselves trouble by filling it up.

For decades builders, engineers, politicians, and journalists all seemed to be of one mind about Many Mind, a creek that has continued to be either neglected or tortured even up to the present day. However, the 1916 bathtub gave initial form to an idea that took off in the late 1930s to build a harbor that would provide safe anchorage and attract boaters to town.

The World War Hits Home

On July 29, 1916, a sultry Saturday night, Dollie Vanderbilt Reiter was staying in Atlantic Highlands at the Bay View House hotel with her husband and her mother-in-law, Julie Reiter, who was the hotel manager for the season. All 80 guests had gone to bed after a dance that evening. In 1982 Dollie remembered what happened a little after 2 a.m.:

> All at once the chairs rocked, the sky lighted up at the end of the pier and there was a terrific explosion. In 30 seconds every bedroom door opened and heads peered out adorned with curl papers to see what had happened. Nearly all of us donned coats over our night clothes and rushed down to the pier. We were joined by others in the same disarray.

Looking north across the bay toward Jersey City, what they saw was a succession of explosions with fiery bombs bursting and soaring 1,000 feet into the air. The flashy pyrotechnics eventually subsided, but roars and rumbling continued until dawn.

The explosion was at a mile-long pier on Black Tom Island just off Jersey City. It was a storage and shipping center for two to four million tons of explosives, ranging from small arms ammunition to TNT in bulk, destined for export to the Allies fighting Germany. During the days, ships loaded with explosives buzzed around the pier, and as many as 100 railroad freight cars on land waited to be unloaded. The explosions here, once started, fed each other and were felt strongly in a radius of 50 miles. Many suspected German sabotage, but it was not proven until 1930.

Not long after the Jersey City disaster, Atlantic Highlands changed from a distant, awestruck, but unengaged observer of a war supplies explosion into a direct participant in the World War that was raging in Europe. The town took an earnest and active role starting right away on April 6, 1917, when the United States declared war against Germany. Its young men began to volunteer for overseas service, going into the ambulance corps, aviation, cavalry (later heavy field artillery), and naval branches. They joined even before June 5, the day when men of military age from the area—together with ten million others across the country—had to register for compulsory service under the Selective Draft Law.

To commemorate Registration Day and honor the enlistees, on June 15 the town held the greatest civic, patriotic, and military parade in its history, and probably the greatest in Monmouth County to that date (illustration no. 53). Known as a "Loyalty Day" event, the parade marched and rolled by on First Avenue with a number of floats, over 1,000 children, and 69 decorated autos. The volunteer spirit was exemplified by two local enlistees in uniform, Private Ashley Roop, and Major Brayton E. Falling, M.D.; they rode in an open-top buggy draped with a large sign reading "We Went, We Were Not Sent" (illustration no. 54). About 8,000 people attended ceremonies at the bayfront Amusement Park.

As hundreds of thousands of new military men nationwide, including 118 from Atlantic Highlands, went off to training camps and then to European battles, the home front experienced the economic and social impact of the war effort. Construction almost ground to a halt because labor was in short supply. The available workers commanded higher prices and the cost of many goods rose abruptly. Coal, which had cost $3.25 a ton before the war, went as high as $15. By the fall of 1917 a coal shortage hit the country, and the government impounded train cars with coal supplies headed for Atlantic Highlands. The embargo was lifted, however, when federal authorities realized that the coal was fuel for the town-owned water, light, and sewer plants, and finally gave priority to municipal needs.

Everybody at home was engaged in supporting numerous levies for war loans, thrift saving, food saving, war stamps, the Red Cross, united war work, and other drives. The borough "went over the top every time," according to Thomas Henry Leonard. Local Boy Scouts helped conduct such patriotic ventures as scrap drives for metal, paper, rope, and other vital materials needed in the war effort. The boys also promoted the sale of War Savings Stamps and seven successive campaigns that urged people to buy Liberty Loan bonds. At many local events, war bonds and stamps were sold during intermissions: buy $18.75 worth of stamps, go to the post office and get a bond worth $25 at maturity.

The Red Cross chapter for Atlantic Highlands and vicinity, organized in town just days before the United States declared war, was very active in both providing services to soldiers and organizing local events. More than 1,100 volunteers joined the chapter from Atlantic Highlands alone—equal to the rest of the membership coming from eight localities of Middletown Township, Keansburg, and Highlands. Among the women chapter leaders from town were Mrs. Charles Snyder, the mayor's wife, and Clara Hendrickson, daughter of Thomas Henry Leonard. In the first War Fund Drive by the national Red Cross, the chapter was asked to raise $500 but brought in $19,225; a second drive in May 1918 had a target of $12,000 and raised $16,000, with almost half the contributions coming from Atlantic Highlands.

The chapter volunteers made burlap sandbags for the defense of Fort Hancock, surgical dressings that were used during frontline battles in France, and garments for the wounded in hospitals. Melvyn Rice, owner of today's Croyden Hall in Leonardo, advanced $10,000 in mid-1918 to buy raw materials for this production. The chapter's rooms on First Avenue were always full, even late on raw snowy evenings. An *Atlantic Highlands Journal* reporter wrote that one cold night the Red Cross rooms had the only lights on First Avenue and he "counted 57 women and girls making surgical dressings . . . to be used in No Man's Land on the Verdun front." To boost morale and comfort, they knitted woolen socks, sweaters, and scarves for soldiers, made and distributed Christmas packets, and gave a Christmas celebration in 1917 for 3,300 soldiers at Fort Hancock.

The Red Cross women also were instrumental in the organization of three large parades in town, starting with one on April 1917. The second parade was held along First Avenue on April 26, 1918, to promote the buying of Liberty Loans, and afterward the Red Cross served dinner to 250 soldiers.

The biggest civic event ever was the third parade, a Welcome Home Celebration for the troops returned from war, held August 21, 1919, and joined in by neighboring towns (illustrations no. 55 and 56). Again there were floats, decorated autos, and lines of children passing on flag-bedecked First Avenue. On one float were nurses in white uniforms and head scarves and a sign reading, "The girls behind the men behind the guns." The main focus was on the ranks of officers and men marching in uniform and being cheered by the crowd. A citizens gift committee offered a special medal and a framed testimonial to each veteran, presented by General William Barclay Parsons of the famous fighting engineers in ceremonies held on the slope of Amusement Park. After the parade, the Red Cross served supper to 300 soldiers in the Majestic Theatre on First Avenue.

An Honor Roll was erected in 1918, listing the name, rank, and branch of the 118 young people who served in the war from Atlantic Highlands. Included were three women from Atlantic Highlands who were uniformed nurses or camp workers overseas, Florence E. Case, Doris N. Cutler, and Margaret B. Purvis. The greatest honor was attached to Paul Brunig, the one hometown boy with family in town who gave his life in the war as a soldier (see box at right). Also killed in the war was a summer resident, William Friedlaender.

The Rum-Roaring 1920s

The long-running Temperance movement in the United States, which had been particularly strong in Atlantic Highlands since the 1800s, finally had its victory in outlawing alcoholic beverages nationwide. Few people remember that World War I was also instrumental in that ban. To preserve grains and labor for the war effort, the federal Food Control Act of September 1917 forbade the use of food materials to produce distilled beverages, malt, and wine. In December 1917 Congress passed the constitutional amendment prohibiting intoxicating liquor altogether, and in January 1919 enough states had ratified it that it came into effect a year later, on January 16, 1920.

Fast-forward to October 16, 1929 when federal agents raided an isolated ridge-top house in the Hillside section above Atlantic Highlands with an outlook over Sandy Hook Bay. Before 1920 the house had been owned by the operatic and music hall impresario, Oscar Hammerstein Sr. In the house agents found a powerful short-wave radio station, a cellar full of submachine guns, automatic rifles, revolvers and ammunition, and 16 men who denied any knowledge of the radio and the weapons.

Despite the denials, the house was the headquarters of a huge bootlegging operation. In fact it was "the heart of the system" of rum-running along the northern coast of New Jersey, according to the *Asbury Park Press*. This base office "kept in touch with each fleet of liquor-laden ships and its own speedboats by radio," with a transmitter that flashed messages from Maine to Florida. The smugglers it directed used airplanes to handle rush orders.

The house had bulletproofed walls and a blinker on a bedroom balcony to signal when it was safe for rum-running boats to dock. Its six-car garage was equipped with a hydraulic lift going down two levels to a hidden storage place for liquor, where a later resident found excellent old French champagne buried. Reportedly there was a rum-delivery tunnel under the tennis court. At one point, the man said to be the ring leader of the bootlegging, Al Lillien, was found shot to death on a stairway landing leading to the garret, where he reportedly was reaching for a door to escape. The murderer was never found.

The rum-running business at this house managed the illegal import of 10,000 cases of liquor a week. Priced at $50 to $100 a case, this haul was worth up to $35 million a year wholesale. Because bartenders in speakeasies generally cut drinks by a third, the estimated retail sales commanded by this one center totaled more than $100 million a year.

What happened to the 16 men caught in the raid at the hilltop house? In June 1931 they and 43 others were brought to court for rum-running. During the trial, it often seemed that the Prohibition agents and Coast Guardsmen were on trial, rather than the bootleg ring. According to one report, all the bootleggers were found not guilty. Another report, however, says that "one of the upper-echelon figures in the Atlantic Highlands enterprise

Paul Brunig, Hero at the Hindenburg Line

Paul Brunig was an original member of Atlantic Highlands Boy Scout Troop 22 when it was commissioned in December 1911. He was one of its 25 members who served in the armed forces during World War I. After the war, 24 of those Scouts returned home, but Paul did not. He was the only Atlantic Highlands resident out of 118 who went to war but did not survive. In September 1918, the eve of his twenty-first birthday, he was killed in France while leading his platoon in a bold attack on German forces at the Hindenburg Line.

As a boy, Paul went to school in Atlantic Highlands, played tennis, and took part in theatrical events. At 18 he joined the National Guard and in 1916 went with his unit to patrol the Texas-Mexico border and protect against raids by the Mexican rebel leader, Pancho Villa. When the United States declared war on Germany, Paul was one of the first to volunteer. In May 1918 he departed for France as First Sergeant, Company B, 107th Infantry, 27th Division, in the American Expeditionary Forces (illustration no. 57).

Paul asked to be put in charge of a platoon as a line sergeant. Since a lieutenant was not available, the entire leadership of the platoon eventually devolved upon him. His commanding officer called him a "very efficient" platoon leader, and a fellow soldier said he was "very calm and fearless." In late September 1918, the company moved up to the Hindenburg Line, 80 miles of trenches, barbed wire, artillery posts, and machine gun block-houses that were almost impregnable. The Allies planned a gigantic offensive there, with eight Allied armies converging on the Germans.

Beginning at 4 a.m. on Sunday, September 29, Paul's company led in the attack. In the first wave, his platoon captured three strong lines of German trenches. American tanks then rolled up under a heavy smoke screen, and the low visibility enabled Paul's platoon to approach very close to the German machine guns before being seen. Calling for his men to follow him and firing his pistol, Paul advanced towards a trench filled with Germans and about six machine guns.

When the battle ended three days later, the Hindenburg Line had been breached and the Prussian Guards had been smashed. Paul's body was found on the field with 128 others out of the 180 in his company—a very high casualty rate. They were all buried there. Five weeks later on November 11, an armistice was declared, all forces stopped firing, and the war was over.

On December 8, a memorial service was held for Paul at All Saints' Memorial Church in Locust, where he was a member. A stone was erected in the graveyard reading, "For Home and County—Greater Love Hath No Man Than This."

was a young man named Felix Bitter;" when the feds raided its headquarters, Bitter was caught and eventually "served his time."

Every inlet, bay, and pier had its operators in Atlantic Highlands and elsewhere along the bay from Highlands to Matawan. Small local boats made night-time runs to meet smuggling ships waiting a few miles offshore beyond the bay. Between ten and fifteen old tramp steamers and large schooners laden with rum from the Caribbean islands or scotch from Canada lay at anchor at any given time, a line-up of boats that became known as "Rum Row." They stayed in international waters beyond the three-mile limit and could not be apprehended. Typically these ships carried from 2,500 to 3,000 cases of liquor. However, during the last of Prohibition's 14-year life span (1920–1933), the offshore fleet included a number of diesel-powered coastal freighters up to about 175 feet long and carrying as many as 5,000 cases of liquor.

Estimates are that between 25 and 75 percent of bayshore fishermen were enticed into becoming rum-runners by the syndicates running the illegal operation. Paid $100 for each load brought in, they got much more profit from liquor than a haul of cod or porgies. One observer of the scene, Kenneth Bahrs of Highlands, told the *Asbury Park Press* in 1982 that "when Prohibition first started, anybody with even a rowboat could get in on the game if he had the cash. He could go out and buy 10 cases or whatever he could carry in his boat. . . . Later on we went to a specific ship for each load." Sometimes the smugglers slipped a bottle of the "good stuff" into the tops of their foul-weather boots for future imbibing—the basis of the term "bootlegging."

Coming back into the bay, runner boats had to dodge the Coast Guard almost constantly, sometimes managing to outrun the slower Guard vessels. And sometimes, in collusion with the smugglers, other boats equipped with illegal radio transmitters sent out false distress signals to draw Guardsmen away from the liquor-laden boats. Other times, they had to dump liquor bottles overboard, faced gunfire from the Guard ships, or were stalled by ropes the Guard threw into their propellers to jam them. In later Prohibition years, big-city mobsters cornered the rum-running trade where there was big money to be made, and there were gang battles for bootlegging rights, frequently ending with the losers buried under water with sashweights as shrouds.

Pick-up boats from the ports included sloops and skiffs used in bay fishing. But, eventually, most were specially constructed boats with high-speed engines. Some were powered with three airplane engines. Many had false bottoms and hidden compartments for stashing liquor.

One of the fastest and most clever boats was the *Lucky Strike*, which operated out of Atlantic Highlands. Coming into shore, it unloaded directly on to ramps that ran into a built-in garage in a bayside house. The great speed of the *Lucky* was such a special secret that, during a Coast Guard chase that risked its capture, the owners pulled the boat up from the water and set it on fire rather than let the feds board it and inspect its engine.

The rum boats returned to secret slips, and nuzzled up to the base of coastal cliffs where tunnels reportedly led into building basements along the water. Burlap bags filled with cases of booze were stored in cellars, secret cupboards, and rooms behind false walls in many houses and restaurants. Cases of beer were sold from the building at the southeast corner of First and East Highland Avenues, and home delivery was even done by kids in town—innocently, as a paid errand. One house in Atlantic Highlands, "Forest Cottage" high up on Prospect Circle, had a brick-walled "hooch cellar" 6 feet wide and 10 feet deep just off a gazebo on the front corner of a porch that was discovered in the 1990s.

During the entire 14 years of Prohibition, illegal hooch was quite common. Entire back seats of cars were converted to transport liquor, covered by women wearing long skirts; when the police stopped them, they dared inspecting officers to lift their skirts and bear the shame of a wrong accusation and offended modesty. In Atlantic Highlands, it was rumored that the underground "well" of the hydraulic lift in Romeo's auto-service station at First Avenue and Highway 36 was used for liquor storage. Andy Richards, who owned Andy's Tavern on First Avenue, was thought to have a big role in the gathering and distribution of liquor off the ships. Locals actually believed he dug a tunnel between his First Avenue store and the garage, later a box factory, that he built seven blocks to the southwest (today's Firemen's Field House). Edward F. Conover in a 1974 interview said that Andy transported liquor in sham oil trucks and "Butter, Eggs & Cheese" trucks.

Once the boats had landed their cargoes, the main distribution job was to fill trucks with the liquor, transport it to warehouses, and distribute it to trustworthy outlets. There were reports that some police, including the chief and one officer in Atlantic Highlands, were nice enough to guide the trucks on late-night and early-morning trips through their towns. Atlantic Highlands in those years had its own electric power station that, conveniently but not coincidentally, shut down frequently between 10 p.m. and midnight so that liquor could be unloaded unseen at the waterfront and trucked to local storage and more distant distributors. Some nights the lights were turned off for a half-hour in the town's social hall, the casino on Ocean Boulevard, while a truck from the eastern bayshore came over the hill and headed to Newark and New York. Even with the power turned off, rumrunners could not operate on moonlit nights, leaving them only about 14 work nights per month.

In addition to certain police, some other officials were also less than diligent in enforcing Prohibition—even Coast Guard personnel, sheriffs, state troopers, and federal revenue agents. Many personally opposed Prohibition and others viewed it as an opportunity to make money for themselves. Some actually became employees of rum-runners and bootleggers, and many accepted bribes to look the other way. But some either could not be bought or would not stay bought. As a result, the rum runners often were chased and were targets for gunfire.

One incorruptible politician in Atlantic Highlands was William Burdge Mount, who ran for mayor in the 1920s. Interviewed in 1973 at age 89, Mount spoke directly about the "Bootlegging Paradise" that had been Atlantic Highlands. A teetotaler who never drank in his life, he was opposed in the election campaign by the liquor interests. These opponents "brought racketeers up from Atlantic City, bus loads, and down from Jersey City. . . . We had to let them vote and try to catch them afterwards. Well, after they voted they went back and you couldn't get them anyhow. So that's how the other side won the election."

During prohibition, bootleggers took advantage of the Mandalay pier at the Atlantic Beach Amusement Park by unloading contraband liquor in the middle of the night. Several times, the park gate was rammed and knocked down by trucks involved in the delivery and had to be replaced. Mount said that one time when the bootleggers ran booze in at the Mandalay Pier, the police chief guided delivery trucks through the town and diverted one into the garage of a First Avenue business, which paid him for the haul. As a result, the bootleggers "wanted to bump him off, but Andy Richards—he was the head of the boot-legging gang here—knew there would be a big mess. He wasn't a pretty bad guy, why, when I lost the mayor vote, Andy put his arms around me and said 'you should have had that job, but you wouldn't listen to reason.' Well, I didn't care whether I won it or not, but I certainly wasn't going to be bossed around by the bootleggers."

Not all contraband liquor supplies coming to town left town. Local restaurants, halls, houses, and underground locations set up illegal bars, called "speakeasies," that sold lots of booze by the drink. They often had a steel door with a peephole, a code word to gain entry, or in elite locations you showed a special card. One reported speakeasy in Atlantic Highlands was in a house called Cliff Lodge on Ocean Boulevard next to today's entry to Mount Mitchill Scenic Overlook park near the Highlands border. In the Highlands, one estimate was that over 70 speakeasies were operating at the height of Prohibition.

Prohibition ended when the 21st Amendment to the Constitution was repealed in December 1933. In the decades since then, many local residents have been afraid to talk about townspeople (even those long deceased) who had been active in bootlegging. They would only offer sideways remarks that this rumrunner donated lots of money to the church and that bootlegger gave out candy to kids. In the 1990s, however, a woman named Spira Bennett, then in her 80s and living on Bayside Drive, told what she knew to an inquiring reporter, Muriel Smith. She said her three brothers had all been bootleggers. The richest—the one who passed out candy—also had a diamond in his tooth. Their house had had lots of nooks and crannies for hiding booze, and no inspectors ever found liquor there. Scariest of all, she knew that two mysterious murders had taken place, connected somehow with rumrunning operations but never solved.

Refuge and Recreation: the Harbor

The 1930s in Atlantic Highlands began another movement that, unlike Prohibition, had a lasting, positive, and pleasurable impact on the town and dramatically redefined a big chunk of its future life and livelihood. In those years, some local visionaries had the idea of building a "harbor of refuge" where boats could find sanctuary during storms, an anchorage that would also be a center of marine recreation where yachts, fishing boats, and tourist excursions could be based. The "refuge" part of the dream enabled the borough to acquire funds for most of the construction from the federal government, the Works Progress Administration, and the State of New Jersey within their mandates. The recreation vision led to the building of a significant tourist and recreation resource, a revenue producer for the town government, and, in effect, the largest industry in Atlantic Highlands.

The coastline waterfront along Sandy Hook Bay has always been the biggest, most visible, and most appreciated feature of Atlantic Highlands. The waterfront stretches 2.5 miles from west to east along the southern edge of the bay. Behind this shore, the territory of the town is a relatively narrow strip ranging in width from only a half mile to one mile maximum. Seen from many vantage points, whether above on the highland ridge or down at the tidal flats, the coast is an important defining factor in the environment and life of the borough. What the harbor did was to add a major new focus of activity along the coast east of its intersection with First Avenue and the railroad pier, which were the central and active thoroughfares of the town since at least the late 1870s.

As early as 1685, the virtues of the bay as a boat harbor were recognized in a document written by John Reid and published in Britain that encouraged settlers to come. It described:

> That noted Bay for Ships within Sandy Hook, very well known, not to be
> inferior to any Harbour in America, where ships not only harbour in greatest

storms, but there Ryde safe with all Winds, and sail in and out thence as well in winter as in summer.

Aiming to get a major boat harbor built in town, businessmen in the borough's board of trade called a citizens' meeting on the subject in January 1895. The consensus was that a breakwater was needed for the safe anchorage of all kinds of vessels. Among the backers were the two boating groups in town, the Pavonia and New York Yacht Clubs. A committee of five was selected to propose that the federal government build the breakwater with an appropriation for the estimated construction cost of $250,000. The delegation visited two congressional representatives from the area: Benjamin F. Howell, who was said to favor it; and John J. Gardner, who reportedly had "property interests in this place and would therefore exert his influence." The initiative did not succeed.

In 1897 the Pavonia Yacht Club abandoned its pier and 40-boat anchorage in the bay offshore from its clubhouse at 48 Ocean Boulevard (between Fourth and Fifth Avenues). Their reason was the absence of a breakwater, which, the local newspaper said, had left many boats of Pavonia members at the mercy of storms that wrecked them.

In the 1930s the leading force in bringing about the creation of the harbor was the Atlantic Highlands Lions Club. Among its key promoters were Thomas McVey (later mayor), Earle Snyder, Eugene Crowell, and Oscar Lichtenstein. In the mid-1930s, these men and others traveled often to Washington, D.C., pleading the case for the harbor. Its development was finally authorized by the federal government in 1937. It became known as "The Million Dollar Harbor, "with its total cost rounded up. The Works Progress Administration (WPA) largely paid for it, with the borough contributing only $53,000.

Construction took place in 1939–1941, starting with a massive landfill operation. The rounded bay cove east of First Avenue was filled in and made into flat land, with a straight edge to which piers would be attached. The Army Corps of Engineers brought in 250,000 tons of quarried traprock to lay down an outer breakwater wall 4,000 feet long. Then the anchorage area inside the breakwater was dredged to eight feet below mean low water and berthing facilities and upland support facilities were provided. The handsome houses on the Terrace lost their waterfront to the landfill.

The work was just about completed when the United States entered the war against Japan, and the Navy took over the harbor for its duration. Sandy Hook Bay was reserved for military use because it was vital for the defense of New York harbor and the protection of the ocean coast. It provided passage for the many troop ships and supply ships heading to Europe. As a result, the harbor, known as the Atlantic Highlands Yacht Basin, was not opened for its intended civilian uses until the dedication ceremony of July 11, 1946.

In its early years, the harbor had six piers each 400 feet long, with berths for 320 boats. A brochure described it as "an exclusive yachting port." Offering numerous waterways for boaters, it is near the meeting point of Sandy Hook Bay and the Atlantic Ocean, south of the Hudson and East Rivers, just north of the Navesink and Shrewsbury Rivers, and southeast of the Raritan River. Extolling its location, the brochure noted that the bay:

> is well protected by the Sandy Hook spit, free of shoals, free of fogs, and entirely uncommercialized. It is also possibly the most popular sports fishing region on the coast. The Highlands of Navesink, which form its southern shore, is still undeveloped. Here are opportunities for the yachtsman desiring a summer home

with a magnificent view of the sea and yet within a few minutes ride of his boat and easy commuting distance to his office. Monmouth Park Race track is 15 minutes away by motor car.

By 1970 day visitors were launching as many as 500 boats a day, in addition to resident sailors leaving from their rented moorings and berths. That year construction was started on a new restaurant. A very ambitious master plan was drawn up, providing for a total of 17 piers extending far to the east, 1,185 new berths, a lee breakwater perpendicular to the eastern end of the existing jetty, and parking for 1,740 cars. Criticized as oversized, the plan was never implemented and harbor growth in the subsequent 30 years never matched its scope. As of 2000, there were 168 moorings and 480 docking slips at ten piers; the harbor also hosted nine party fishing boats and 15 charter boats that could be booked for private parties.

At the western end of the harbor, the railroad and ferryboat pier continued operating until 1965. Between 1879 and 1965 at least 21 boats made regular runs between Atlantic Highlands and New York. For almost all of that time, the Central Railroad of New Jersey ran the boats to serve its railroad terminal on the pier. Their names included *Jesse Hoyt*, *Chauncey M. DePew*, *Grand Republic*, *Restless*, and *Susquehanna*. The queen of the fleet was the 297-foot *Asbury Park* (1903–1918). Two of the best known were the *Monmouth* (1888–1941) and the *Sandy Hook* (1889–1943). As sister ships, they were each 260 feet long and had two stacks. The *Sandy Hook* became a troop ferry during World War II.

In the mid-1930s, after a day's ferry duty, the boats would take passengers for three-hour $1 cruises around New York Bay. The "dinner sail" offered steak for $1 and lobster for $1.50. A "moonlight sail" followed.

During World War II, service was interrupted by government fuel conservation orders that banned ferry competition with railroads and by restrictions on all but military uses of the harbor. After the war, the borough bought the pier from the Central Railroad of New Jersey and it stood idle for several years. It was rented during the summers of 1948 and 1949 by the Sandy Hook Boat Line, but two disastrous fires caused the borough to condemn the property and then sell it to the Atlantic Wharf Company. Boat service resumed in about 1950, with trips timed to coincide with buses taking horse-race fans to and from the Monmouth Park track.

The last ferry to New York left the Atlantic Highlands dock on Labor Day 1965. The big pier finally came to a fiery end when two blazes of undetermined origin destroyed it. The first fire, on May 6, made it impossible for summer boat service to restart. The second fire, on July 4, 1966, started during the Fourth of July firemen's fair being held at the harbor. At its outbreak, the town firemen went to the pier and fought the fire until companies from neighboring towns arrived and began getting it under control, at which point the town firemen returned to the fair. Many curiosity seekers who came to see the fire stayed on for the fair, increasing its receipts dramatically. The firemen believed that fishermen's cigarettes were the cause of the July fire. Only two vestiges of the railroad and steamboat era remain: rows of pilings still in the water at the end of the peninsula extending into the bay, and a section of railroad track still embedded in that strip of land.

In the late 1970s, when an estimated half of the borough work force was commuters, there was talk of starting hydrofoil service but it came to nothing. In the mid-1980s, ferry service finally returned when large catamarans began plying the route to New York, with docking alternating between Highlands and Atlantic Highlands.

In December 1992, a nor'easter packing hurricane-force winds and exceptional tides slammed Atlantic Highlands and its municipal harbor. The storm caused an estimated $3.5 million in damage to the piers, bulkhead, and promenade, with the worst damage to pier 6. Following major reconstruction, all piers were back in operation by late spring 1993, but building a new pier 6 took longer. By 1998 an entirely new bulkhead of coated steel was installed on 1,180 feet of waterfront, and a new macadam promenade with fencing, old-style lighting, and benches was laid out.

Erosion from the land and shifting bottom sediments in the bay waters silt up the navigation channels, which require periodic dredging. In 1988, an upland disposal site for dredged materials was built at the eastern end of the harbor. Since then it has received dredged materials periodically inside mounded earthen berms that rise about 22 feet above sea level, where water eventually drains out and the remaining solids dry out.

World War II

On December 7, 1941, Japan attacked Pearl Harbor, provoking the United States into World War II. Already the next day soldiers were dispatched to guard the harbor in Atlantic Highlands and the huge oil and gas storage tanks in the Esso yard at Avenue D along the bay.

Soon thereafter, young men from Atlantic Highlands started going off to war in Europe or the Pacific. Many of them had first gone to 121 First Avenue to report for a draft call by the Selective Service System. Until 1944, that address was the headquarters for Local Board 2, which covered the Bayshore from Highlands to Keyport, as well as Middletown and Holmdel townships. They left for training camps from the Atlantic Highlands railroad station, with send-offs that were a mixture of patriotism and apprehension.

A total of 346 men and women from town served as draftees or volunteers in the war, sometimes including several from the same family. Five brothers from the Rich family of Avenue A served in different branches—Jerry, Henry, and Ralph in the Army, Tony in the Navy, and George in the Air Force. George was a propeller specialist for B-29 bombers that regularly struck at Japan's war industries from a huge superfortress base in the Marianna Islands. Henry was wounded at Okinawa and Ralph was killed in Germany. Three Posten brothers were in the service: John, James, and Bill. John, a major, was a fighter plane pilot in the Philippines and Australia whose exploits were honored in a hometown parade in 1942. Caspar and Stanley Joslin from South Avenue were also military brothers. Caspar was so eager to fight that he joined the Royal Canadian Air Force before the United States entered war, and then transferred to the U.S. Air Force and did combat service in North Africa and Sicily. The Nystroms, father and son, were both in overseas service; the father, Lieutenant Colonel R.A. Nystrom, commanded a Signal Service unit in France while his son Raymond was active in French Africa, Sicily, and Italy, and was a D-Day fighter-bomber pilot.

Two Air Force lieutenants from town, Anthony Carbona and Aram Kantarian, were navigators for B-17 planes in the European theater and both received the Flying Cross and Air Medal, among other awards. Carbona flew with a D-Day mission and 35 missions over Germany.

The war took away townspeople from many roles. Three teachers went on military leave from the Atlantic Highlands High School and served overseas: Lieutenant John J. Daly Jr., Ensign Henry Kaftel, and Lieutenant Stephen Halata. Daly, the school's physical education director, became a paratrooper and was killed during the invasion of Normandy. The pastor of the Central Baptist Church, Captain William R. Schillinger, became the chaplain of a Field Hospital Unit that landed on D-Day with the first United States troops and worked with doctors and nurses many times under enemy fire.

It was the infantrymen who fought on foot in the most difficult places, including Private Joseph N. Caruso, who slogged with his company through the Vosges Mountains in eastern France, breached the Siegfried Line, and drove the Germans back across the Rhine. The forbidding mountain country between Florence and Bologna, Italy, was the battleground for Corporal Louis V. Rapa, a former star basketball player at Atlantic Highlands High School; he and his unit had also fought the Afrika Korps of German Field Marshal Erwin Rommel in Tunisia and then invaded Italy at Anzio.

On the home front, in 1943, the Earle Naval Weapons Station was built inland at Colts Neck and on the bay at Leonardo, its 2.2-mile long pier visible from all over Atlantic Highlands. Construction crews were housed in Atlantic Highlands in the Hollywood Lodge at Eighth and Mount Avenues. At times Earle stored enough explosives to blow up all of New Jersey and New York City. Each month Earle sent nearly 130,000 tons of munitions to the European front. Also helping with weaponry in the war effort, the present Firemen's Field House was a factory for the production of ammunition boxes made of wood and cardboard under government contract with Andy Richards.

Coastal defenses took on urgency when German submarines started sinking ships off the Jersey shore in 1942. Globs of oil, evidence of ships that were sunk, appeared on local beaches. Artillery units were beefed up at Fort Hancock. A 16mm firing battery was established on top of Rocky Point overlooking the ocean; when it was fired one day, it broke all the windows in the Highlands. Fear and defense measures escalated when a warning was issued in August 1944 about possible German robot-bomb attacks on the east coast. There was also initial fear that German saboteurs were behind the blow-up of a destroyer escort, the USS *Solar*, while loading ammunition at Earle Naval Weapons Station, but it was found to be an accident.

At the height of the submarine menace, the Coast Guard enlisted some private boat owners into a Reserve Coast Guard, including some in Atlantic Highlands harbor waters. Their boats were painted gray, got CG numbers, and filled up at a huge fuel barge in the harbor. Called "the hooligan navy" by some in town, they were on tap in case evacuation was needed, helped with air-sea rescues, and went out to look for German submarines. Encountering a German sub south of Montauk, one reservist boater dropped a depth charge, stayed put, and blew himself up.

Kids went to Mount Mitchill's lookout over the bay to watch dozens of troop and supply ships threading their way through the bay. Lots of troops were at Sandy Hook for training, and then left by boat for Jersey City and Hoboken piers where they embarked for the European Theater of Operations. There were rules against being on ocean beaches and bay shorelines after sundown. One old-timer remembers "an unofficial rule about no kite flying at the Mount Mitchill overlook because it might be taken as a signal."

Beginning in March 1942, a growing number of products were subjected to government rationing. Eventually, at the peak, it covered gasoline, heating fuel, sugar, coffee, canned and bottled goods, meat, butter, and other foods. Once a month residents went to the elementary school on First Avenue, which kept records and distributed ration books containing different colored stamps for different foods with different point values. Nylon stockings were not available. Fuel shortages curtailed travel, and no school trips were held, not even the annual civic learning excursion to Washington, D.C.

Blackouts occurred every day. Newspapers announced the time when lights had to be turned off and blinds closed, though for some reason the amusement parks in Asbury Park and Long Branch kept their lights on. There were periodic air raid drills, with air raid wardens patrolling the streets and kids running around the street ahead of them. Some people wondered why they were asked to prepare for air attacks when Japanese and German planes could not reach the United States. They looked at air raid drills only as exercises in building awareness and support of the war effort.

Secret War Research in Atlantic Highlands

An acre surrounded by barbed wire. Armed sentries on patrol. Inside this perimeter: three houses, perched on bluffs 100 feet above Sandy Hook Bay. To one side: a tall structure that looks like a water tower. One house has a line-up of strange machines on its porch, all pointed at the waters of New York harbor (illustration no. 59).

This strange ensemble at 60, 66, and 72 Bayside Drive in Atlantic Highlands was a site for what has been called "the nation's most secret military planning next to the Manhattan project" that developed the atomic bomb. The compound served as a research lab and test site for the development of radar between 1941 and 1945. Up to 20 engineers worked day and night trying out and improving different radar models that Bell Laboratories developed under contract to the Army. The guest register of the lab recorded the names of practically all the famous radar engineers, scientists, and officers of the United States, as well as visiting British specialists.

The researchers' goal was to demonstrate that radar—then a new and untried technology—could accurately direct ship guns toward an enemy target. Radar, the acronym for "radio detecting and ranging," projects a beam of radio impulses that bounce off objects and rebound to the observer. At this location they scanned a 16-mile radius from the bluffs to the Brooklyn shoreline, aiming radar at moving ships in the harbor as if on an open sea. Several systems they worked on later were used effectively against enemy ships. Radar helped detect German planes in the Battle of Britain and put the Navy on target to discover and destroy German submarines.

Work here started in early 1941, before the attack on Pearl Harbor and the United States' declaration of war. The first lab was the small four-room bungalow at 66 Bayside Drive. By spring of 1942 they built the house at no. 72 to be the main lab, and the antennas of units being tested were arrayed on its front porch. At no. 60 was a storage building.

To ensure secrecy for a special experiment, an antenna was enclosed in a water tower 100 feet high. That caused some area residents to mutter in wonder at the new owner's foolishness; the municipal water system seemed just fine, they said. Secrecy was also protected by FBI and Army Intelligence specialists who policed the surrounding hills.

After the war, Bell Labs sold the lab building, dubbing it "Bel-Aire." All three buildings were subsequently remodeled into private residences.

The war came forceably home when Atlantic Highlands soldiers returned to town after suffering in prisoner-of-war camps and being wounded or killed on battlefields of Europe and the Pacific. For 23 months Staff Sergeant Thomas Ryan was imprisoned in Menz, Austria, after his Flying Fortress plane was grounded following a raid in occupied territory. He was finally liberated by Russian troops in April 1945. Colonel Alfred Olivier, a Methodist Chaplain from Sixth Avenue, was among 513 gaunt, ragged men rescued by United States Rangers and Filipino guerrillas in a daring prison-camp raid in the Philippines in March 1945. The same month, Frank Swan, a civilian employee of Manila-based General Electric and Gas Company, was freed after many months in a concentration camp on the island of Luzon. Among others whose sacrifices are not forgotten were Corporal Joseph Spicer Jr., wounded in his third Pacific mission; Private Leon D. Platky, wounded in the European theater of war in May 1945; and Private First Class Vincent Nappa, who received the Purple Heart for service with the 9th Armored Division in Europe.

Finally, 12 men from Atlantic Highlands gave their lives in the war, as listed on the memorial stone in Veterans' Park. Included, as already mentioned, were John Daly and Ralph Ricciardelli (a.k.a. Ralph Rich). The others were David Bashaw, James Brady, Edward Finnigan, John Gallagher, John Joy, James Latta, William McLaughlin, Corval Mosley, and John Pape. A thirteenth name on a different list was Albert T. Buchhop, who enlisted as an airplane radioman and died at age 23 in the June 1944 invasion of Saipan.

On a lighter note, one bomber pilot from Atlantic Highlands offered special greetings to his hometown from the sky in September 1944. Having flown many war missions against Nazi industrial and military installations, Lieutenant Jack Oakes of Memorial Parkway was returned to Mitchell Field on Long Island. On a routine flight from there, he flew his plane over Atlantic Highlands and buzzed the whole town from a couple hundred feet up along First Avenue, the bay, and the hills. John Phair remembered this as "a great day for Atlantic Highlands" and for him as a 12-year-old. He said everyone knew that the plane was piloted by Jack, who was the son of Honey Oakes, the owner of Honey's Tavern on First Avenue.

Oakes' overflight was the town's happiest day of the war years, except for May 6, 1945, when final victory was achieved in the European battlefields and an armistice was announced. On V-E Day, the town was buzzing because everyone came out in the streets and cars drove around honking their horns in a cacophony of celebration.

BIBLIOGRAPHY

Adelberg, Michael S. *Roster of the People of Revolutionary Monmouth County*. Freehold, NJ: Monmouth County Historical Association, 1977.

Applegate, John A. *A History of Monmouth County, 1664–1920*. 3 vols. New York: Lewis Historical Publishing Co., 1922.

Atlantic Highlands Journal.

Barber, John W. and Henry Howe. *Historical Collections of the State of New Jersey*. London: Board of General Proprietors of the Eastern Division of New Jersey, 1844.

Beekman, George C. *The Early Dutch Settlers of Monmouth County, New Jersey*. New Orleans: Polyanthos, 1974 [1901].

Bierhorst, John, ed. *Mythology of the Lenape: Guide and Texts*. Tucson: University of Arizona Press, 1995.

Bill, Alfred Hoyt Bill. *New Jersey and the Revolutionary War*. Princeton: D. Van Nostrand Company, Inc., 1964.

Black Birth Book of Monmouth County, New Jersey 1804–1848. Freehold, NJ: 1989.

Condon, Thomas J. *New York Beginnings: The Commercial Origins of New Netherland*. New York: New York University Press, 1968.

Cunningham, John T. *Colonial New Jersey*. New York: Thomas Nelson, Inc., 1971.

Danckaerts, Jasper. Journal of Jasper Danckaerts 1679–1680, in *Original Narratives of Early American History*. ed. J. Franklin Jameson, vol. 13. New York: Charles Scribner's Sons, 1913 [1680].

Ellis, Franklin. *History of Monmouth County, New Jersey*. Cottonport, LA: Polyanthos, Inc., 1974 [1885].

Gerlach, Larry R., ed. *New Jersey in the American Revolution 1763–1783: A Documentary History*. Trenton: New Jersey Historical Commission, 1975.

Heckewelder, Rev. John. *An Account of the History, Manners, and Customs of the Indian Nations, Who Once Inhabited Pennsylvania and the Neighbouring States*. Bowie, MD: Heritage Books, Inc., 1990 reprint [1876].

Hodges, Graham Russell. *Slavery and Freedom in the Rural North: African Americans in Monmouth County, New Jersey, 1665–1865*. Madison, WI: Madison House Publishers, Inc., 1997.

Hornor, William S. *This Old Monmouth of Ours*. Freehold, NJ: Moreau Brothers, 1972.

Kobbé, Gustav. *The New Jersey Coast and Pines*. Short Hills, NJ: 1889.

Kraft, Herbert C. *The Lenape-Delaware Indian Heritage: 10,000 BC to AD 2000*. Union, NJ:

Lenape Books, 2001.

Leonard, Thomas Henry. *From Indian Trail to Electric Rail*. Atlantic Highlands: Atlantic Highlands Journal, 1923.

Mandeville, Ernest W. *The Story of Middletown: The Oldest Settlement in New Jersey*. Middletown: Christ Church, 1972.

Manumission Book of Monmouth County New Jersey 1791–1844. Freehold, NJ

McCormick, Richard. *New Jersey: From Colony to State, 1609-1789*. Newark: New Jersey Historical Society, 1981.

Monmouth Press.

Morford, H.T. *Fifty years Ago, A Brief History of the 29th Regiment N.J. Volunteers in the Civil War*. Hightstown, NJ: Longstreet House, 1990.

Nelson, William, ed. *Documents Relating to the Colonial History of the State of New Jersey*. Calendar of Records in the Office of the Secretary of State 1664–1703. Paterson, NJ: The Press Printing and Publishing Co., 1899.

Pomfret, John E. *The New Jersey Proprietors and Their Lands 1664–1776*. Princeton, NJ: D. van Nostrand Co. Inc., 1964.

Ryan, Dennis P. *New Jersey in the American Revolution, 1763–1783: A Chronology*. Trenton: New Jersey Historical Commission, 1974.

Salter, Edwin and George C. Beckman. *Old Times in Old Monmouth: Historical Reminiscences of Old Monmouth County*. Baltimore: Genealogical Publishing Co., Inc., 1980 [1884].

Smith, Samuel Stelle. *Sandy Hook and the Land of the Navesink*. Monmouth Beach, NJ: Philip Freneau Press, 1963.

Stewart: R. Michael. *Ceramics and Delaware Valley Prehistory: Insights from the Abbott Farm*. Federal Highway Administration and NJ Department of Transportation Bureau of Environmental Analysis, and Archaeological Society of New Jersey, 1998.

Valentine, David T. *History of the City of New York*. New York: G.P. Putnam & Company, 1853.

Van der Donck, Adriaen. *Description of New Netherland*. 2d Ser. New York Historical Society Collections: 1849 [1656].

Van Laer, A.J.F. *Documents Relating to New Netherland, 1624–1626*. San Marion, CA: Henry E. Huntingdon Library and Art Gallery, 1924 [1624].

Wacker, Peter O. *Land and People, Culture and Geography in Pre-Industrial New Jersey: Origins and Settlement Patterns*. New Brunswick, NJ: Rutgers University Press, 1975.

Wacker, Peter O. and Paul G.E. Clemens. *Land Use in Early New Jersey: A Historical Geography*. Newark: New Jersey Historical Society, 1995.

Weslager, C.A. *The Delaware Indians: A History*. New Brunswick, NJ: Rutgers University Press, 1972.

Whitehead, William A. *East Jersey Under the Proprietary Governments*. Newark: Martin Dennis, 1875.

INDEX